THE CENTER FOR RESEARCH ON
LANGUAGE AND LANGUAGE BEHAVIOR
Ann Arbor, Michigan
October 17-18, 1966

Proceedings of the Conference on

LANGUAGE

and

LANGUAGE BEHAVIOR

Ann Arbor, Mich., 1966.

Edited by

Eric M. Zale

New York

 APPLETON-CENTURY-CROFTS

Division of Meredith Corporation

Library of Congress Catalog Card No. 68-28144

Q 18149

PREFACE

When the Conference on Language and Language Behavior
was originally conceived by Harlan L. Lane, director of
the Center for Research on Language and Language Behavior,
some thought was given to the publication of the proceedings. However, the reasons which influenced our decision
not to attempt it were that the CRLLB staff and dissemination funds were already committed to the development of
our new quarterly journal, Language and Language Behavior
Abstracts, the first issue of which was scheduled to appear
(and was published) late in January, 1967.

However, the caliber of the papers offered and the
enthusiasm of the capacity audience that attended each of
the sessions prompted Charles Walther, vice president of
Appleton-Century-Crofts (the company which is co-sponsoring
the publication of LLBA), to offer his firm's facilities
for the publication of these Proceedings.

Because of the delay resulting from the decision to
publish after the conference had concluded, and because
nothing had been said earlier about publication of the
proceedings, it was decided that all participants would
be offered an opportunity to revise their contributions
to take advantage of the opportunity to have their papers
appear in print. Most of the participants accepted the
opportunity to revise their manuscripts and to bring
their data up to date, to add illustrations, tables, and
important footnotes and references. In the few instances
where manuscripts were not revised, the Editor took the
liberty to delete phrases that were obviously included for
the benefit of the listening audience, but which would
have no value to a reading audience. However, all of the
papers included in these Proceedings are essentially the
same as those read at the Conference. As for proof-
reading, the Editor undertook this responsibility for the
authors who were not immediately available in Ann Arbor
at the time this work had to be done.

The Program of the Conference, plus certain necessary
changes and additions, constitutes the Table of Contents
of the Proceedings. The program for the morning of
October 17 was given over to the Inaugural Ceremonies for

the new CRLLB facilities in the City Center Building, 220
East Huron St., Ann Arbor, Mich. These Ceremonies were
held in conjunction with the Conference.

The introductory remarks of the chairmen of the
various sessions, and the discussions which followed each
of the presentations were not included in these Proceedings because it was concluded that the real value of the
Conference was in the contents of the papers.

The Editor wishes to express his sincere thanks to
the following persons for their help in preparing the
material for the Proceedings: George Smith, who was in
charge of arrangements for the Conference; Miss Jill
Calsibet, for reproducing duplicates of all papers (as
a safety measure in case of loss or destruction of
originals): Jane R. Zale, for help in reading copy;
Mrs. Autumn Kuehne, for her typing and correction of all
manuscripts, and, especially, for her wonderful sense of
congenial cooperation; Emmanuel (and Mimi) Companys, for
help in preparing transcriptions of the French tapes of
the papers read by Companys and Guy C. Capelle; Capelle,
for his assistance in revising the transcription of his
presentation; Franklin Philip, for translating the
abstract of the Companys paper (included on the suggestion
of the author); John F. Hemdal and George D. Allen, for
help in overcoming some difficulties with the content of
papers in Session E; and, most of all, to Mrs. Lydia
Peterson, for her help in preparing illustrations, in
filling in for me during my absence, and, generally, for
the extremely pleasant and efficient way in which she
handled every assignment.

ERIC M. ZALE[1]

Center for Research on Language and Language Behavior
University of Michigan
Ann Arbor, Michigan, 48108

[1]Currently Director of .Remedial Studies and Professor
of English, Wilberforce University, Wilberforce, Ohio

PROGRAM AND TABLE OF CONTENTS

2:30 p.m.   Chairman, William P. Livant
                 Research Psychologist, Mental
                 Health Research Institute, and
                 Human Growth and Development
                 Center, University of Michigan.

2:45 p.m.   Edward S. Klima, "Knowing Language   25
                     and Getting to Know It"
                 Associate Professor of Linguistics,
                 Massachusetts Institute of Tech-
                 nology

3:15 p.m.   Ursula Bellugi, "Linquistic Mechanisms   36
                     Underlying Child Speech"
                 Senior Research Assistant,
                 Harvard University

4:00 p.m.   G. David McNeill, "A Question in   51
                     Semantic Development: What
                     Does a Child Mean When He Says
                     'No'?"
                 Associate Professor of Psychology,
                 University of Michigan, Member,
                 CRLLB

4:30 p.m.   Sheldon Rosenberg, "Language Habits   63
                     and the Recall of Connected Discourse"
                 Research Associate, Member, CRLLB

Session B: Controlled Acquisition of First-
                 Language Skills

2:30 p.m.   Chairman, Daryl Bem
                     Assistant Professor of Psychology,
                     Carnegie Institute of Technology,
                     Research Associate, CRLLB

2:45 p.m.   Donald E. P. Smith, "Behavioral   75
                     Engineering: Problem Readers"
                 Professor of Education, University
                 of Michigan; Chief, Reading Improve-
                 ment Service, University of Michi-
                 gan; Member, CRLLB

3:15 p.m.   George L. Geis, "Two Paths to   87
                    Innovation: Imposition and
                    Evolution"
                Assistant Professor of Psychology,
                University of Michigan; Member,
                CRLLB

4:00 p.m.   O. K. Moore (Unable to attend because
                    of death in the family)
                Professor of Social Psychology,
                University of Pittsburgh

4:30 p.m.   Ernest Z. Rothkopf,[1] "Research
                    Approaches to Instruction"
                Supervisor, Learning and Instruc-
                tional Processes Research Group,
                Bell Telephone Laboratories

                Tuesday, 18 October 1966

8:30 a.m.   Second Major Address

                James J. Jenkins,[2] "Thought and
                    Language"
                Director of Research, Center for
                Research in Human Learning,
                University of Minnesota

Session C: Second-Language Learning

9:30 a.m.   Chairman, James McClafferty
                    Research Associate, CRLLB
                    Director, FLICS (Foreign Language
                    Innovative Curricula Study)

9:45 a.m.   Emmanuel Companys, "Discrimination   97
                    Auditive et Apprentissage des
                    Langues"
                Research Associate, CRLLB

11:30 a.m.   Richard Ohmann, "Mentalism in the   188
                    Study of Literary Language"
               Associate Professor of English,
               Wesleyan University, Conn.

1:30 p.m.   Third Major Address

               John C. Carroll, "Word-Frequency   213
                    Studies and the Lognormal
                    Distribution"
               Professor of Educational
               Psychology, Harvard University

Session E: Phonology and Phonetics

2:30 p.m.   Chairman, Herbert H. Paper
                    Professor of Linguistics,
                    University of Michigan; Member,
                    Executive Committee, CRLLB

2:45 p.m.   John F. Hemdal, "Some Simple Rules   236
                    for Self-Adaptive Mechanical
                    Recognition of Vowels"
               Research Associate, CRLLB

3:15 p.m.   Alexander Z. Guiora, "An Exploration   261
                    of Some Personality Variables
                    in Authentic Pronunciation of
                    a Second Language"
               Associate Professor of Psychology
               and Psychiatry, University of
               Michigan, Member, CRLLB

4:00 p.m.   George D. Allen, "Towards a Descrip-   267
                    tion of Stress-Timing in Spoken
                    English"
               Research Associate, CRLLB

4:30 p.m.   Peter Ladefoged, "What is Happening   283
                    in Phonetic Research"
               Professor of Phonetics, University
               of California, Los Angeles

<u>Session F</u>:   Language Impairment

Footnotes

[1]The paper read by Ernst Z. Rothkopf had been promised for the publication of the proceedings of the Symposium on Research Approaches to Instruction held at the University of California, Berkeley, on 28-29 November, 1966.

[2]The paper read by James J. Jenkins had been previously promised to the report of proceedings of a conference at the University of Pittsburgh on language.

[3]The paper read by Alton L. Becker was based on the research project which he is conducting with Frank M. Koen and Richard E. Young. Therefore, his comments are included in the Koen paper.

DEDICATION ADDRESS

A. Geoffrey Norman[1]

We are met today to mark the inauguration of activities of the Center for Research on Language & Language
Behavior, in fine new quarters, which you can visit
shortly. I could wish it were possible to dedicate a
University building as the Center's home, and perhaps some
day that can be done. But for the present, we must take
advantage of space provided by private initiative, fur-
nished to meet the requirements of the new program to be
housed there. Dr. Lane and his staff have been most
patient these last few months, during which time they
lived in what could only be described as gentile squalor--
a condition more frequently encountered in academic world
than is generally recognized. The compression forces
operative there were also substantial, but just as with a
gas, the human molecules expanded instantaneously to fill
the container to the much greater volume to which they
were transferred. Collision frequency has certainly been
reduced, and no doubt also they find it cooler, as the gas
laws require. When you inspect the new quarters, you will
no doubt be struck by the fact that there is a good
comfortable fit, but those of you with experience in such
matters will know that the next compression cycle has
already started.

The Center is young, with many of the attributes of
youth: vitality, rapid growth, and incessant activity. I
would not want to predict when a cry of overcrowding will
be raised and relief again sought, but that is the
inevitable and self-inflicted result of success, the
success we know will come.

I have been turning over in my mind what remarks
would come appropriately from an administrative officer of
the University, whose ignorance of the professional fields
represented in the Center was complete, until Dr. Lane
undertook to provide me with some elementary or perhaps
kindergarten-level instruction--enough to approve a budget,

1

but not so much as to enable me to ask awkward questions. For I am professionally a biochemist--and, as yet, the biochemisticans contributes little to the problems of language, language acquisition and language structure. Indeed about all the biochemist has done has been to contribute some dandy new words--probably with mixed roots, repugnant to a scholar in linguistics. But, of course, we are confident that ultimately biochemical mechanisms will be found for all human characteristics and senses. Learning and memory, vision and speech, all are the resultants of complex, interacting biochemical systems. Some day these will be identified; as yet we are only at the beginning of this aspect of human physiology.

Human genes and the genetic code they carry determine the apparatus of speech and of communication between individuals, but do not transmit anything about the medium of communication-language. That has to be learned and is a remarkable feat which is performed by every young child in a two- or three-year period. Most adults acquiring facility in a second language find this not an easy matter and moreover encounter some impediments in enunciation and accentation that carry over from the first, or native, language. Clearly, the process of language acquisition is something about which much more should be known, and this is one of the Center's objectives.

I have always been fascinated in a baffled sort of way by language itself--that words which are just sounds can be used to transfer information from one person to another--to express abstract thoughts or concepts, to describe objects or phenomena, or to depict processes or events. Precision in word choice is a most valuable skill. Most accomplished scientists are articulate and precise in their choice and use of words, because their findings or theories are accepted by their peers only if they can be understood. But all scientific fields develop their own language--within-a-language--readily understood by the votaries, but only partially comprehensible by the stranger, because in a language-within-a-language the meanings of words are restricted or modified by sequence or context. For example, I find almost incomprehensible some papers emanating from the Center, as no doubt their authors might find the writing of a cell biologist or radio astronomer.

Then, again, there is the fascination of language competence and use. Words can be combined in innumerable ways, but some combinations are more powerful than others in influencing others. Our assessment of those we meet is greatly affected by what they say and how they say it. Phrasing and intonation can add to, detract or modify the thoughts expressed. We can all recollect speeches that sounded fine, but were dull to read, and, conversely, fine words debilitated by delivery in a monotonous, disinterested manner. To be articulate is not necessarily to be eloquent--the distinction is subtle and not easily explained--and to those who are neither these are twin peaks that are formidably difficult to scale.

These näive remarks, though well-intentioned are, I suspect, becoming less and less suitable to the occasion. So let me conclude by performing the function for which I was presumably invited--to express on behalf of the University of Michigan our appreciation of the substantial support provided by the Office of Education for the programs of the Center, to thank the Office of Education for its understanding of the goals towards which Dr. Lane and his associates are reaching, and, finally, to say to the Director and staff of the Center that they have made an impressive beginning. We expect great things from them, and have every confidence that their efforts will result in new knowledge and new skills which will improve the abilities of men everywhere to communicate with one another.

Footnote

[1]Dr. Norman is vice-president for research and professor of botany at the University of Michigan.

INAUGURAL ADDRESS

Harlan L. Lane[1]

I propose this morning to tell you something about
the Center for Research on Language and Language Behavior:
past, present, and future. Now the concept of a center is,
of course, an abstraction applied to the concrete activities of a group of people, their tools, and their products.
Hence, I propose, in fact, to tell you about the inhabitants of this language community and about their artifacts;
and, of course, I shall also discuss their language and
language behavior.

The community of the Center for Research on Language
and Language Behavior, which numbers about 120 inhabitants,
is situated on a pleasant peninsula in Midwest America--
more specifically, at the corner of Huron Street and Fifth
Avenue in Ann Arbor, Michigan. Although it is uncommon
for similar communities in this region, a single structure
affords shelter for all the inhabitants. The shelter is
a brown brick construction and is hermetically sealed,
presumably to provide protection from the extremes of heat
and cold, and the heavy precipitation normally experienced
in this region. The economy of CRLLB, based on the
exploitation of Federal funds, has been expanding rapidly
and approached one million dollars in trade during the
past year. Most of the income derives from the preparation
of written documents: more than 6,000 pages were issued
during the year; and from the oral presentation of long
stories, usually rendered in a monotone: there were some
100 of those recorded during the year. Both oral and
written style are characterized by intricate narrative
structure rendered in one of several trade jargons.

Socially, the community of CRLLB is rather close knit,
but the family is not the basic unit, due to a taboo on
nepotism. Marriages are extra-tribal, and most inhabitants
are monogamous. Few of the CRLLBians are indigenous.
Almost all come from other tribes, many of them neighbor-
ing, but others as distant as Europe and Asia.

CRLLB sprang up in February, 1965, in an area that was heavily populated by other communities whose subsistence was also based on the preparation of written documents, and many of the inhabitants merely changed tribal affiliations. Consequently, the structure and activity of CRLLB must be understood in the context of the activity of these other language-oriented communities which I should like to describe briefly to you now.

Perhaps not every member of this audience is aware of the international reputation for excellence that our University of Michigan community has sustained in the language field. This is due in part to the quality and quantity of modern language instruction.

The bulk of this instruction at the University goes on in the seven language departments: English, Far Eastern, German, Near Eastern, Romance and Slavic Languages, and Speech.[2]

According to the number of elections in the more than one hundred courses offered by these departments, it is estimated that approximately 14,000 students participate in nearly 17,500 different course elections.

By far the biggest and most active is the <u>Romance Language Department</u> which registered nearly 6,000 students this fall [1966] for courses in French, Spanish, Italian, Portuguese and Romance Linguistics, as well as for graduate courses.

The second most active group in terms of enrollment is the <u>Speech Department</u>. There were nearly 5,700 elections this fall, including those for the 53 courses, both graduate and undergraduate, offered in speech pathology, audiology, and speech and hearing science.

A close third is the German Department, with nearly 5,000 elections for three semesters.

The <u>English Department</u> had over 1,000 elections for its 11 undergraduate and graduate language courses, with nearly one-third enrolled in the Teaching of the English Language course which is offered every semester.

There are a like number of elections, nearly 1,000, in the various Slavic language courses. Instruction in this area has been offered on a regular basis for the past 40 years.

The 425 elections in the Far East Department reflect the development of this department with the establishment of the Center for Japanese Studies in 1947 and the Center for Chinese Studies in 1961.

Like the other Asian departments, the Near East Department has grown under the impetus of the Center for Near Eastern and North African Studies (established in 1961), and it lists 200 elections during the past year.

These offerings in the more popularly enrolled languages are supplemented by those in the Department of Linguistics.

Almost every one of the nation's leading linguists have either studied or taught here at the University of Michigan, at one time or another!

You name them--Leonard Bloomfield, Edward Sapir, Charles Fries, Hans Kurath, Albert Marckwardt, Edgar Sturtevant, Kenneth Pike--and a whole host of others have either been involved with the graduate division of linguistics here, or have been members of the faculty of the Linguistic Institute on the Ann Arbor campus.

This same Linguistic Institute, which annually offers the latest advances in all phases of linguistic science, taught by the nation's outstanding linguists, has been conducted at the University campus 18 times, far more than at any other campus in the nation, and was offered here again for the summer of 1967.

The Graduate Linguistic Committee (now functioning as a Linguistics Department) lists such distinguished linguists as Charles Fries, Hans Kurath and Albert Marck-wardt, as its past chairmen. They have also served as past presidents of the Linguistic Society of America.

Foreign language courses are supplemented by the University's Language Laboratory. Established in 1949 by the Department of Romance Languages, the Lab became associated with the English Language Institute in 1950, the German Department in 1951 and eventually each of the seven language departments at the University.

Originally set up with six listening positions, a record player and a wire recorder, the lab now has 140 student positions, and a dial distribution system controlled by a PDP-8 computer.

One of the best known language organizations in the world--and the first of its kind in the United States--is the University's fine English Language Institute.

First established in 1941 by Charles C. Fries, ELI has grown in size and prestige under its directors whose names read like a page from the "Who's Who in Linguistics": Fries, 1941-1956; Robert Lado, 1956-1960; Albert Marckwardt, 1960-1963; Edward Anthony, the acting director, 1963-1964; and now John C. Catford, who is a member of CRLLB and its Executive Committee.

One of ELI's outstanding current achievements is its language testing program in more than 50 different countries of the world, with approximately 7,500 tests per year administered to foreign students.

At present there are nearly 500 students studying English as a foreign language at ELI. Upon graduation, they will bring the total number of ELI graduates from Michigan to nearly 10,000.

The teacher training program, another phase of ELI activity, lists nearly 1,500 graduates. Next summer [1967], for example, 25 Russian teachers will study here for 10 weeks as part of the Soviet-American Cultural Exchange Program.

Language is, of course, intimately bound up with culture and those scholars who seek an understanding of Asian culture have the opportunity to study at one of five area centers for Asian Studies:

The Center for Japanese Studies (created in 1947), the Centers for Chinese, Near Eastern and North African, South and Southeast Asian, and Russian Studies all created (1961). Among them, they cover the continent of Asia and the northern area of the continent of Africa in nearly 300 courses.

In keeping with its long-established traditions of leadership in linguistics and the social sciences, the University approved, last January, the first formal Ph. D. program in the world devoted exclusively to psycholinguistics and appointed Dr. Ronald Tikofsky, a member of CRLLB, as chairman of the new Psycholinguistics Division.

Psycholinguistics represents the integration and application of skills and knowledge of the psychologist and linguist to the study of language and language behavior. The core program focuses on the student's acquisition of initial competence in experimental design, lab and field research methodology, usage, and knowledge of language features and structures. Upon completion of this phase, the student can concentrate in one or more of five special areas: developmental or experimental psycholinguistics, language disorders, second-language learning and testing, and socio-linguistics.

Another rather recent academic program in the language area, created by the University in response to a growing body of knowledge and method, is the Communications Sciences Department.

Although the Communications Science graduate program has been in effect only since 1958, and as a literary college department since 1965, its growth has been remarkable. Since the program was actually launched in 1959, there have been 21 Ph. D.'s awarded.

Com Sci is concerned with understanding, on a theoretical basis, the communication and processing of information by both natural and artificial systems in two general areas of study: (1) the technical study of natural and artificial languages as modes of communication, and (2) the investigation of information processing, both in natural systems and in automata.

Com Sci is interdisciplinary, with foundations in five areas: mathematics, electrical engineering, physiology, psychology, and linguistics. Com Sci and Linguistics have developed jointly a Phonetics Laboratory under the direction of Professor Catford.

Another instructional, research and clinical service unit is the Speech Clinic. Its instructional programs in speech pathology and audiology provide for about 80 undergraduate students annually enrolled for the teaching major in speech correction. Its graduate programs serve about 40 graduate students annually. Its research activities include faculty and student projects in various phases of communication disorders. Each year, its diagnostic and therapy services benefit more than 700 children and adults who have some form of speech or hearing defect. The clinic also operates a speech and hearing camp with an enrollment of 96 youngsters.

Individual members of various other departments at the University have been, or are currently, involved with projects in the areas of language, speech or hearing. They include <u>Anthropology</u>, <u>Electrical Engineering</u>, <u>Mathematics</u>, <u>Philosophy</u>, <u>Physics (acoustics)</u>, <u>Sociology</u>, <u>Neurology</u>, <u>Otorhinolaryngology</u>, <u>Pathology</u>, <u>Pediatrics</u>, <u>Physiology</u>, <u>Psychiatry</u>, <u>Psychology</u> (<u>Child</u>, <u>Clinical</u>, <u>Experimental</u> and <u>Social</u>).

The language orientation of the University of Michigan community is to be found not only in its academic departments but also in its research centers.

The University's <u>Mental Health Research Institute</u> focuses on three major objectives: (1) integration of the various disciplines in physical, biological and social behavioral sciences into a unified body of knowledge; (2) a program of basic research on various aspects of mental health, including how information is processed within the living body and among human beings in health and disease; and (3) the application of findings to the prevention, diagnosis and cure of mental illnesses and mental retardation. The pursuit of these objectives includes a number of projects in the language area.

The <u>Center for Human Growth and Development</u>, organized nearly two years ago, has as an objective the study of the development of language functions as a part of the complex matrix of the growing organism. Studies are underway to investigate the individual's language as it interacts with the development of cognitive and motivational factors which allow him to function effectively in his environment.

Another area involves the application of experimental methods and strategies in the area of language and cognitive development. A third area of research involves

cognitive and associative theory and deals not only with
the learning of words or other linguistic elements but
also with the acquisition of concepts, and with chains or
nets of intervening stimuli and responses.

Although only four years old, the Kresge Hearing
Research Institute operates with a staff of some 75
persons, including academic, administrative, support and
consulting personnel. There are approximately 20 research
projects currently in progress.

In addition to the various centers, institutes,
clinics, laboratories, and departments described above,
there are various other organizations in the University
community involved with language research, learning, and
teaching.

One such area is the Veterans Administration Hospital
where staff members are carrying on research in speech
pathology, stuttering, aphasia, the psychology of the
communication of words and their meaning, and audiology.

Thirty years of research in general pattern recognition has led to some significant developments in single
pattern and word recognition at the University's Institute
of Science and Technology. These studies are also steps
in the process of automatic computer abstracting with the
use of key words.

Research on the detection and recognition of signals
(including phonetic, phonemic, lexical, and grammatical
signals) is in progress at IST's Sensory Intelligence
Laboratory.

This, then, is the community from which the Center
for Research on Language and Language Behavior drew its
inspiration, its context, and some of its personnel, and
in which it is now a distinguished member.

It was the thinking and efforts of a small group of
scientists about two years ago that has culminated in this
inauguration today. These scientists were disturbed by
the lack of coordination among language teachers, linguists,
phoneticians, educational, experimental and child psychologists, speech pathologists, communication scientists and
the representatives of many other allied disciplines.
They observed that the integral field of language and

language behavior had been fenced off into disciplinary areas, with largely impenetrable boundaries along lines that were arbitrary rather than functional. They observed that, as a consequence, new techniques and findings were adopted primarily by those who were taking the same approach to language research, rather than by those who were concerned with the same or related problems. These scientists were disturbed to find that promising techniques and relevant findings uncovered in the laboratory were rarely elaborated and modified into workable instructional practices. They observed, in complementary fashion, that little of the basic research was undertaken with a view toward instructional problems in the long-term advancement of language fluency.

These scientists were determined to put an end to the daily reenactment of the parable of the blind men and the elephant. You know the parable, according to which one man grabbed the leg and said the elephant was round and rigid, one the trunk and said, it was hollow and flexible and so on. So too, the psychologist sees largely the elephant's behavior, the linguist its form and structure, the pathologist its deficits, the engineer its mass and so on. Let's get a complete picture, these scientists said, and so they proposed--first to their colleagues, then to the University Administration, finally to the federal government--that a new Center be created; and in all quarters their reasoning was received with agreement and support.

These scientists proposed a Center that would carry out comprehensive and closely integrated research, development and dissemination activities that would make it more possible for people of all ages and abilities to learn languages effectively. They proposed to accomplish this three-fold objective by providing the funds, facilities and intellectual climate within one functional unit that would ensure fruitful interaction among the scientists and educators concerned with the several facets of language and language behavior.

The CRLLB has functioned as an integrated multi-disciplinary organization for research, development and dissemination for about one and a half years.

Its staff has grown from a small nucleus of seven to more than 100 full- and part-time persons, utilizing equipment valued at more than a half-million dollars.

11

Basic research, one of the Center's three major objectives, in divided into four fundamental areas (language processes, language acquisition, language modification and language structure).

Development activities, a second objective, have kept pace. The Center's record shows: a Pilot Project in the teaching of French using special electronic equipment; research on teaching a standard dialect of American English to students in southern Negro colleges; the establishment of a clearinghouse in the LLB area; the development of an alliance with major European agencies to develop the flow of language information from all foreign sources; the development of the Center's own quarterly journal, LANGUAGE AND LANGUAGE BEHAVIOR ABSTRACTS [the first issue was published in January, 1967]; collaboration with the Ann Arbor Public School system in a planning activity to develop supplementary educational centers and services to improve language education, to develop and conserve bilingual and bicultural resources in the State; and to modernize use of learning laboratories for language instruction; a computer-based information storage and retrieval system, in conjunction with LLBA; and a program to train grad students in language research, with special emphasis on second-language learning.

The third objective, dissemination, is directly involved with LLBA, the computer storage and retrieval system, the presentation of conferences, workshops, symposia, etc.; the publication of a monthly NEWSLETTER; and the development of a steady input of transient LLB information; and the output of reprints and preprints of articles and reports prepared by CRLLB personnel (more than 1,000 during the past year).

These, then, are some words about the deeds of men concerned with words. If I have been a bit wordy, it may be--at least in this context--forgivable.

Footnotes

[1]Dr. Lane is director of the Center for Research on Language and Language Behavior and an associate professor of Psychology, University of Michigan.
[2]The University's excellent Department of Classical Studies offers all levels of Greek and Latin.

SCYLLA AND CHARYBDIS
OR
THE PERILOUS STRAITS OF APPLIED RESEARCH

A. P. van Teslaar[1]

It's a sage recommendation that every cobbler should mind his own last. In so distinguished and varied a company as this, such an injunction becomes doubly compelling. The trouble is, of course, that, in the final analysis, everyone turns out to be working on the same pair of shoes.

I confess to irritation when I read or hear phrases like "in this day and age", "in this modern world of ours", "nowadays, for the first time", all of which express the too facile and antihistorical assumption that the past, to those who lived it, was simpler, better organized, freer from care, less dangerous, or, for that matter, more stupid than our own age. In most cases such rhetorical flourishes are a manifest absurdity. Mutatis mutandis, the black plague is an efficient substitute for the H-bomb as a source of anxiety and a symbol of the apocalypse.

However, we must not deny our age all claim to originality. Among many others, there is one respect in which a quantitative change has become so great as to make a qualitative difference. I refer to the organization of knowledge and research in the 20th century.

Formerly compartmented areas of research have lost their traditional outlines and defining walls and have become a series of communicating chambers. There are numerous domains--verbal behavior is one--before which a warning sign should be fixed: "Enter only at your risk and peril." In proposing this notice I've been optimistic; in another mood, one might think that the Dantean sign-post: "Abandon all hope, ye who enter here" would be more apropos.

Actually, a single sign-post would not suffice; as the Center for Research on Language and Language Behavior so eloquently testifies, many are needed. What is characteristic of these disciplines and areas of investigation, become suddenly so permeable, is the multiplicity of ways of access and the odd juxtapositions to which they give rise. One man enters by the gate marked "electronics" and ends up wrestling with schedules of reinforcement. The psychologist is called upon to adjudicate, or at least to have an opinion, about IC, transformational and stratificational language models. And it is not long before the inherent logic of the situation drives the conscientious language teacher—to cite a humble example—to familiarize himself with the reactivity of the basilar membrane and the Weltanschauung of the Hopi Indians.

This multiplicity gives rise to heady sensations. Amidst the plethora of investigations and reports, one has the feeling that basic problems are being resolved, fundamental options being clarified, and clear guidelines for enlightened practice being laid down.

The theme of my remarks can be encapsulated in a cautionary tale or anecdote. This past summer I was associated with a five-week seminar held in Germany for a mixed lot of experienced modern language teachers from the United States, Germany and Scandinavia. One purpose of the seminar was, banally enough, to survey the aspects and doctrines of linguistic and psychological theory that could illuminate the practice of foreign-language instruction. Verbal learning obviously fell into that category. Accordingly a psychologist from a German university read several papers summarizing, very competently indeed, the experimental literature on verbal learning and retention.

Our group learned or was reminded of the classic studies of massed vs. distributed practice, whole vs. part learning, mobilization and attention, proactive and retroactive inhibition, etc. A question from the floor on meaningfulness elicited a long but cogent explanation of mathematical information theory and the construction of texts showing successively higher degrees of statistical approximation to natural language.

Other questions followed. What were the optimal practice rhythms? How frequently should one revert to the same learning material? How much vocabulary should

14

one present at a single session? How could one count the bits of information in a foreign language text so as to dole out the suitable number of bits per unit time to the pupil? Ad infinitum.

The pattern of the lecturer's responses was set with his first answer. The facts and conclusions he had presented were derived from studies with meaningless CVC-syllables; the results, while suggestive, could not simply be taken over and applied in the language classroom or in the construction of language courses. Repeated questions from the audience met similar admirably cautious and professional disclaimers. In the end, whatever suggestive value the experimentation on paired-associate learning may have had for the assembled teachers was lost in their growing conviction that learning theory was no very useful guide to classroom practice.

On hearing such a tale--one that is surely not unique in its sort--the psychologist, according to his temperament, is likely to smile or squirm at the naiveté of the audience, at their search for the magic formula--the foolproof device from the man in the white coat. They just don't understand, he'll say, what psychology and psychological research is all about. This search for teaching panaceas is but one step removed from the folk superstition that looks to the psychologist for "five keys to successful living."

Well, yes and no. I can't help wondering whether this misconception on the part of the layman isn't in some measure matched by a subtler set of preconceptions on the part of the specialist, be he a linguist or a psychologist. True, the audience of teachers expected too much, on a far too <u>ad hoc</u> basis, from the lecturer. But I'm not sure that when he started his lecture series, he didn't, for his part, feel that paired-associate learning <u>was</u> the appropriate paradigm for second-language acquisition. In fact, from a few unguarded early remarks, I gather that he did: foreign language acquisition was for him mainly, or at least importantly, the matching of new foreign words with familiar native-language ones. If his audience was guilty of over-simplification, so was he. The only difference was that his vocabulary was more abstruse.

At this point, I'm sure, you're tempted to interject that our psychologist was not particularly well up on

15

psycholinguistics and that few American students of verbal behaviour still entertain such primitive notions.

Perhaps. But, even then, is it so certain that one is avoiding the twin dangers of synecdoche and inadequate specification?

By "synecdoche" I mean the tendency to take the part for the whole, a valid poetic and rhetorical device, certainly, but a dangerous one in the sciences. The researcher, confronted with the booming, buzzing confusion of the phenomenal world, posits certain hypotheses, establishes certain categories of observation and modes of analysis as convenient devices permitting an initial organization of data. At the start, the partial, contingent nature of the guiding hypotheses may be recognized; but as they give results, as other investigators adopt them, as the framework for widening explorations of the domain, their contingent nature is lost sight of. It is not that the investigator feels that all questions have been answered; otherwise he would not be investigating. But inplicit in his work is the assumption that what he finds will be of the same sort as what the controlling hypotheses have already made it possible to discover. And, in fact, what he does discover is of the same sort, because that's what he was looking for. Reinforcement strengthens response and eventually a resonating system of research and confirmatory findings is set up that quite drowns out the still small voice of doubt about the universality of the explanation given.

The lecturer whom I have chosen as a monitory example did, I think, tacitly equate paired-associate learning with verbal behavior generally, and only when the teachers assailed him with their admittedly naive questions--but questions arising from an intimate if unsystematic experience of language-learning behavior--was he to some extent jolted from his dogmatic slumbers.

One may smile at his discomfiture. But does not the interpretation of verbal behavior in terms of operant conditioning represent a similar, if less gross, mistaking of the part for the whole? The elegance, imaginativeness and precision of the experimental technique associated with operant-conditioning research have given it wide authority, and for a time permitted it to overflow its

banks, so to speak, and flood the entire field of verbal
behavior. Chomsky's 1959 review marks a reaction that in
retrospect was inherent in the situation. It's the voice
of outraged intuition protesting against the credo qui
absurdum.

Another example of synecdoche is provided by the
interpretations that have been made of the semantic
differential, and the uses to which it has been put. It
represents a significant stride forward in the techniques
for objectively evaluating the affective, noncognitive
connotations of words. But in the heady enthusiasm engen-
dered by this advance, many have identified affective
meaning with meaning überhaupt and lost sight of the
necessary distinction between denotation and connotation.

Decades ago, cognition, plan-making, intuition and
other hypothesized mechanisms of the little black box were
expelled first from psychology and then from linguistics.
We are now witnessing their triumphant return under the
banner of, say, Bruner, Miller and the transformationalists.
But hybris follows in the train of too glorious a triumph.
It seems to me that if the proselytizing zeal of the
transformationalists will allow us, we must, for the fore-
seeable future live with a dual interpretation of verbal
behavior; we don't, after all, accuse physicists of flaccid
eclecticism simply because they are obliged for the time
being to put up with the dual interpretation of light as
wave and quantum.

I see--only dimly yet, I confess--these two explanations operating at different levels--or on different
substances? At a molar level one would have transformational analysis, explaining the individual's capacity for
language and providing the plan, the rationale by which
he generates utterances. And at the molecular level,
exploring the immanent contingencies, the probabilistic
constraints that control the moment-to-moment verbal
behavior of the individual, one would have the "psychological", "behavioristic", operant-conditioning analysis.
I throw out for your consideration the possibility that
the transformational analysis is the appropriate one for
language as langue, whereas the behavioral one more faith-
fully reflects the reality of language as parole.

By way of parenthesis, let me state that I am far from being convinced of the psychological reality of the transformational system. Experiments have been performed to demonstrate this reality--for example, by means of the increased latency accompanying multiple, as against single, transformations. But to my knowledge, none has been reported that is not capable of an alternate interpretation in probabilistic terms, that is, in terms of the relative degree of prior conditioning. Transformational grammar represents, I suggest, a convincing statement--<u>ex post facto</u> and therefore capable of neat and compact formation-- of the rules that the speaking subject has internalized and that make speech possible. But I have not been able to get a clear indication from a practitioner of the trans- formational art whether or not his long sequences of rules, carefully pruned with Occam's razor, were intended to represent steps actually gone through by the speaking subject each time he generated an utterance. If that is indeed the claim, then in the name of the same intuition that plays so large a role in transformational theory as the judge of grammaticality, I protest.

All these considerations serve as parerga to my main point: unless we restrain transformational theory to the sphere where its application is licit and necessary, it will make, and for a time succeed in imposing, the same claim to absolute universality as the theories it presently derides.

As Barrutia points out in a recent <u>IRAL</u> article, we are already beginning to feel the impact of transforma- tional grammar in the resurgence of pedagogical doctrines of questionable validity. Specifically, we are hearing arguments in favor of abandoning inductive, discovery procedures in second-language instruction in favor of a deductive, rule-oriented exposition. To my knowledge the experimental evidence in favor of discovery learning was not suddenly annulled with the advent of transformational grammar. The insight into deep grammar that transformation provides has been a source of great and legitimate excite- ment: to some it has come with the force of revelation. But this same excitement, this Lucretian sense of having burst out to the <u>flammantia moenia mundi</u>, engenders a kind of coronal effect, a blurring of the vision for distinc- tions and appropriate spheres. The arrival of the New Testament should not cause us to forget or ignore the Old.

So much for now about the perils of synecdoche. As you may remember, I coupled them with those of inadequate specification, which, paradoxically enough, can also be labelled inadequate generalisability. I approach this phase of the discussion with the mixed feelings of the man who sharply feels the problem but has no reasonable solution to offer.

Let me present to you the terms of my antinomy.

You will remember that when pressed for specific pedagogical recommendations our German lecturer took refuge in the impossibility of generalizing his data. The plain fact of the matter is that practically all "pure", current laboratory research in psychology is capable of only the most limited generalization or transfer. This is so for necessary and obvious reasons, inherent in the nature of psychology as an experimental science. To achieve meaningful results in the laboratory, one simply has to eliminate or cancel out variables extraneous to those one is investigating. As with the immense body of work on paired-associate learning, one achieves results that are clean but of limited applicability because they fail to take into account the specifics of the pedagogical situation, for example. Hence my use of the term "inadequate specification."

At the other end of the spectrum we have "educational research," so called, that tries to come to terms with the experiential reality of the classroom, with its alarmingly uncountable interweaving of variables. I'm not betraying any secret, I think, if I suggest that such research all too often suffers from the fault of excessive specification. The ambitious project aimed at comparing the efficacy of programmed and traditional instruction ends up as a comparison of one particular teaching program, warts and all, with one particular textbook in one particular school with one or more extremely particular teachers, again warts and all.

Now if one approached the laboratory psychologist and said: "I've seen your results on the practice and retention of nonsense syllables and I should be most grateful for equivalent data on second-language vocabulary items," I rather imagine the answer would be either, "Life

19

is short and art is long," or else, "All right, provided we limit ourselves to CVC combinations having no cognates in the subject's native tongue."

In trying to visualize the response of educational researchers to an equivalent request, I cannot help thinking, grimly, of a footnote to a paper I read some time ago. Though the details have grown vague, the paper described, I think, a controlled investigation with foreign-language school classes to help determine the optimal ratio of language-laboratory to classroom instruction. In his introduction the author briefly discussed the independent variables--the place of laboratory drill before, during or after the class session, the type of drill, etc.--that were involved in the investigation. And in his footnote appeared the observation that the permutations and combinations of the variables described constituted a total of 1024--at least I think it was 1024--different instructional patterns, each of which would have to be explored singly and in comparison with the others in order to arrive at a satisfactory answer to the question: how much laboratory drill where and when. With seemly modesty the author went on to say that his present paper represented an attempt to provide a partial comparison of the first two or three of these thousand-odd situations. One admires his unflappability, his tranquil assurance that others will join him in the patient exploration of this labyrinth. Nonetheless, the mind boggles, particularly when one reflects that once the task was done, one would need only introduce a differently-structured laboratory drill program in order to generate another 1024 explorable situations that might or might not parallel the first set.

Seriously, though, I don't think I'm overstating the point if I say that the experimental psychologist tends to provide masses of precise information of uncertain practical relevance, while the educational researcher provides masses of relevant information of uncertain validity.

Large areas of teaching and learning as they are currently organized are still inaccessible to systematic analysis and control. That fact, as much as any real or fancied superiority in the results, helps explain the intense current interest in self-instructional and computer-controlled learning programs. In that way at least, some of the pesky variables represented by the teacher, and the social interactions of the class are eliminated, and, in general, the learning steps themselves become more transparent, more amenable to examination.

Let me play the devil's advocate, though, by suggesting that this revolutionary reorganization of the educational process, while it may simplify, does not abolish the problem of ameliorating teaching strategies. Teaching is going on in accordance with an explicit algorithm, but the algorithm itself had to be developed. And at some point a human programmer has been making decisions, hosts of decisions, from the wording of the learning step to the criteria for acceptability of response, that in the final analysis depend on what he knows experimentally or what, like most teachers and course writers, he can plausibly guess about the most effective combination of learning factors for the subject matter in question and the individuals for which it is intended. The assumptions and corollaries of such an algorithm have to be all the more explicit and all the more complete in that the pedagogy has to be built in in advance. Although I know cynics who would dispute this, a human teacher can in general reprogram himself more expeditiously than one can a teaching program.

In any case, even if we advance fully into the Brave New World of educational technology, we shall not thereby be able to evade the need for the kind of experimental information on learning factors that reflects the constraints and contingencies of the subject matter and the specific learning milieu.

I've argued in this paper that such information is unavailable to the language teacher in much greater measure than is generally recognized, and I've pointed out that neither from educational research nor from experimental psychology has he got the kind of guidance that he looks for. The difficulties of emerging with clean experimental results from the complex field of the foreign language class, with its variegated learning tasks spread out over a long temporal trajectory, are such as to give pause to the stoutest. Salvation must come, I feel, from the experimental psychologist rather than the educational researcher; and in spite of all the difficulties on which I've been dwelling, the prognosis is undoubtedly favorable. It's favorable because certain prerequisites are gradually being met.

In the first place, the student of verbal behavior is acquiring, through close interdisciplinary association with linguists, a much more nuanced and sophisticated view of the nature of the language system.

Secondly, this growing awareness of the complexities of language has endowed various sub-areas of the field with a heightened theoretic interest. The road to central insights into cognition and behavior now leads through such matters as first- and second-language acquisition, aphasia, stuttering, learning to read—to name only a random few. One can give oneself over to these and similar pursuits without having to fear a loss of prestige and with good hope of a significant contribution.

And, finally, I suppose one should mention the quantum advances in experimental equipment and techniques that make it feasible to attack ever more complex functions. It's a reciprocal process. An interest in second-language learning makes it desirable to develop an instrument like the Speech Auto-Instructional Device here at the CRLLB. And the SAID device itself now promises a rich reward in the way of precise information about speech behavior in general.

With so many conditions being met it would be churlish to ask for more. Yet let me give voice to one further desideratum: that the man pursuing research pertinent to second-language learning, for example, occasionally make contact by visiting and sitting in on a language class or program. Some fresh, first-hand experience of the realities of a more or less loosely structured learning situation can prove a useful corrective and spur to laboratory experiment. I was much cheered by the work described in a recent progress report of this Center, for which videotape recordings of actual class sessions provided the starting point. It's a precedent that could and should be generalized.

I trust I'm not being unduly sanguine if I see in the Center, whose creation we are here celebrating, the place where my optimism will be justified, where theory and practice join hands, and where intellectus becomes sapientia. Or let me be less flowery but more realistic by saying that, like Voltaire's God, if the CRLLB hadn't existed, it would have been necessary to invent it. For only out of such an intimate conjugation of specialists whose competence and interests span the huge and diverse domain that is language can we look for the emerging synthesis that does justice to the need to understand the complexity of language and the need to use these insights to better the human condition.

* * * * *

My last utterances sound suspiciously like a peroration--as they were intended to. But in the age of the New Yorker and the "whimper, not the bang", perorations can be disconcerting. Let me dissipate the effect by proposing a weighty problem for your consideration.

It concerns the name of the new Center. I am, myself, a partisan of pronounceable acronyms, as my editorship of IRAL, and my position with SHAPE should demonstrate, if not my directorship of the SKF (or "skuffy"?).

Now, when I look at the monogram of this Center, I'm perplexed. How the devil are we supposed to pronounce the damned thing? C-R-L-L-B is much too ponderous and circumstantial. Several possibilities suggest themselves, which I propose to you with annotations.

First, and most unlikely, is the Welsh interpretation, that takes the double -l as the sign for the unvoiced monolateral fricative--[krəɬb] or [kərɬb].

Using [r] as a syllabic nucleus as in Sanskrit, Czech or Serbian, we emerge with [kr̩lb].

Or perhaps we should do homage to one of the scholars with us today, the pioneer of psycholinguistics, the man who has made the seminal ideas of Benjamin Whorf available to us all. In that case, the name of the Center becomes Carrollbee.

Whatever our choice, whether among these or other possibilities, I adjure you, ladies and gentlemen, not to separate without agreeing on some common appellation.

Footnote

[1]The author is editor of IRAL (<u>International</u> <u>Review</u> <u>of</u> <u>Applied</u> <u>Linguistics</u>), director of SKF (Sprachkyberne-tisches Forschungszentrum) in Heidelberg, Germany, and Director of Education for SHAPE (Supreme Headquarters Allied Powers of Europe), located in Belgium.

KNOWING LANGUAGE AND GETTING TO KNOW IT[1]

Edward S. Klima[2]

This paper and the one by Ursula Bellugi, which
follows, form a unit. Our objective is to point out some
facts that we hope will be suggestive about the nature of
the grammar of a child's language. The modus operandi of
this paper will be to pose some linguistic questions that
clarify what we consider to be the main issues.

Now obviously, the goal of the child's acquisition of
a language--let's say English--is when he knows English.
But what do we mean when we say: "John Smith knows
English"? What is involved in this concept of knowing a
language? Knowing English is not the same thing as knowing some text by heart. Knowing Sanskrit is a different
thing from knowing the Veda. The thing known--when we
speak of knowing the Veda--is a particular group of
objects, that is, sentences in a fixed order. The thing
known--when we speak of knowing English--is clearly not all
the sentences of English, for there are indefinitely many
of them. "Indefinitely many" is a radically different
thing from "a great many". Knowing English is not the
same thing as knowing the telephone directory--but it does
have certain things in common with knowing the system of
national phone listing by area code--where the first three
of the ten digits comprising the number refers to the area
and the rest to the local number. Take some listing like
617-267-6686: Edward S. Klima in the Boston area. In
anticipation of an analogy with natural language, consider
the complete number as the <u>form</u> of the listing and the
name and area as its <u>content</u> or meaning. Now, aside from
the national local number for information (555-1212
preceded by the area code), there is no predictability--no
direct relationship--between the <u>form</u> of the number and
its meaning; i.e., from some arbitrary number like
617-267-6686 one cannot, by some mental process, conclude:
Edward Klima in the Boston area. One has to know it as a
fact, look it up in a reverse phone book, or resort to the

vagaries of reality by dialing and, if there is an answer, asking under what name the phone is listed. I would probably answer "Ed Klima", rather than "Edward S. Klima", or, suspicious of your intent, I might say "None of your business". In neither case would my response yield what you were after. In fact, from any arbitrary ten-digit number, you can't even tell if there is such a listing. This is not to say that there is no information in the presence of 617 before the number. But this information amounts to no more than: "if there is such a listing then the party is in the greater Boston area". The nature of the information is similar to that of finding your name in a Chinese text, when you don't know Chinese. You might conclude that the sentence has something to do with you or, if you're a linguist, with the sounds of your name; but this does not constitute an understanding of the sense of the sentence. The listings in a national phone directory-- if there were one--do involve a system, but at the same time they are at heart a group of objects of finite number, i.e., a collection of listings with a system.

Now let's look at the English language. Again, as with the national telephone listings, we have a system-- and knowing English means knowing a system. But there is a difference between knowing the system in national telephone listings--which is a collection that involves a system--and knowing English, which is a system with indefinitely many objects, i.e., sentences, representing it.

That is, knowing a language represents competence in an infinite process. Symptomatic of this is the fact that indefinitely many novel sentences (ones you have never heard or spoken before) make sense in the same way as the finite number of sentences you have already heard or spoken. Language is creative within itself. Above and beyond this is individual creativity of expression-- creating around language. This is language in the hands of the poet, or the ordinary speaker as a poet. We shall not speak further about this aspect of linguistic behavior, though it is an important factor in child language, and a disturbing factor for a linguist attempting to characterize the child's grammar from his undifferentiated utterances.

Let us return now to language--for example, English-- as a system. The realizations of this system are English sentences. Recalling the analogy with telephone listings, consider the sentence also to be a form associated with a content, in this case the sound-structure of the sentence associated with the sense of the sentence. By the sense of a sentence I mean roughly all that the sentence has in common with the sentences it implies, independently of the circumstances under which it has been or might be uttered. For example, the sense of the sentence "Frankie has slain Johnnie" would contain all the semantic features that are contained in the sense of the sentence "Johnnie is dead". The linguistic system provides for the association of sound-structure and sense for each one of indefinitely many sentences. And a sentence has its appropriate sense, no matter what the situation is in which it is uttered. There is an expression in ordinary English which captures the notion of the autonomy of the sense of a sentence: we speak of sentences themselves as "making sense or not making sense". Provided that it is one of the indefinitely many realizations of the system, a sentence makes sense whether we've heard it before or not. Of course, the hearer can make sense out of what he assumes to be an intended sentence, with varying ease, depending on its degree of predictability, from, among other things, the system we are referring to as the English language. Jabberwocky does not make sense, which is not to say that the sound of the words and their familiar grammatical endings, like your own name in a Chinese text, do not yield information. But one can certainly make some sense out of Jabberwocky. Of course, to some degree and at some level we have to make sense out of every sentence we hear. For example, in understanding any given utterance of "Frankie has slain Johnnie", the association of the utterance with the sound-structure of a sentence means making sense out of a unique stretch of accoustical effects. But this is a matter of our more inclusive total linguistic competence. In the remarks that follow we restrict ourselves to just one aspect of total linguistic competence. We restrict ourselves to the competence involved in the association of sound-structure and sense in any one of the indefinitely many sentences representative of the English language. We might call this grammatical competence. Knowing English, then, is having grammatic competence in English, in this sense.

Let us now consider some superficial characteristics of the realizations (i.e., the sentences) of the system one knows when one knows English.

As examples, look at the following sentences:

1. Frankie has slain Johnnie.
2. You think Frankie has slain Johnnie.
3. Frankie's friends think that you think Frankie has slain Johnnie.
4. Is it Johnnie you think Frankie has slain?
5. Johnnie has slain Frankie.

Let's say that the sense of (1) and (2) are something like the following:

6.

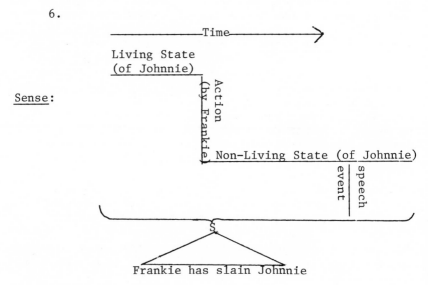

Frankie has slain Johnnie

Sound-structure

7.

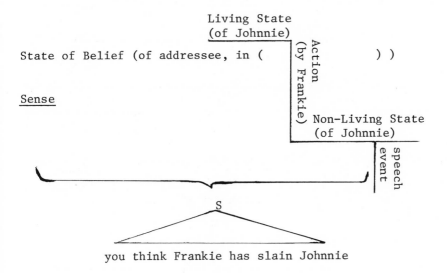

Sense

you think Frankie has slain Johnnie

Sound-structure

The second and third sentences indicate that one sentence may contain another sentence, which itself may contain a sentence, and so on indefinitely.

A comparison of sentences (1) and (5) indicates that the order of forms in the sound structure is related to the sense of the sentence.

Sentence (4) indicates that the occurrence of forms and their order is related not only to the sense of the sentence but also to one another--presenting a complicated interrelationship.

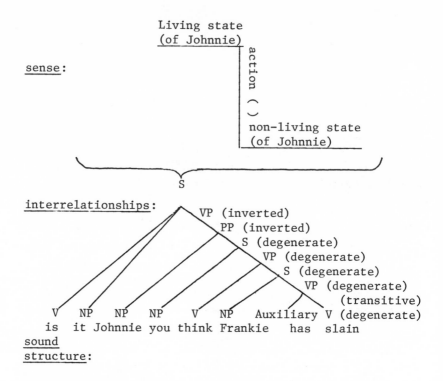

Consider the provisos on occurrence of elements, order, and relationship to sense when a sentence such as (4) ("Is it Johnnie that you think Frankie has slain") is viewed as a sequence of forms or even group of forms (i.e., even allowing some parsing).

A description of sentence (4) that would also apply to the other example sentences would go something like this:

A sentence may be a Noun Phrase (NP) followed by a Verb Phrase (VP) or it may be of the inverted type (the case at hand) with a Verb followed by a NP and a VP. The Verb is one of a small class including be and have. Provided the sentence is the inverted type and its Verb is be, the next constituent may be a NP which may be represented by it. The VP in an inverted type sentence with be as Verb, and it as NP may be a Predicate Phrase (PP) consisting of a NP followed by a degenerate

sentence which itself has a missing NP or which
includes a degenerate sentence with a missing NP.
The degenerate sentence may have a degenerate VP
consisting of a transitive Verb, like <u>slay</u>, in
which case the meaning of the verb is completed by
the Predicate Noun of the sentence.

The wider the range of sentences considered, the
more complex the interrelationship between occurrence of
forms, their order, and the sense of the sentence. The
significance of such a description, however, is that this
is the nature of such complexity when sentences are
considered as elements, or even groups of elements, in a
string. And, of course, the raw material which constitutes
the physical part of our utterances, and thus serves as the
source for the child's acquisition of English, is even less
differentiated.

Let us return to grammatical competence in English,
i.e., competence in the system which a child knows when he
has finally learned the English language. What is it then
to write a grammar of the English language? Writing a
grammar is an attempt, through explicit statement, to
capture the nature of this system--to crystalize the
general principles that account for the regularities in
the complex interrelationships mentioned above. Earlier,
we spoke of a sentence as the association of a sound-
structure and a sense. The language system is represented
by indefinitely many sentences. In this light a grammar
can be thought of as one part of a device which, if
presented with a sound-structure and a sense, can at
least answer the following questions about the sentencehood
of the pair: Is the putative sentence well-formed and, if
so, is the sound form well-matched with the sense? The
grammar, if it is to reflect the language system, must
have just the right machinery to generate, i.e., to account
for, the indefinitely many well-matched, well-formed
sentences, and only these.

Earlier, we spoke of the characteristics of the
sentences representing the system: the complex inter-
relation between the occurrence of forms, their order, and
the sense of the sentence and the fact that there are
indefinitely many sentences. The machinery of the grammar
(the finite set of rules and symbols) must be so conceived
as to account for these characteristics.

In current transformational grammars the principles of the interrelatedness exemplified by "Is it Johnnie you think Frankie has slain" are represented by assuming a binary structure for each sentence: there is an underlying structure which specifies (i.e., whose rules describe) the grammatical categories that occur in each sentence (e.g., Noun Phrase, i.e., Noun and accompanying Modifiers). The underlying structure also indicates the function of the categories (e.g., Subject of the Verb). It is the underlying structure that provides the basis for relating the meaning of the words to the sense of the sentence. There is, secondly, a transformational structure which, by a restricted set of rules of deletion and rearrangement of categories specified by the underlying structure, relates the sense of the sentence to its final shape.

So far we have spoken only about the system that the child eventually knows sometime before puberty. Let's turn now to questions pertaining to the grammar of a child's English at such and such a stage in learning English. Now the grammar of a child's English, as a representation of the aspects of the English language system he knows at a certain stage, i.e., as an indication of his grammatical competence, is clearly not a catalogue and systematization of everything he has uttered during that period. For, if factors outside the linguistic system tint everything uttered by adults, then such factors must nearly adumbrate the language of children. If memory restricts the clausal complexity of adult-uttered sentences, then the restricted word-length of the child's sentences is not surprising. Add to this the fleeting span of interest and the small vocabulary. To attempt to delineate the grammatical competence of a child on the basis of what he utters, mutters and stutters is ambitious, to say the least.

Why not just suppose, a linguist might wonder, that the basic principles of language are there all the time-- all the basic categories and their functions, as well as all the relations that an underlying structure can have to the final form of the sentences--but that the child simply makes a lot of mistakes in associating the particular relationshpps between sense and sound-form that are correct for English. Take, for example, the relationship found in subject-verb inversion. English

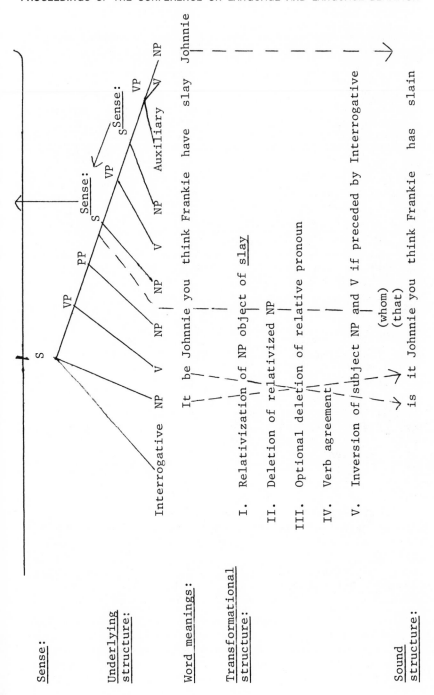

has subject-verb inversion with initial negatives and questions: "Never have I seen such a thing before", "Have I seen such a thing before?"; French has inversion with questions and with a certain class of adverbs but not with negatives; Russian does not obligatorily invert with either. The mechanism involved may well be general but its assignment to particular constructions seems to be language-dependent. Why not assume that the child has all the mechanisms but must learn their correct assignment? Who knows to what extent such an assumption may be true? But across the case studies of a variety of children, there are certain regularities, in the form of systematic errors and lack of errors, that suggest that additional factors are operative. The variations in word order that we _might_ expect do not occur. The final shape of the sentence seems to relate first directly to the sense, in the very constructions like negation and interrogation where this is not the case in adult English. (See Ursula Bellugi for more information on this matter.) The progressive steps in learning the system are not random.

While it may not be possible to delineate the total grammatical competence of the child at any given point during the acquisition period, it is certainly possible to characterize the grammatical mechanisms underlying the systematic errors and to investigate what seems to be the systematic growth of grammatical complexity, i.e., the step-by-step increase in the complexity of the inter-relationship of occurrence of forms, their order, and their function (their contribution to the sense of the sentence). In a sense, the child is like a linguist, making and rejecting hypotheses about the language. However, there is a difference. After ten years of passionate hypothesizing, I still don't know the correct principles for an English _grammar_, whereas, after ten years, the child knows all the principles of the English _language_. The child obviously poses the right questions and in the right order. The child is an underage linguist-cool and systematic, and with all the right insights.

Footnotes

[1]This work was supported in part by the Joint Services Electronics Project under contract BA 36-039-AMC-03200(E), in part by The National Science Foundation Grant GP-2495, The National Institute of Health Grant MH 0473-05, The National Aeronautics and Space Administration Grant NSG-496, and the U. S. Air Force ESD contract AF 19(628-2487)

[2]The author is a member of the teaching-research faculty at Massachusetts Institute of Technology.

LINGUISTIC MECHANISMS UNDERLYING CHILD SPEECH[1]

Ursula Bellugi[2]

What do we mean when we say we are writing about the grammar of children's language, or even that we write a description of children's speech? First of all, it is fair to consider what psychologists before this last decade have been able to achieve in studies of child language. If one examines the child development texts, discussions of language development were in terms of counting parts of speech, number of words, mean utterance length, number of clauses, and so forth, as if each child sentence were the equivalent of an adult sentence with some omissions. With the advent of psycholinguistics a little more than ten years ago, and with recent strides made by transformational grammar in the direction of specifying precisely the character and the rules involved in language systems, we have been able to make a fresh start on all questions of language acquisition. We will try to provide an answer to the question we have raised by giving some examples of the process of analysis of child language.

Our data consist of the recorded speech of three children, each visited by a different observer in the home. We recorded interactions of mother and child, from two to four hours per month over a period of one to three years. Our starting point was the period when children began to produce structured utterances. The children were unacquainted, the families never encountered one another. Our methods have included investigation of comprehension of grammatical constructions by testing and by examining aspects of the mother-child interchange tracing developmentally stages of progress in the grammatical subsystems of the language and periodic total grammars of each child's speech.

Our general claim, and it is still in the form of a question, is that there is an orderly progression to grammatical development across children which may be represented by stages, and which is not precisely correlated with age, but, rather, with rate of development. This orderly development is not only represented in gradual accumulation of language abilities and in an orderly progression of milestones, but is reflected in syntactic regularities of children's language systems throughout the process of acquisition. These regularities may be thought of as the systems that children ascribe to language at various stages.

We are interested in describing and characterizing the stages of language acquisition, in investigating children's language abilities, and, eventually, in discovering something about the mechanisms which underly these linguistic abilities.

The early stages of language acquisition have been frequently described by Brown and Bellugi (1964), McNeill (1966), Slobin (1966), and others. And some aspects of the intermediate stages (for example, the period of development of transformational operations) have been considered by Brown (1966), Bellugi (1965), and Klima and Bellugi (1966) in papers on the development of negation and interrogation. We want to suggest some types of hypotheses which are beginning to emerge from these studies, and give some illustration of the process by which we study these problems. We will take two sets of facts about child language and discuss interpretations suggested by linguistic analysis.

"WHAT WE WILL PLAY WITH?"

If you listen carefully to the speech of children of three or four years of age, you may hear certain question forms like these:

What he can ride in?

What he wants?

Where I should put it?

Why he's doing it?

37

These questions, which form part of the record of child speech in our study, along with many other examples like them, have a common structural aspect which makes them different from questions an adult would ask. That is, in this set of questions, if an auxiliary verb is present it is in its normal sentence-order form, and is not inverted with the subject noun-phrase. As McNeill (1966) put it, these questions are only an inversion away from being well-formed.

The questions occurred to a varying degree in our three children, but, in general, there was a stage in the speech of each one of the children when the auxiliary verbs of wh word interrogatives were either missing, or present but non-inverted. At the same time, the children were producing questions with inverted auxiliary and noun-phrase components in another type of question, the yes/no question. So that we found at the same time:

Can he ride in a truck? and What he can ride in?

In older grammatical studies, these sentences could be catalogued, counted, and forgotten. Our effort has been to try to account for the particular form that children's questions take at a stage. In order to do that, it is necessary to examine other parts of the children's grammar at this period. We looked at yes/no questions, declarative sentences, development of tense marking, negativity, transitivity, the child's responses to adult questions, and so forth.

It must be clear that this form is not an imitation of the speech the child hears around him. An adult would not say, "What the words are doing?" During this period, when we asked the child to repeat sentences, he would often repeat the sentence filtered through his own rules.

Adult: "Adam, say what I say:

Where can I put them?"

Adam: "Where I can put them?"

It is not the case, as it seemed to be in an earlier stage, that the wh questions are simply an interrogative word before a sentence. The children did not produce

sentences like these, which are his questions without the
<u>wh</u> word:

> He can ride in.
>
> He wants.
>
> I should put it.
>
> We will play with.

Let us summarize the operations relevant to questions
which the child did perform at this stage. Well-formed
questions involve two operations (with a good deal of
complication and special consideration for adult English):
the inversion of the noun-phrase and the auxiliary of a
sentence, and an interrogative word associated with a
missing element which is being questioned. See Klima
(1964) or Brown (1966).

The children at this stage did invert noun-phrases and
auxiliary elements in <u>yes</u>/<u>no</u> questions (<u>Can I go out?</u>).
And they were not just producing interrogative words with
sentences attached, but, each time, a particular interrogative and a sentence with a missing element, as in
<u>What he wants</u>? These are the two basic operations
involved in the formation of questions.

Our suggestion is that the children are able at these
stages to perform the operations necessary for <u>yes</u>/<u>no</u>
questions and <u>wh</u> questions, but not when auxiliary inversion and <u>wh</u> preposing are both required. In other words,
there may be a limit, not only on the number of words in
a child's sentence at a particular stage, or on the number
of constituents a child's sentence may have, but on the
number of operations per sentence he can perform, as a
measure of permitted complexity in the relationship
between occurrence of the forms, their order and the sense
of the sentence. This is a suggested performance limit
to account for the shape of some of the children's
structures. It may not be a correct account but it is a
plausible hypothesis which could be checked and which <u>may</u>
begin to account for children's speech at varying stages.

At a later stage, at least with some of the children, a further variation appeared. Inversion appeared in the <u>wh</u>-word questions which were affirmative, but not in the negative <u>wh</u>-word questions (<u>Why can he go out</u>? but <u>Why he can't go out</u>?). We tested this by the following procedure. Using puppets, we asked the child to form <u>wh</u>-word questions, affirmative and negative, by giving him an instruction with an indirect (non-inverted) question. The game went like this (notice the order of the auxiliary verbs and noun-phrases in the question and the response):

Adult has a puppet in the shape of an Old Lady on her hand:

> "Adam, ask the Old Lady where she can find some toys."

Adam: "Old Lady, where can you find some toys?"

Adult: "Adam, ask the Old Lady why she can't run."

Adam: "Old Lady, why you can't run?"

We gave a mixed set of twenty questions to a child at this stage. In his responses, all affirmatives were inverted, all negatives were not. The interpretation again fits with the notion of a limit on the permitted complexity at one stage.

We could also test this notion in other ways. We could take sentences with operations which the child can perform separately at various stages and combine them to see whether this limit holds; for example, negative and passive, negative and relative, relative and passive, etc.

"ME AND HIM ARE FRIENDS"

OR A NOTE ON THE DEVELOPMENT OF CASE-MARKING

Let us look at another set of facts about children's language. Again at four years or so, you may hear sentences like the following, which were produced by our children:

Mom, me and Paul fight, huh?

He wants to do everything that me and Robin do.

Can me and him play with this?

Let us consider only children who have been exposed to what we might call "educated" English, for lack of a better term, so that we are not dealing with problems of dialect differences. In so-called educated English, of course, one finds pronouns in the nominative form in conjoined subject relations like these. We would say, if we would say anything of the sort, <u>Paul and I fight</u>, <u>Can he and I play with this</u>?, and so forth. The facts which we want to describe here are the occurrences of these types of sentences in the children's speech. In addition, we want to trace the occurrence of case-marking in children's speech as a developmental study.

What we are investigating here is a late-appearing problem, beyond anything so far discussed in our papers. These structures have appeared in two of the three children, but in the same non-changing form which is deviant from the educated English to which the children have been exposed. Once sentences of this sort (i.e., with objective case pronouns in conjoined noun-phrases) appeared, there were some examples in almost every session of speech. This "step" phenomenon has not been frequently discussed. In the children's productions, once a construction of a particular type appeared, it was often produced frequently and regularly for a period of time, and then perhaps replaced by a later form. This is characteristic of our data, and gives us some confidence that we are investigating some systematic aspects of child language, and not just random appearances of particular sentences.

<u>Characteristics in Adult Speech of Case-Marking</u>

First, we need to point to the reflexes in adult grammar of case-marking (let us consider only nominative and objective case here) and limit the discussion to the form of personal pronouns. There is little left to indicate case in English, although historically the system was richer. Among the personal pronouns, <u>you</u> does not change in form for nominative, objective, singular or plural. We have then:

Nominative	Objective
I, we	me, us
he, she	him, her
they	them

In adult English, it is obvious to all of us that the nominative form of a pronoun is used in subject relation of a sentence, and the objective form of a pronoun in object relation. Thus we have: I bumped her and She bumped me, not any variant like: I bumped she or Her bumped I, etc. Although this is the general rule (without defining here object relation, etc.), there are other considerations, as we can see if we examine the passive. Take the sentence: The dog bit me. It is clear that the dog is the subject and me is the object of the verb bit. These relations do not change when we passivize the sentence: The speaker is still the object of the biting dog, but the form of the pronoun has changed. That is, we do not say Me was bitten by the dog but rather I was bitten by the dog. As another example, it is not the case that all pronouns in subject position, or even in the position immediately before the verb, are in the nominative form. Consider: All of us are going and not All of we are going. Whatever rules and order of rules we establish for the single pronoun, however, would apply also to the conjoined pronoun. As we have suggested, in educated English, we would say: He and I were elected by the class, not Him and me were elected.

We are dealing with children whose input (or the language which they heard) is educated English, and whose constructions at a late specifiable stage are deviant in a particular way from this English.

What the Children Hear

The parents offered to the children sentences like:

Grandma and I are going to shop for socks for you.

Those sandwiches are for Papa and me.

> Baby Sarah wants some of your cake. Can she and I
> have some?

We need to note further, however, that these constructions in the speech addressed to the child were extremely
rare in our data. In 52 hours of recorded speech of
mother to child, there were no examples of a conjoined
subject noun-phrase in the mother's speech which gave
indication of case-marking. There were interchanges like
the following:

> Adam: "Can me and Robin share?"

> Mother: "Yes, you and Robin can share."

In this example, you does not give the child information
about nominative or objective case. The point of interest
here is that this construction seems to have a low
frequency in terms of the sentences the child hears
ordinarily. In our data the children's constructions of
this type are not imitations of adult structures, nor are
they corrected by the adult when produced. So, to
summarize, we are dealing with a construction in child
speech which is deviant from standard English, presumably
rarely heard in adult speech as input, but heard in
standard English form when it occurs. It occurs in the
same form, not like the adult form, in two of the children
at a relatively late stage of grammatical development.

It is possible to go beyond spontaneous speech in
investigating regularities of this sort, and we have begun
to construct tests which can be used with adults and
children to test for these syntactic phenomena. In the
meantime, we use the data from spontaneous interchanges
of mother and child to direct us in our search.

Characteristics of Children's Sentences

Let us take a set of child's sentences produced
during one period of his language development, and
examine grammatical aspects of these sentences and the
whole language system at the period which might lead us
to an interesting description of these facts.

> Me and Paul have string, huh?

43

Were me and Paul there?

That me and everybody's color.

Me and him are drum makers.

Me and Diandres are working, aren't we?

Can me and Robin share?

Me and you put the clay away because me and you were playing with it.

Without any further information we could not try to account in any serious way for the appearance of these sentences in the children's speech. We need to look beyond this set of sentences at at least the following grammatical information:

What other reflections of case-marking are evident in the children's sentences?

What reflections of singular-plural relationship hold?

Other aspects of sentence-conjoining?

Noun-phrase conjoining?

Complex noun-phrases?

How are these facts ordered with relation to other types of sentences, for example, transformations?

We can then begin to suggest alternative hypotheses to account for these phenomena and see what evidence there is for each. As an example, the objective case could be accounted for by:

1) the distance from the finite verb,

2) the position in the underlying string, and

3) appearance in conjoined noun-phrases.

What is the procedure of analysis? We looked at conjoined sentences in the children's speech, and found that the system of conjunction was already quite varied. Not only is there sentence conjunction (as in Cromer comes and Fraser comes, or You have one and I have one), but also constituent conjunction, and, specifically, noun-phrase conjunction. There are grammatical reasons to consider some of these examples as more than two separate sentences combined. Me and Robin are friends is not just a conjunction of I am friends/ a friend and Robin is friends/ a friend. The conjoined noun-phrase in this set of sentences always occurs with the appropriate plural or unmarked form of the verb. That is, there are no sentences of the form Me and Papa has some sale or Me and Robin is friend. To find out whether this is a reflection of a general rule or is specific to this type of construction, we looked at the rest of the children's sentences at this stage and found that almost invariably the subject and verb agreed in number, even with quantifiers like each, both, all. Notice the subject-verb agreement in:

He wants to do it.   Here they are.

Why doesn't he go?   Are they steam things?

Each one gets it.   We both have guns.

There are some special cases like complex noun-phrases: all of us do it; a pronoun with numerical adjectival noun-phrase, we two little gentlemen. Most of the children's sentences were of the form, "Me and proper noun," but there were some cases lik: Can me and him play with this? Me and him are drum makers. Some sentences in which there were constructions different from the basic subject-verb-object relationship were: Were me and Paul there? He wants to do everything that me and Robin do.

From this wider range of facts, what can we suggest about this particular construction in children's speech? Let us take three alternative hypotheses, and the evidence surrounding each.

1) We can suppose that the shape of these noun-phrases is motivated by the distance of the pronoun from the verb (that is, that only the pronoun immediately preceding the verb is in the nominative case). This

could not account for sentences like: <u>Can me and him play</u> <u>with it</u>? where the pronoun adjacent to the verb is also in the objective form.

2) Perhaps, only the pronoun as simple subject (and not as a member of a compound subject) occurs in the nominative case. As evidence against this notion we have complex constructions like: <u>We two little gentlemen</u> and <u>All of us do it</u>.

3) We would see that the facts suggest that these particular case-markings are related to noun-phrase conjoining specifically, before transformational operations on the noun-phrase constituent take place. Notice that the conjoined noun-phrase operates as a single constituent in the following sentences:

<u>Can me and him play</u>?

<u>He wants to do everything that me and Robin do</u>.

<u>Could we have juice, me and Ursula</u>?

What we have suggested here is one sort of system the child may have postulated on his road to mastering the language. To put this in a little more focus, we would like to outline some stages toward this late development in child speech, to clarify that none of the linguistic concepts can be taken for granted (like pronominalization, case-marking, transitivity, and the like), but must be demonstrated developmentally as a part of the child's linguistic capacities.

A brief statement on the development of case-marking is appropriate now. Children and the adults near to them often avoid certain grammatical complications at the onset of structured speech by using proper names instead of pronouns. The child often refers to himself with his own name, and the mother does the same, so that one finds interchanges like:

Adam: "Adam want milk."

Mother: "No, dear, Adam can't pour the milk yet. Let Mommy do it."

Adam: "Where Adam milk go?"

Among other linguistic problems this circumvents
(while the mother wipes up the milk from the floor) is the
problem of case-marking. At this stage, the child may say
both <u>Adam watch</u> and <u>Watch Adam</u>. These sentences have at
least two quite distinct meanings, although the words are
the same. We can infer that the child has notions of
"subject of" and "object of" from sentences like these
used appropriately.

At a later stage, once the child has learned to
overcome the linguistic problems relevant to pronouns, we
find a new version of these sentences, namely, <u>I watch</u>
and <u>watch me</u>, where <u>I/me</u> have the same meaning, but two
variants, depending probably on the position before or
after a verb.

At a still later point in the developmental sequence,
we found an interesting regularity reflected in all three
children. Each had some instances of questions of the
form to be considered, but not all the questions were of
this form. We found:

What me fold?

Why me careless?

Why me got some chocolate?

Where me sleep?

Why me sitting on it?

During this same period, any pronoun which occurred
as sentence initial (disregarding adverbs, vocatives, and
so forth) was in the nominative form. Any pronoun which
appeared after a major constituent of the sentence was in
the objective form (where major constituent includes verb,
<u>wh</u> interrogative word). So that we found sentences like:
<u>Ready me go</u>? <u>Let me do it</u>. <u>Paul push me</u>. <u>Give me some</u>.
And the type discussed above: <u>Why me break it</u>?

At this point we might consider that the children
have revised their original simple notion about case-marking and replaced it with a slightly more complicated form.
This is at least a way of accounting for the shape of
children's sentences at this stage. It is still a long

way from the complexity we have suggested in the child's system of case-marking for conjoined noun-phrases. (During these early periods there is no evidence of sentence or noun-phrase conjoining in the children's utterances.)

We have considered some steps in the child's development of case-marking as a set of changing hypotheses about the structure of the language they are hearing. Roughly, the first may be something like the following: pronoun is nominative if first in the sentence. The second is not very different, but includes further analysis of sentential elements. That is, pronoun is nominative if first in the sentence, where "sentence" does not include adverbs or vocatives, but does include the interrogative word. (There are independent reasons to consider the interrogative word as part of the analysis of sentence at this period, so that this explanation is not ad hoc.) The third hypothesis we discussed occurs as a very late development in children's grammar (one could discern a number of steps in between). This is after indirect questions, direct questions, relative clauses, negatives and so forth have appeared in the children's speech. At this point we would have to consider the child's hypothesis as considerably changed. The relationship of the position and form of the pronoun to its function (and thus to its meaning) is more complex. This complexity is reflected by the assumption of several intervening operations: adverb and question-word proposing, subject-verb inversion. But the nominative form of the pronoun has not yet been extended to the conjoined noun-phrase. We could say that there is a special constituent, a conjoined noun-phrase constituent, which has the marker plural, and which promotes the objective case. We are suggesting here, as a very preliminary hypothesis, that the child's language system develops as a function of increasing conditions on the applicability of rules. What we are groping for is some systematic statement of the step-by-step increase in the complexity of the interrelationship of the occurrence of the pronoun, its form, its position, and its contribution to the sense of the sentence in the spirit of these notions, as mentioned in the preceding paper.

SUMMARY

We have been discussing language acquisition in terms
of new approaches to linguistic theory. Our attempt has
been to account for and describe the particular systematic
regularities found in successive stages in children's
speech. In part, this paper is meant to be an illustration
of the psycholinguistic process as applied to child
language.

We have suggested an accounting for the shape of
children's questions at the stage of: "What I will read?
as a limit on the complexity of a string at a particular
stage.

We discussed very briefly the development of case-
marking in children's grammar, and suggested a preliminary
accounting in terms of increased conditions on the
applicability of rules.

It should be clear that we are only at the beginning
of serious studies of development of language in children.
To account for steps in language development, it must be
obvious that we need more than the notions which have
seemed crucial in the past: imitation, habit-strength,
reinforcement, corrections by parents, frequency, and
expansions. Our emphasis has been on descriptions of the
children's systematizations of language and the milestones
of language development which these reflect.

References

Bellugi, Ursula. The development of interrogative
    structures in children's speech. In K. F. Riegal
    (Ed.) The development of language functions.
    Report No. 8 of Univer. of Mich. Center for Human
    Growth and Development, Nov. 30, 1965, pp. 103-137.

Brown, Roger. The dialogue in early childhood. Paper
    presented at A. P. A. meetings, Sept., 1966,
    manuscript.

Brown, Roger and Bellugi, Ursula. Three processes in the child's acquisition of syntax. In E. H. Lenneberg (Ed.) New directions in the study of language. Cambridge, Mass.: M. I. T. Press, 1964, pp. 131-162.

Klima, Edward S. Negation in English. In J. A. Fodor and J. J. Katz (Eds.) The structure of language. Englewood Cliffs, N. J.: Prentice-Hall, 1964, pp. 246-323.

Klima, Edward S. and Bellugi, Ursula. Syntactic regularities in children's speech. In Proceedings of the Edinburgh Symposium on Psycholinguistics, Edinburgh, Scotland: Univer. of Edinburgh Press (in press, 1966).

McNeill, David. Developmental psycholinguistics. In F. Smith and G. A. Miller (Eds.) The genesis of language: a psycholinguistic approach. Cambridge, Mass.: M. I. T. Press, 1966.

Slobin, Dan I. The acquisition of Russian as a native language. In Smith and Miller. The genesis of language.

Footnotes

[1] The Language Acquisition Project is supported by Public Health Service Research Grant MH-7088 from the National Institute of Health, under the direction of Professor Roger Brown.

[2] The author of this paper is a member of the Psychology Department faculty at Harvard University.

WHAT DOES A CHILD MEAN WHEN HE SAYS "NO"?[1]

David McNeill and Nobuko B. McNeill[2]

The emergence of negation in English is a portrait of a child's resolution of complexity. Very roughly, negation in English requires two transformations--one to remove an underlying negative element from where it is located in the deep structure of a sentence, and the other to introduce an auxiliary verb (do or can) to support this element in the surface structure (Klima, 1964). This sketch omits most significant matters, but it reveals an important part of what a child must acquire in order to negate in the English manner.

One hypothesis about language acquisition is that it rests on a set of specific cognitive capacities. These may be innate and may be described by the so-called theory of grammar, or linguistic theory (Chomsky, 1965; Katz, 1966; McNeill, in press). The suggestion is that the universal form of language reflects children's capacity for language--language has the form described by the theory of grammar because of the innate capacities of children to acquire language. Children's capacities everywhere in the world impose the same features on language, which, therefore, appear as linguistic universals.

An advantage of this view is that it accounts for the existence of linguistic abstractions, features in adult grammar that are never included in the overt forms of speech. Such features, of course, cannot be presented to children; yet, they exist as a part of adult linguistic knowledge. On the capacity hypothesis, such abstractions are held to be linguistic universal, deriving from children's capacity for language, and they are made abstract through the acquisition of transformations.

An example of a linguistic abstraction, never
presented as an overt form of speech, is the location of
NEG at the beginning of the deep structure of English
sentences. On the capacity hypothesis, this abstraction
is <u>possible</u> because the location of NEG on the boundary of
a sentence reflects an aspect of children's capacity for
language. The principle would be, roughly, that every
proposition can be denied by attaching to it a minus sign.

In this light, it is interesting that Bellugi (1964)
finds the earliest negative sentences from children to be
NEG + S and S + NEG--i.e., sentences in which a negative
element (usually <u>no</u> or <u>not</u>) is placed outside an otherwise
affirmative sentence. Examples are <u>no drop mitten</u>, and
<u>wear mitten no</u>. This form of negation persists until a
child shows independent evidence of having the two transformations mentioned above, at which time it completely
disappears--having now presumably become abstract (McNeill,
1966). The same is true of the primitive negation of
children learning Russian (Slobin, 1966) and French (our
records).

The Syntax of Negation in Japanese

We mention these findings with children exposed to
English and other languages in order to compare them to
the development of negation in Japanese. Syntactically,
negation in Japanese is rather simple. Except for order,
the relevant part of the deep structure is identical to
the deep structure of English sentences:

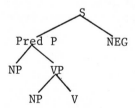

In Japanese, however, there are <u>no</u> order-changing transformations involved in carrying the negative aspect of
this structure to the surface. The surface structure of
a negative Japanese sentence is also <u>NP NP V NEG</u>. On the
capacity hypothesis, therefore, the development of negation
in Japanese should be likewise simple. Indeed, on the
capacity hypothesis, Japanese children should not be <u>able</u>
to make syntactic errors.

We thus take it to be consistent with the English
findings and the capacity hypothesis that neither of the
two children we have been following has <u>ever</u> uttered a
grammatically-deviant negative. Their negative sentences
are identical to some of the negatives that Bellugi
described, i.e., S + NEG, and this is entirely correct in
Japanese.

Syntactically, the development of negation thus poses
no problem in Japanese. The language does not require
more from children than is already available in their
general capacity for negation. In Japanese, the problem
is of a different sort.

The Semantics of Negation in Japanese

Although syntactically simple, negation in Japanese
is <u>semantically</u> complex. In contrast to English, for
example, the language provides several distinct forms; it
is here that one can gain some insight into the process of
development.

There are four common forms of negation in Japanese:
<u>nai</u> (aux), <u>nai</u> (adj), <u>iya</u>, and <u>iiya</u>. <u>Nai</u> (aux) is the
form introduced into the phrase-marker given above. It
is attached both to verbs, as indicated, and to adjectives.
<u>Nai</u> (adj), like all adjectives in Japanese, has verbal
force, so that one can say, for example, <u>peace-nai</u>, meaning <u>there is no peace</u>. <u>Iya</u> stands alone, and means,
roughly, <u>I do not want</u>. <u>Iiya</u> also stands alone and means
that what was just said is wrong <u>and</u> something else is
right. There are other forms than these four, but they
are restricted to special situations--formal speech, for
example.

These four forms--<u>nai</u> (aux), <u>nai</u> (adj), <u>iya</u>, and
<u>iiya</u>--embody three dimensions of meaning. <u>Nai</u> (adj) is
used in such sentences as "there's not an apple here,"
said after someone has asked about a place where there is
no apple. The use of <u>nai</u> (adj), therefore, depends on the
<u>non-existence of objects and events</u>.

<u>Nai</u> (aux) is used in such a sentence as "that's not
an apple," said after someone else, pointing to a pear,
said, "that's an apple." The use of <u>nai</u> (aux), therefore,
depends on the <u>falsity of statements</u>.

Iya is used in such sentences as "no, I don't want an apple." Iya by itself conveys the idea of "I don't want," and its use, therefore, depends on internal desire, or the lack of it.

Iiya is used in such sentences as "No, I didn't have an apple, I had a pear." Contrastive stress can convey this idea in English: "No, I didn't have an apple, I had a pear." The import of iiya is that one alternative (already mentioned or somehow in mind) is false and another is true. We will call this type of negation entailment, since, in this case, the negation of one statement entails the truth of another.

The four kinds of negative in Japanese thus involve three dimensions, or contrasts: Entailment-Non-entailment, External-Internal, and Existence-Truth (the last to be understood as indicating the condition of negation--the existence, or lack of it, of some thing, versus the truth, or lack of it, of some sentence).

One can organize the dimensions of negation into a cube, always a mark of progress in this area, and locate the four negative terms in Japanese at the appropriate corners.

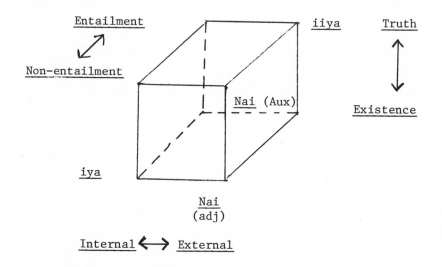

Alternatively, one can define the terms of negation in Japanese by means of feature matrices:

	Nai (adj)	Nai (aux)	Iya	Iiya
Existence	+	–	+	–
Entailment	–	–	–	+
External	+	+	–	+

According to these matrices, iya and iiya are diametrically-opposite kinds of negation, and the two kinds of nai are identical, except that one depends on the non-existence of objects and the other on the falsity of sentences. Both implications accord with native intuition.

The matrices also help explain what always strikes English speakers as a bit of oriental exotica when they first learn how Japanese affirm or deny negative questions. If someone asks, in English, "Is there no pear?" and you wish to give an affirmative answer, the correct response is "no, there is no pear," or some more idiomatic variant. In Japanese, however it is the reverse. If one wishes to give an affirmative answer, the reply should be, "Yes, there is no pear". A similar reversal exists for denial. In English it is "yes, there is a pear," but in Japanese it is "no, there is a pear."

The difference is that "yes" and "no" in Japanese are (–Existence), whereas "yes" and "no" in English are (+Existence). Thus, the Japanese "yes" refers to the truth-value of the sentence, whereas the English "yes" refers to the existence of the pear. Similarly for "no" in the two languages: in Japanese it signifies a false statement, whereas, in English it signifies non-existence.

The cube indicates that there are four other negatives possible but not used in Japanese. One, for example, would be a negative that denies the truth of statements on the grounds of internal desire, but which does not entail a true alternative. It would be a negative for existentialists: What you don't desire is false, but nothing in particular is thereby true. This is despair.

55

These three dimensions can be found in English negation also, but English is ambiguous with respect to them. The English "no" is (+Existence) when discussing the physical environment, but it becomes (-Existence) in other contexts: for example, "three plus two is six", "no". And when one says, "No, anything but that!", presumably the left side of the cube is evoked. But English does not have separate terms sorted out in the analytic Japanese manner. When a child says, for example, no dirty in English, he is at least four-ways, and possibly eight-ways, ambiguous.

Japanese, since it distinguishes among words along the three dimensions of negation, makes it possible to trace the order in which the dimensions emerge. We have looked for patterns of confusion--which negatives replace others--and from these patterns have attempted to infer the sequence of development. In effect, we have asked, how is the cube built up? Or, equivalently, in what order are the rows of the feature matrix added?

The Development of Negation in Japanese

We have worked with tape-recordings of the speech of two Japanese children. Both children are girls and both live in Tokyo. To date, there is some seven months' accumulation of speech. One of these children presents very little data, and what she does present so far eludes our understanding. The other child, whom we call Izanami, will be described here.

At 27 months, the youngest age at which we have recordings, three of the four negative forms occur. These are nai (adj), nai (aux), and iya. Iya is always used alone. Nai (adj) is used alone and after nouns, and both are correct syntactic contexts in Japanese. Nai (aux) is used with just one verb--shira-nai--meaning "I don't know".

Of the two forms abundantly present at 27 months, nai (adj) is always used when called for, as far as this can be judged from context. That is, whenever non-existence is referred to, Izanami uses nai (adj). Iya, however, is often replaced by nai (adj). For instance if Izanami's mother said, "Let's give you some," Izanami would sometimes apparently reply, "There's no giving," instead of "I don't want". Nai (adj) intruded thus into as many as 40 per cent of the contexts appropriate for iya. Iya, on the other hand, never intruded into contexts appropriate to nai (adj).

This pattern of confusion would arise if Izanami did not yet know any of the dimensions involved in negation, but reacted instead only to non-existence. Then nai (adj) would be used whenever called for, and iya (being in her vocabulary) would oscillate with nai (adj) in contexts calling for an expression of personal desire, but not involving non-existence. Let us assume then that Izanami began with the registration of simple non-existence as the occasion for negation. In effect, she began with the nai (adj) termini of each of the three dimensions, but did not yet have the dimensions themselves. She built from Existence, Non-entailment, and External. We have called this Stage 1.

About two months later, two things happened to iya. First, it began to appear in contexts calling for nai (aux). For example, if Izanami's mother said (falsely), "This is an apple," pointing to a pear, Izanami would reply with iya, apparently meaning "I don't want it." This is only apparently odd. We will return to it shortly. The second development with iya is that it began to appear in contexts calling for iiya.

The last intrusion, iya in place of iiya, is totally inexplicable on the feature analysis. These terms share no features--they are at opposite corners of the cube--and so should never be confused, so long as at least one dimension has been acquired. Moreover, iya has been present in Izanami's vocabulary since the beginning, but it appears in contexts calling for iiya only now, after two months. We are fairly certain, therefore, that the intrusion is the result of a new development.

Let us suppose that it is not iya but really iiya that appears in contexts calling for iiya. Vowel-vowel sequences are common in Japanese, but Izanami has none at this time. Since iya and iiya can be distinguished only through a difference in vowel length, it is at least possible that Izanami intends to say iiya, even though she

actually says iya. In support of this interpretation is
one further fact. From the beginning, nai (adj) has
appeared in contexts calling for iiya, but the intrusion
ends at this same time--again, indicating that Izanami has
acquired iiya. If we accept the interpretation that
Izanami says iya when she intends to say iiya, we can
conclude that Izanami has added the Existence-Truth, or
the Entailment-Non-entailment dimensions, or both.

Of the two, the evidence favors Existence-Truth.
Recall that contexts calling for nai (aux) begin taking
iya about this time. Instead of saying, "It's not an
apple," Izanami apparently says, "I don't want an apple."
However, if it is really iiya appearing in place of nai
(aux)--so that she is saying, "It's not an apple (but
something else)"--we then know that Izanami has acquired
the Existence-Truth contrast only. It could not have been
Entailment-Non-entailment because iiya and nai (aux) are
distinct on this feature--one being Entailment, the other
being Non-entailment. They could not be confused, if this
dimension had been acquired. However, they are alike on
Existence-Truth, both being marked for Truth, and so
could be confused if Izanami had acquired this dimension
alone.

Thus, the first dimension to emerge is Existence-
Truth, and its appearance marks Stage 2, at which time
Izanami's knowledge of negation presumably is as follows:

	Nai (adj)	Nai (aux)	iya	iiya
1. No contrasts				
2. Existence	+	-	+	-

Stage 3 took place two months later. The replacement
of iya by nai (adj), which had been present from the
beginning, stops altogether. Izanami no longer apparently
says, "There isn't an apple," when she should say, "I
don't want an apple." The new development must signify
acquisition of the External-Internal dimension, as well as
the virtually certain appearance of iya (as opposed to the
truncated iiya). No other possibility exists, given our
semantic analysis, since External-Internal is the only
dimension on which iya and nai (adj) contrast. There is
no problem here of distinguishing iya and iiya, of course,
since the observation involves the pronunciation (or lack

of it) of <u>nai</u>. For the same reason, no assumptions are
made about the meaning of <u>iya</u> when Izanami uses it, but
only about the existence of <u>iya</u>-contexts.

Thus, Izanami has two dimensions by Stage 3, and <u>iiya</u>
and <u>nai</u> (aux) are synonyms:

	nai (adj)	nai (aux)	iya	iiya
1. No contrasts				
2. Existence	+	−	+	−
3. External	+	+	−	+

About a month later, Izanami apparently acquired the
Entailment-Non-entailment dimension. The evidence is that
she distinguished <u>nai</u> (aux) from <u>iiya</u>, and so eliminated
the remaining confusion: (i)<u>iya</u> no longer appeared in
<u>nai</u> (aux) contexts. Thus, Izanami developed the entire
system of negation in Japanese in some five months' time.

At the moment that Entailment-Non-entailment emerged,
an interesting further development occurred. A new word,
<u>chigau</u>, appeared, and did so in considerable numbers. It
had been completely absent from Izanami's speech before
this time.

<u>Chigau</u> is not a negative. It is variously translated
as "different", "wrong", or "disagree"--and so is different
from such words as "no", "not", or "no-but". Syntactically, it is a verb.

However, Izanami uses <u>chigau</u> in none of the senses
just given. For her, <u>chigau</u> is an omnibus negative, used
in completely diverse contexts. It appears in situations
calling for <u>iiya</u> and <u>iya</u>--even though <u>iiya</u> and <u>iya</u> share
no features of negation at all--and possibly appears also
in contexts appropriate to <u>nai</u> (adj) and <u>nai</u> (aux),
although we have not observed this. If we assume that
Izanami's use of <u>chigau</u> has not demolished the system of
negation just developed--as, indeed, it apparently has
not, since she continues to use the four terms of negation
as well--we must conclude that <u>chigau</u> has negative import
but is marked on none of the dimensions of negation.
Thus, it appears in contexts calling for Truth as well as
Existence, External as well as Internal, and Entailment

as well as Non-entailment. In fact, Izanami's use of chigau resembles most closely the use of un-uh in English: "Do you want some?" "Un-uh"; "Did you have a pear?" "Un-uh, I had an apple"; "Springfield is the capitol of Massachusetts." "Un-uh"; "Does she have a wart on her nose?" "Un-uh". Un-uh, too, represents omnibus negation.

How are we to account for the sudden appearance of an omnibus negative? It seems most plausible to suppose that Izanam's use of chigau reflects the concept of negation, as opposed to the particular forms of denial (iya, nai (adj), etc.), or the particular dimensions of negation. As such, chigau adds the idea of general denial, as an abstract possibility, and so liberates negation from the semantic constraints represented in the three contrasts of Truth-Existence, External-Internal, and Entailment-Non-entailment.

However, the interesting fact is not so much that Izanami eventually developed a form of omnibus negation, but that she did so after having developed the various special forms of negation. For Izanami's parents' use chigau in the omnibus sense, too. Chigau, as a kind of featureless denial, has been presented to Izanami as a model throughout the five-month period we have studied (and doubtlessly before), yet Izanami resisted developing chigau precisely until she had acquired the last of the three contrasts of negation. On this evidence, generic negation is not primitive, as often claimed. It is, instead, a late development, constructed from, and possibly summarizing, the three features of negation discussed above. It is these features that are preliminary. If anything in Izanami's history of negation reflects some aspect of children's capacity for negation, it is the features of negation and not the general concept of denial.

We can summarize our findings, and answer the question, "What does a child mean when he says 'no'?", by setting down the following five points:

1. At first, Izanami had no features of negation at all. At this point "no" meant something did not exist, and nothing more. Subsequent development consisted of forming contrasts with the ends of the dimensions represented in nai (adj); that is, with Existence, External, and Non-entailment.

2. The first such contrast to emerge was between Existence and Truth. In addition to marking the existence and non-existence of events and objects, Izanami came to mark the correctness and incorrectness of statements. By Stage 2, "no" had come to mean false, as well as not here, creating an order of development that appears to be quite natural. Izanami judged relations about language only after she had judged other relations about the external world.

3. The next contrast to emerge was between External and Internal. Besides registering the non-existence of events, Izanami began to mark her desires concerning events. By Stage 3, "no" meant disapproval or rejection, as well as false and not here. Another direction of development, therefore, was from outside to inside, and this, too, seems to be in a natural order. Note that Izanami had the idea of linguistically registering the truth of statements before she had the idea of linguistically registering her inner states in relation to outer ones.

4. The last contrast to emerge was Entailment-Non-entailment. With this dimension, "no" also came to mean "no but," which requires an ability to organize statements into mutually exclusive pairs. Because Entailment-Non-entailment requires a child to hold in mind two propositions at once, it would naturally follow either of the other two contrasts, both of which involve judgments about single propositions or events.

5. The last step was the formation of an abstract concept of negation--the equivalent of un-uh. If chigau is a construction, its appearance last is also natural.

It is possible that these same steps, insofar as they follow a natural order, are also taken by English-speaking children. As pointed out above, the three dimensions of Japanese negation are used in English as well. Hopefully, future work will discover some way to investigate this possibility.

References

Bellugi, Ursula.   The emergence of inflections and negation
    systems in the speech of two children.   Paper pre-
    sented at New England Psychological Association, 1964.

Chomsky, N.   Aspects of the theory of syntax.   Cambridge,
    Mass.:   M.I.T. Press, 1966.

Katz, J. J.   The philosophy of language.   New York: Harper
    & Row, 1966.

Klima, E. S.   Negation in English.   In J. A. Fodor & J. J.
    Katz (Eds.), The structure of language.   Englewood-
    Cliffs, N. J.:   Prentice-Hall, 1964.

McNeill, D.   Developmental psycholinguistics.   In F. Smith
    & G. A. Miller (Eds.), The genesis of language: A
    psycholinguistic approach.   Cambridge, Mass.:   M.I.T.
    Press, 1966.

McNeill, D.   On theories of language acquisition.   In T.
    Dixon & D. Horton (Eds.), Verbal-behavior theory and
    its relation to S-R theory.   Englewood-Cliffs, N. J.:
    Prentice-Hall, (in press).

Slobin, D. I.   The acquisition of Russian as a native
    language.   In F. Smith and G. A. Miller (Eds.),
    The genesis of language: a psycholinguistic approach.
    Cambridge: M. I. T.   Press, 1966.

Footnotes

[1]This report is a slightly revised version of the
paper presented by the major author, David McNeill, at the
Conference on Language and Language Behavior. It is based
on research supported by a contract with the Office of
Education, U. S. Department of Health, Education & Welfare,
under provisions of P. L. 83-531, Cooperative Research,
and Title VI, P. L. 85-864, as amended.

[2]The authors are members of the research staff at the
CRLLB. Dr. McNeill is also a member of the University of
Michigan Psychology Department faculty.

LANGUAGE HABITS AND THE RECALL OF CONNECTED DISCOURSE[1]

Sheldon Rosenberg[2]

Evidence from developmental and linguistic studies
(McNeill, in press; Chomsky, 1965) suggests that when we
acquire a language, we acquire a system of phonological,
syntactic (grammatical), and semantic habits (or implicit
cognitive rules, as many psycholinguists would prefer to
call them). This system of habits represents the basic
linguistic competence that underlies our ability to speak
and understand a language. This is by no means the entire
story, however. Other language habits--some idiosyncratic,
such as those that characterize individual differences in
style, and some cultural, such as those that are revealed
by word-frequency counts and word-association norms--are
the result of experience in the use of a language. Habits
of the latter type and non-linguistic variables, such as
noise, the presence of appropriate objects in the environment, motivation, reinforcement, memory capacity and
physical health, act as constraints upon the use of our
basic linguistic competence in actual performance situations.

It should be clear, of course, that the term habit is
being used here in the very general sense of input-output
constraint, so as to include, for example, such phenomena
as simple word-class dependencies (e.g., adjective-noun)
and fundamental grammatical relations (e.g., subject-object,
main verb) under the same concept.

One of the most interesting sources of constraint
created by language habits is the result of the fact that
they are hierarchically organized. The hierarchic structure of language habits is reflected in the dependency
that exists between syntax and meaning. For example, the
sentences John hit Mary and Mary hit John differ in meaning, and the difference between them can be seen to be the
result of a difference in word order. In sentences of
this type, word-order is a fundamental, syntactic cue to

63

the identification of subject-object relations. A detailed
discussion of the relationship between syntax and meaning
can be found in Katz and Postal (1964).

A few examples will suffice to indicate the interest
that is developing in the study of the role of language
habits in verbal learning and verbal behavior. Underwood
(1965) has reviewed some of the work on the role of
language habits in traditional studies of rote verbal
learning, and Miller (1962) has reviewed some of the early
work on grammatical structure as a variable in language
processing. Miller and Isard (1963) have demonstrated the
importance of syntactic and semantic constraints in
sentence perception. Similarly, Marks and Miller (1964)
have shown the importance of syntactic and semantic
constraints in sentence memorization. Their findings, with
respect to the effects of syntactic habit, were confirmed
by Rosenberg (1966d), who found, in addition, that sentences that contain associatively-related words (as determined
from free-association norms) are easier to recall than
sentences that contain associatively-unrelated words.
Mehler (1963) has reported that transformed declarative
sentences are more difficult to memorize than active
declarative sentences, but his findings have been questioned by the results of research by Martin and Roberts (1966)
who used a different measure of sentence complexity.

Johnson (1965) raised the question of the "psychological reality" of linguistic phrase structure rules and
used a sentence-learning task to evaluate it. He reasoned
that if in processing a sentence the words are recoded
into noun- and verb-phrase units, the probability of making
a transitional error (TE) between phrases--the probability
of making an error on a word, given the preceding word in
a sentence is correct--should be greater than the probability of a TE within phrases. His data supported the
hypothesis. Other data presented by Johnson, and the
results of a subsequent study (Johnson, 1966) led him to
conclude that his results could not be accounted for in
terms of differential intra- and inter-phrase associative
constraints between the words in his sentences. He established (1966) an association between an adjective and a
noun (within phrase) and between a noun and a verb
(between phrase) prior to the learning of sentences that
contained these adjective-noun and noun-verb transitions.

Rosenberg (1967) argued, however, that Johnson's failure to find a significant effect of associative habit upon the probability of a TE at the phrase boundary may have resulted from the fact that the associations Johnson established in the laboratory were not as strong as the natural-language associations revealed by word-association norms. The results of Rosenberg's study confirmed his expectations: the probability of a TE between phrases was greater than the probability of a TE within phrases, only when the between-phrase transition was marked by a weak associative constraint. Controlled association norms were used by Rosenberg to vary associative strength. The results of Rosenberg's study suggested further that the presence of strong associative constraints between all of the words in a sentence makes it possible to process such sentences in units larger than the phrase.

From Johnson's and Rosenberg's research it is possible to conclude that phrase structure and associative habits interact with each other in determining the way in which the words in a sentence will be organized for recall. What is interesting about this conclusion is that it emphasizes the fact that language habits are organized on several levels of linguistic structure simultaneously.

While interest in the role of language habits at the level of the sentence is growing, psychologists have generally neglected the problem of connected discourse. The only consistent work in the area has been on the effects of approximation to the statistical structure of English (e.g., Miller and Selfridge, 1950; Lachman and Tuttle, 1965) upon the recall of passages. From a structural standpoint, connected discourse should arouse all of the habits that are aroused by sentence structure, but, in addition, such factors as serial organization of sentences, pronominalization and equivalence chains (Harris, 1952) should arouse habits that extend beyond the sentence. The term "equivalence chains" refers, among other things, to the presence of identical items in different sentences in a discourse. Recent research by Koen, Becker and Young (1967) has been concerned with identification of the cues that Ss use in discriminating paragraphs from nonparagraphs, and thus will be useful in identifying factors that arouse extra-sentence habits.

In an attempt to gain some understanding of the role of language habits in the recall of connected discourse, this writer has undertaken a series of investigations of the recall of associatively-related words embedded in connected discourse, some of which have already been completed (Rosenberg, 1966b, 1966c, forthcoming). The method used in most of these studies can best be described with reference to an example. The following two narratives--a high-association passage and a low-association passage--are modified versions of passages used previously.

High-Association Passage

It was a Sunday afternoon in March and the air was clear and brisk. The (man) walked to the corner to meet the <u>woman</u> who was looking at a <u>boy</u> and a <u>girl</u> across the way. After exchanging a few words, they went to a restaurant, and as they entered, they passed someone who was examining a (table), a <u>chair</u> and a <u>desk</u>, and someone with a <u>cloth</u>. After they ordered, there was time to look at a newspaper, where there was a story about a (king) and a <u>queen</u>. It concerned a <u>ruler</u> who had just been given a new <u>crown</u>. There was also a story about a (priest) whose <u>church</u> was in difficulty, which went on to discuss <u>God</u> and <u>religion</u>. The front page contained an item about a (lion) that had a fight with a <u>tiger</u> in a <u>zoo</u> and had its <u>mane</u> pulled. It also contained an article on (justice), <u>law</u> and <u>peace</u> written by a former <u>judge</u>. Their order arrived, and everything was good: the (cheese), the <u>bread</u>, the <u>crackers</u> and the <u>milk</u>. After they finished, they headed toward a (city) which was located near a <u>town</u> on the other side of the <u>state</u>. The <u>country</u> they passed through on the way was nice. When they arrived, they went directly to a (house) where a <u>home</u> used to be. They had to check up on the <u>roof</u> and the <u>garage</u>. There was a (river) nearby, and the <u>water</u> was visible on a clear day. A <u>lake</u> and a <u>stream</u> were nearby also. The caretaker was outside with a (hammer) and a <u>nail</u>. A <u>tool</u> of some sort and a <u>saw</u> were on the ground. There were some (shoes) on the grass, and there was dirt on the fellow's <u>feet</u>. His <u>socks</u> and <u>laces</u> were discolored. Someone had left a (needle), some <u>thread</u>,

a <u>pin</u> and their <u>sewing</u> about, and there were some
(kittens), <u>cats</u>, <u>dogs</u> and <u>mice</u> outside, as well.
It grew late and they decided to leave.

Low-Association Passage

It was a Sunday afternoon in March, and the air
was clear and brisk. The (man) walked to the corner
to meet the <u>guest</u> who was looking at a <u>horse</u> and a
<u>bird</u> across the way. After exchanging a few words,
they went to a restaurant, and as they entered, they
passed someone who was examining a (table), a <u>door</u>
and a <u>post</u>, and someone with a <u>glass</u>. After they
ordered, there was time to look at a newspaper,
where there was a story about a (king) and a <u>nurse</u>.
It concerned a <u>leader</u> who had just been given a
new <u>plane</u>. There was also a story about a (priest)
whose <u>friend</u> was in difficulty, which went on to
discuss <u>life</u> and <u>industry</u>. The front page contained
an item about a (lion) that had a fight with a <u>hound</u>
in a <u>pit</u> and had its <u>fuzz</u> pulled. It also contained
an article on (justice), <u>age</u> and <u>doubt</u>, written by a
former <u>sailor</u>. Their order arrived, and everything
was good: the (cheese), the <u>corn</u>, the <u>lettuce</u> and
the <u>fish</u>. After they finished, they headed toward a
(city) which was located near a <u>road</u> on the other
side of the <u>valley</u>. The <u>region</u> they passed through
on the way was nice. When they arrived, they went
directly to a (house) where a <u>store</u> used to be.
They had to check up on the <u>gate</u> and the <u>plaster</u>.
There was a (river) nearby, and the <u>forest</u> was
visible on a clear day. A <u>grave</u> and a <u>station</u> were
nearby also. The caretaker was outside with a
(hammer) and a <u>bell</u>. A <u>stem</u> of some sort and a <u>pan</u>
were on the ground. There were some (shoes) on the
grass, and there was dirt on the fellow's <u>porch</u>.
His <u>wrists</u> and <u>knees</u> were discolored. Someone had
left a (needle), some <u>metal</u>, a <u>hat</u> and their <u>violin</u>
about, and there were some (kittens), <u>guns</u>, <u>rocks</u>
and <u>oars</u> outside as well. It grew late and they
decided to leave.

Each passage contains the same context materials and
the same series of stimulus words selected from free-
association norms (e.g., Palermo and Jenkins, 1964). The
high-association passage contains response words that were
selected from the top of the associative hierarchies of

the stimulus words, while the low-association passage
contains response words that were selected from the bottom
of the associative hierarchies for the stimulus words. For
the reader's convenience, the stimulus words have been
placed in parentheses, and the response words have been
underlined. There are three response words for each
stimulus word, and, in all instances, the response words
are the items that follow the items in parentheses. In
general, high- and low-association responses are comparable
in length, in grammatical class and in Thorndike-Lorge
(1944) frequency. In addition, an attempt was made to
avoid semantic anomaly in the selection of low-association
items. It can be seen, however, that from the standpoint
of style and good English, the passages are awkward in
places. This situation was made necessary by the need to
control the variables that traditional studies of rote
verbal learning have demonstrated to be of importance.

In a typical study, one group of $\underline{S}$s is exposed to
the high-association passage and another group to the
low-association passage. There is only one exposure, and
it is followed immediately by a written recall test.

An important part of the studies that have been
conducted thus far was to collect "cloze" data on the
passages from $\underline{S}$s who had not participated in the recall
studies. In the cloze task, the stimulus words, the
response words, or both were deleted from the passages,
and the $\underline{S}$s' task was to try to guess the missing words on
the basis of the remaining context. The cloze data were
collected to reveal something of the strength of association between the stimulus and response words within the
context of the passages, and also to reveal something of
the strength of association between the context and the
critical stimulus and response words, so as to avoid the
situation in which high-association or low-association
items are favored by constraints from the context. As an
additional check upon the effect of context, list-learning
recall data were collected on the critical stimulus and
response words.

It was anticipated that associatively-related words
would be recalled better than associatively-unrelated
words. The rationale for this expectation was based not
only upon the result of research on the role of associations in learning word lists (Deese, 1959) and word pairs

(Rosenberg, 1965), but upon assumptions such as the following as well:

1. In decoding language materials, we tend to anticipate subsequent items, with the items anticipated being, in part, a function of associative constraints created by words that have already been decoded. For example, if we encounter man in decoding a discourse and anticipate woman, and woman actually occurs later on in the discourse, then woman has, theoretically, occurred twice instead of once. This "frequency" hypothesis predicts that recall of high-strength associates should be superior to recall of low-strength associates.

2. Miller (1956) has made us aware of the importance of "linguistic recoding" in verbal learning and verbal behavior, a phenomenon which has been studied extensively in the verbal learning laboratory (e.g., Rosenberg, 1966a). One of the implications of this notion is that associatively-related words occurring in connected discourse should to a certain extent be recoded into chunks. For associatively-related items, then, the unit of memory in a recall task would be the chunk, whereas in the case of associatively-unrelated items, the unit of memory would be the word. In the sort of task that we are concerned with here, of course, the result of linguistic recoding would be a difference in recall in favor of high-association items.

3. If we fail to recall a word from a passage during a recall test, we are likely to try to guess at it. According to the "construction" hypothesis, our guessing behavior under such circumstances is likely to be influenced, in part, by associative constraints created by the items that have already been recalled. The recall scores of Ss exposed to a high-association passage, therefore, could be enhanced by construction during recall.

The following conclusions were suggested by the results of the studies that have been conducted thus far.

1. Groups of associatively-related words embedded in connected discourse tend to be recalled better than groups of associatively-unrelated words.

69

2. A word, such as <u>king</u>, occurring in connected
discourse, is more likely to be recalled if it is
accompanied by high-strength associates (e.g., <u>queen</u>,
<u>ruler</u>, <u>crown</u>) than if it is accompanied by low-
strength associates (e.g., <u>nurse</u>, <u>leader</u>, <u>plane</u>).
This finding may have resulted from the fact that
associative bidirectionality was the rule for most
of the materials used in these studies. It remains
to be seen whether this finding of mutual facilitation extends to associatively-asymmetrical word
groups.

3. The results of three out of four studies suggest
that probability of recalling a word from a group
of associatively-related items, given that other
words from the group have also been recalled, is
greater than the probability of recalling a word
from a group of associatively-unrelated items under
the same circumstances. The term <u>recall</u> <u>dependency</u>
appears to describe this phenomenon.

4. If a word is deleted from connected discourse, the
probability of constructing it correctly (cloze
test) is greater if the discourse contains a strong
associate of that word than if the discourse contains
a weak associate of that word. In general, associative facilitation in construction was found to be
bidirectional.

These, then, were the major findings of our work on
the role of associations in the recall of items embedded
in connected discourse. After these studies were completed, however, it was hypothesized (Rosenberg, forthcoming) that the presence of associatively-related words
in a passage might make the passage a more integrated
unit. The result would be a higher level of recall of
context-content words from the high-association passages
than from the low-association passages. Another way to
account for such a finding, of course, would be to assume
that in learning a passage, new associations are established between items, the result being that one item can act
as a cue to the recall of another item. The more cues
present during recall, the greater the likelihood of
recall of other items from the passage. Since more
associatively-related words are recalled from passages
than associatively-unrelated words, more context-content

words should be recalled from high-association passages than from low-association passages. This hypothesis was confirmed by data from four studies (Rosenberg, forthcoming).

Current Work

There are a number of questions still to be answered concerning the role of associative habit in the recall of connected discourse. Perhaps the most interesting of these is the question of the source of facilitation in the recall of associates. Theory suggests that high-association items are not only stored more efficiently than low-association items, but are more likely to be constructed during recall, especially when the recall is written and the S has his production before him as he attempts to come up with additional items. At present, we are attempting to evaluate the hypothesis that the superior recall of high-association items does not depend upon opportunities for construction. In other words, even though construction may contribute something to the recall of associates, storage variables, such as "frequency" and "linguistic recoding", should be sufficient to produce a significant difference in favor of associatively-related materials.

This hypothesis is being evaluated through the use of a recognition-memory task which reduces greatly the likelihood of construction. Briefly, the critical stimulus and response words are taken out of the context of the passages and randomized within a long list of distractors. After a passage has been exposed for learning in the usual manner, this test list is presented as a paced successive binary recognition task. Preliminary results with passages that contained 16 pairs of key items suggest that the superiority in the recall of associatively-related word pairs does not depend upon the presence of opportunities for construction.

Another interesting problem is created by the fact that in the learning of connected discourse, performance is heavily constrained by serial organization. It is possible, therefore, that the associative facilitation we have found has been the result of the fact that associatively-related words always occurred contiguously, i.e., in the same or in adjacent sentences. At present

71

an attempt is being made to construct passages in which associatively-related words do not occur in the same or in adjacent sentences. It is anticipated that this manipulation will result--at least in the case of recall--in a condition of associative interference.

References

Chomsky, N. Aspects of the theory of syntax. Cambridge: Massachusetts Institute of Technology Press, 1965.

Deese, J. Influence of inter-item associative strength upon immediate free recall. Psychol. Rep., 1959, 5, 305-312.

Harris, Z. S. Discourse analysis. Language, 1952, 28, 1-30.

Johnson, N. F. The psychological reality of phrase-structure rules. J. verb. Learn. verb. Behav., 1965, 4, 469-475.

Johnson, N. F. The influence of associations between elements of structured verbal responses. J. verb. Learn. verb. Behav., 1966, 5, 369-374.

Katz, J. J., & Postal, P. M. An integrated theory of linguistic descriptions. Cambridge: Massachusetts Institute of Technology Press, 1964.

Koen, F., Becker, A., & Young, R. The psychological reality of the paragraph. In H. L. Lane (Ed.), Studies in language and language behavior, IV. Ann Arbor: The Center for Research on Language and Language Behavior, The University of Michigan, 1967.

Lachman, R., & Tuttle, Abigail V. Approximations to English (AE) and short-term memory: construction or storage? J. exp. Psychol., 1965, 70, 386-393.

Marks, L. E., & Miller, G. A. The role of semantic and syntactic constraints in the memorization of English sentences. J. verb. Learn. verb. Behav., 1964, 3, 1-5.

Martin, E., & Roberts, K. H. Grammatical factors in sentence retention. J. verb. Learn. verb. Behav., 1966, 5, 211-218.

McNeill, D. Developmental psycholinguistics. In T. Bever & W. Weksel (Eds.) Studies in psycholinguistics. New York: Prentice-Hall, in press.

Mehler, J. Some effects of grammatical transformations on the recall of English sentences. J. verb. Learn. verb. Behav., 1963, 2, 346-351.

Miller, G. A. The magical number seven, plus or minus two: Some limits on our capacity for processing information. Psychol. Rev., 1956, 63, 81-97.

Miller, G. A. Some psychological studies of grammar. Amer. Psychologist, 1962, 17, 748-762.

Miller, G. A., & Isard, S. Some perceptual consequences of linguistic rules. J. verb. Learn. verb. Behav., 1963, 2, 217-228.

Miller, G. A., & Selfridge, Jennifer A. Verbal context and the recall of meaningful material. Amer. J. Psychol., 1950, 63, 176-185.

Palermo, D. S., & Jenkins, J. J. Word association norms. Grade School through college. Minneapolis: The University of Minnesota Press, 1964.

Rosenberg, S. The influence of grammatical and associative habits on verbal learning. In S. Rosenberg (Ed.) Directions in psycholinguistics. New York: Macmillan, 1965.

Rosenberg, S. Associative clustering and repeated trials. J. gen. Psychol., 1966, 74, 89-96. (a)

Rosenberg, S. Associative factors in the recall of connected discourse. Psychonom. Sci., 1966, 4, 53-54. (b)

Rosenberg, S. Word associations and connected discourse: a reply to Lachman, Dumas, and Guzy. Psychonom. Sci., 1966, 5, 249-250. (c)

Rosenberg, S. Recall of sentences as a function of syntactic and associative habit. J. verb. Learn. verb. Behav., 1966, 5, 392–396. (d)

Rosenberg, S. Associative facilitation and interference in the recall of sentences. In H. L. Lane (Ed.) Studies in language and language behavior, IV. Ann Arbor: Center for Research on Language and Language Behavior, University of Michigan, 1967.

Rosenberg, S. Associative facilitation in the recall of connected discourse. In Rothkopf, E.Z. Verbal Learning research and written instruction. Forthcoming.

Thorndike, E. L., & Lorge, I. The teacher's word book of 30,000 words. New York: Teachers College of Columbia University Press, 1944.

Underwood, B. J. The language repertoire and some problems in verbal learning. In S. Rosenberg (Ed.) Directions in psycholinguistics. New York: Macmillan, 1965.

Footnotes

[1]This paper was prepared pursuant to a contract with the United States Office of Education under the provisions of P. L. 83–531, Cooperative Research, and Title VI, P. L. 85–864, as amended.

[2]The author is a member of the research staff at the Center for Research on Language and Language Behavior, University of Michigan.

BEHAVIORAL ENGINEERING: PROBLEM READERS[1]

Donald E. P. Smith[2]

Over the past four years, the members of a research
group have been engaged in engineering a learning
environment which will produce literate children. Our
original goal was a programmed literacy curriculum. But
when we attempted to try out programmed material in a
first-grade classroom, our task changed from program
construction to behavioral engineering. That is, control
of behavior in groups precedes the control of literate
behavior. Therefore, discovering what constitutes an
effective classroom and then producing one were necessary
conditions for trying out the program.

Any self-instruction program is incomplete until it
works well within some larger system, such as a classroom.
One must either modify the program to fit the education
system or modify the system to accommodate the program.

Fitting a program to an experienced teacher is a
herculean task. If the program is to teach, it will
necessarily take over part of the teacher's present role.
In the resulting conflict between teacher and program,
the program is likely to lose. For example, a usually
reluctant learner suddenly becomes immersed in a task.
Such task control of behavior is predictable since the
tasks are devised to make successful responses highly
probable. But the teacher is so delighted that he walks
by and smiles at the child, thus preempting a reliable
task-related reinforcer by substituting an unreliable one,
his approval. One characteristic of the classroom loser,
the eventual illiterate, is his vulnerability to the
behavior of persons of authority. While the successful
student enjoys the challenge of the task, much of the
loser's behavior turns upon praise and punishment. In
the present case, the child is likely to stop working and
engage, instead, in other better-established behaviors
designed to elicit approval.

Or again, the child may have before him a satisfying piece of material. He has worked for fifteen minutes and has had enough of this task for the present. He stops working. However, the teacher is challenged by the sight of the non-working child. He may chide, cajole, and, finally, entice the child into working. Thereafter, non-working may be used as a device for manipulating the teacher into playing the game of chide, cajole and enticement. Other, and more complex, games played by children and their teachers help to account for an annual contribution of at least a million children to the national pool of illiterates.

After observing these dynamics, we concluded that we should try to modify the classroom system, rather than the literacy program. Specifically, we have defined a role for the teacher which places him in the position of a monitor, or manager, rather than that of a dispenser of information and reinforcers. The teacher behaviors which define that role have been programmed, and the resulting system is now operating in many public schools[3].

Our present efforts are aimed at the refractory problems: the withdrawn, the passive-aggressive, and the aggressive-acting-out children. Further refinement of the teacher's role may make it possible to ameliorate such problems within the normal classroom simply by increased control of environmental variables. To understand how that may occur, let us consider the components of a controlled classroom environment.

Controlled classroom defined.

A controlled classroom is a learning system consisting of (1) a teacher-monitor whose behaviors are consistent and thus predictable; (2) a set of self-instructional materials requiring no teacher assistance; and (3) one or more learners.

An initial assumption should be made explicit: the organism moves toward increasingly complex skills for dealing with increasingly complex environments; optimum reinforcement contingencies during such change may vary from moment to moment; the learner is capable of arranging his own optimum reinforcement schedule given an optimum supporting environment.[4] In brief, we assume that, given well-designed tasks, all children can learn strictly by themselves. They can determine for themselves when they have done a task correctly, just as they do when swinging at a baseball. Thus, one essential component of the system is well-designed instructional material.

Characteristics of the materials. The literacy program consists of fifteen booklets and a series of tapes which, together, train reading, writing, listening and speaking. They begin with letter and phoneme discrimination and end with cursive writing, word attack and comprehension, roughly equivalent to a third-grade reading level in most skills. Independent work entails approximately 20,000 responses. Certain of the oral materials are carried out as group exercises--word-fluency training, dramatization and the classification component of concept formation. During these activities, the teacher follows a programmed script.

Tasks are, with few exceptions, of the matching-to-sample variety, each having a model and two choices. One choice is equivalent to the model and one is a foil (or S $^\triangle$), different from the model in some critical way.

Administration is such that all tasks are self-selective and self-pacing. Check tests appear from time to time for monitoring.

The Role of the Monitor. The teacher in this classroom is quite different from the cultural stereotypes, the substitute mother, the helper or the strict disciplinarian. He has three functions: rule-maker, rule-enforcer and examiner.

As rule-maker and rule-enforcer, he establishes one or two rules and enforces them absolutely. That is, no extenuating circumstance justifies an exception to the rule. We use three rules in the clinic: (1) "No talking during independent work periods," (2) "No disturbance of others" and (3) "Remain in the room." No other rule is used and none is necessary. Every infraction of the rule must be recognized and the rule is enforced. Enforcement of the silence rule consists of saying, "The rule is no talking." Enforcement of the other rules, disturbance and leaving the room, consists of exclusion for that period. Exclusion may be viewed as punishment. We view it as a

77

predictable event which the child chooses to have occur.
There is no rancor on the part of the teacher. On the
other hand, neither does the teacher praise the child,
either for conformity or achievement, for reasons which
will become apparent.

Aside from rule infractions, all other behaviors are
ignored. That is, the teacher is aware of irrelevant
behaviors, such as sitting on the floor, but he does not
respond to them. Since they have no apparent effect on
the teacher's behavior, they readily extinguish.

The term "independent" work period means exactly that.
A request for help by a child is responded to by enforcement of the silence rule.

The third function of the teacher-monitor is that of
examiner. The child meets check tests periodically. He
is required to perform each task without error before new
materials are provided.

Characteristics of the children. Disabled readers
are, as a group, highly perfectionistic, and they have
little frustration tolerance. That is, they tend to
exhibit high need for achievement and high fear of
failure. Furthermore, they tend to be authority-oriented:
they are peculiarly vulnerable to praise and punishment
by the teacher.

One way in which the child reduces his vulnerability
is to deny that he has a problem, and to reinforce the
teacher for supporting that self-deception. Other teacher
manipulative techniques are common. (1) He may refuse to
work. Thus, he cannot be said to fail since he has not
made an attempt to succeed. (2) He may work very hard on
assigned tasks only and be consistently unsuccessful. In
effect, he is fulfilling the teacher's demands, so the
teacher is responsible for the outcome. He remains
uncommitted. Thus, it is the teacher who is failing, a
satisfactory resolution of the problem for this child.
(3) He may be hostile and aggressive, thus diverting the
teacher's attention from the achievement task. (4) He
may be clever, amusing and loving, another diversionary
tactic. All of these techniques have the effect of
leaving the child uncommitted to the task. He feels that
he must achieve 100% success and that, if he commits himself, he dare not fail. Thus, his safest resolution is
avoidance.

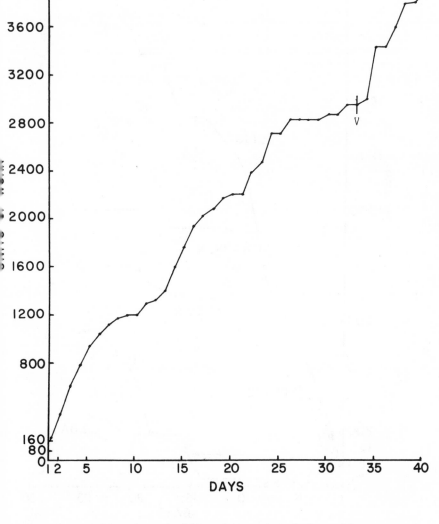

Fig. 1.   Units of work (discriminations) in a literacy
program by a ten year old boy over 40 days under
conditions of self-selection and self-pacing in
a controlled environment.   V designates a
"vacation," i.e., an arbitrarily determined
elapsed time of 21 days.

79

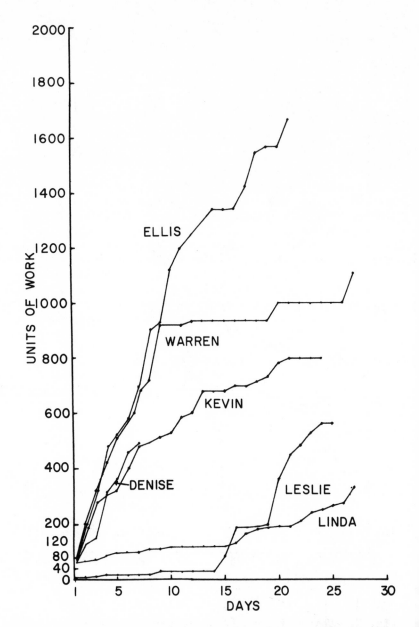

Fig. 2.   Cumulative work curves for six non-verbal, first-grade failures under conditions of self-selection and self-pacing in a controlled environment. Work periods varied from 20 to 35 minutes per day with no discernible pattern.

Let us look now at what happens to such children in the environment described.

Outcomes of a Controlled Environment

<u>Intrinsic reinforcement</u>. All of the instructional material has been constructed in an iterative fashion, with the result that success is virtually assured. Since each task sets a problem, and since children are at least 95% successful in solving the problems, success or "intrinsic reinforcement" is the sole motivator. It has proved to be sufficient in public school classrooms.

For problem readers, the motivation is clearly <u>not</u> sufficient. Sometimes, periods of intensive work are followed by periods of little or no work (extinction), in turn followed by intensive work, in a cyclic fashion (See Fig. 1). Periods of reduced work are characterized by high emotionality, acting-out such behaviors as attacks on objects, peers or teacher, followed by such fearful behaviors as visual pursuit of the teacher, attempts to escape, or hiding in a corner.

Sometimes, periods of work are followed by periods of no work (See Fig. 2). These are six first-grade failures, also designated non-verbal. The following remarks are excerpted from the teacher's report. Below is a summary of the impressions of each child's behavior when he entered:

Linda: highly distractible, manipulating, dependent.

Warren: precariously contained aggression, many neurotic movements, apparently enthusiastic about class.

Denise: frightened, withdrawing.

Kevin: very fearful, hyperactive, distractible, manipulating.

Leslie: extremely angry and withdrawing; spent first two days in tears; refused to work for the first 13 days.

81

The behavioral changes are summarized below:

Linda: Dependency behaviors were extinguished. She stopped asking me for help or praise. She expressed some anger toward me and her classmates. She attended to tasks for longer periods.

Warren: He did a great deal of work, expressed a great deal of anger. After several weeks he stopped working and his acting out became extreme. There was a change in this behavior at the end of the session: his attack behavior was ritualistic, without affect.

Denise: Attended only nine class sessions. She worked very hard and made noticeable gains in fluency; fearfulness diminished.

Kevin: His behavior changed markedly from "hyper-active, distractible" to "hard-working, cooperative" to "angry, aggressive, non-working" to "fearful, infantile, withdrawing."

Leslie: He was very fearful and angry and refused to do any work for 13 days. Then, suddenly, he began working very hard. There was some aggressive acting-out during this last time. There was a noticeable increase in fluency. There were no tears after the first two days.

Behavior changes occurred at the beginning, all in the right direction. Then, in all cases, but one, extinction occurred. We concluded that an alternative solution was necessary.

<u>Extrinsic reinforcement</u>. By a circuitous line of reasoning, reinforcement may be viewed as being analogous to uncertainty reduction. As such, it is equivalent to information. Uncertainty is uncomfortable; the reduction of uncertainty is pleasurable. When a child faces a problem, his uncertainty is aroused; when he solves the problem, his uncertainty is reduced, i.e., he is reinforced.

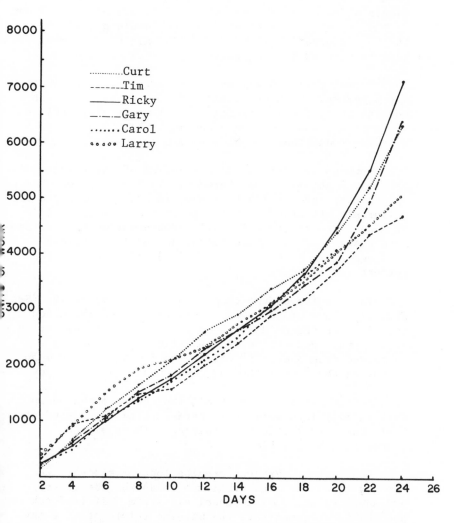

Fig. 3.   Cumulative work curves for six problem readers
under conditions of self-selection, self-pacing
and continuous reinforcement (money) in a
controlled environment.

The extinction curves (See Figs. 1 and 2) indicate a decreasing amount of reinforcement (or information) despite continued success in the work. Why should that occur? Where is the missing reinforcer? Viewed as information, success or failure in the tasks must answer some question, perhaps the question, "Can I succeed in these books?" Within a few days, the answer would become clear: "I can do these tasks." Continuing to work would provide no further information if this child's main concern were his failure. An extinction curve might then be expected.

Normal children appear to be aware of their day-to-day progress. Perhaps, their question is not aimed at success on particular exercises. If uncertainty relates to progress, the question asked might be, "Did I read anything today that I couldn't read yesterday?"

Perhaps, a striking demonstration of day-to-day progress might make a difference. To find out, we changed our unit of information to money, in order to capture the children's attention. They were paid at a rate of 1/10 of a cent per response for all independent work. Performance tasks, such as check tests, and oral and silent readings, were paid at rates of 2, 3 and 4 cents for a perfect performance.

The results of the change were quite impressive (See Fig. 3). Rate of work was consistently high throughout the six-week period and, in some cases, was accelerating at the end. Proportion of class-time spent working increased from a mean of 64% on the first day to a mean of 93% on the fourteenth day, and then remained steady.

Suffice it to say that all the children shaped up very rapidly into efficient, hard-working young students. There was very little rule-testing. There was no competition observable.

Conclusion. Present results look promising. We are now faced with the problem of adapting the pay-off procedure to the public-school classroom. If feedback on progress does constitute the missing reinforcer, it may be possible to substitute a pay-off other than money, perhaps "points". A child who received $ .26 on one day appeared shocked when he received only $ .05 the following day. "Yeah, I didn't work very hard today," he explained, aloud, to himself. Would that occur if he were paid-off

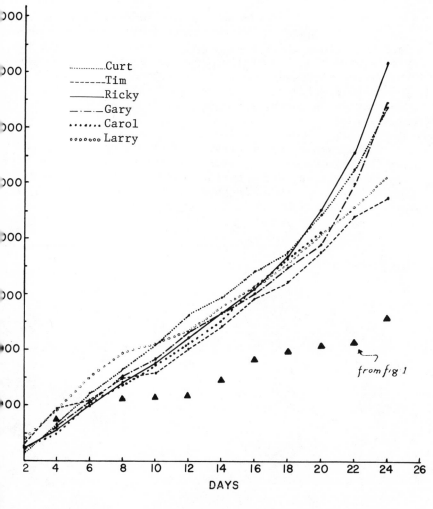

Fig. 4. Cumulative work curves for six problem readers
under conditions of self-selection, self-pacing
and continuous reinforcement (money) in a
controlled environment.

85

with 26 points and 5 points? Present evidence on high
school and special education students suggests that it
would (see Fig. 4).

Footnotes

[1]The work on classroom control reported here has been
conducted by Judith M. Smith, Raymond Cabot, Dale Brethower
Carl Semmelroth and the author. This report is based on
research that was partially supported by a contract with
the Office of Education, U. S. Department of Health,
Education & Welfare, under provisions of P. L. 83-531,
Cooperative Research, and Title VI, P. L. 85-864, as
amended.

[2]The author is a professor in the School of Education;
chief of the Reading Improvement Service, Bureau of Psychological Services; and a senior member of the staff at the
Center for Research on Language and Language Behavior,
University of Michigan.

TWO PATHS TO INNOVATION: IMPOSITION AND EVOLUTION[1]

George L. Geis[2]

A considerable part of the efforts of the Center for
Research on Language and Language Behavior is devoted to
studying problems of language instruction. The Center was
conceived of by both its founders and sponsors as, Janus-
like, looking simultaneously to the laboratory and to the
language-learning student.

One group at the Center is devoted solely to the
problem of the modification of language behavior. Its
members are concerned that their innovative efforts not
end up merely as "another approach to language pedagogy".
They are interested in the problem of educational innovation itself. In this paper I will propose some characteristics of successful and unsuccessful educational
innovation, and describe briefly one project in which
members of the Center and associated groups are involved--
a project which illustrates one present strategy for
innovation.

The problem of educational innovation is commonly
viewed as a rather simple one. Thus, there are really
only two parties to be considered when innovating. On
the one hand, there is the psychologist who works in his
laboratory to produce those basic laws, or principles,
which better enable him to predict and control behavior,
and to develop a system of explanation, i.e., a theory.
On the other hand, there is the teacher who faces the
practical task of producing behavioral changes in a
variety of human beings, and, incidentally, to produce
such changes while allowed only minimal control over the
important variables which affect behavior. Both roles
are clearly encapsulated. The problem, according to this
view, is to build a bridge between the psychologist and
the teacher, and between the laboratory and the classroom.
A great deal of effort has been expended in developing
this connecting link across which principles of behavior

can be transported to the educational engineer. At best, that bridge has been little more than a thin verbal strand across which no idea can safely cross.

It seems that the problem lies not with construction, but with conception. The bridge-building solution requires at least four assumptions, all of which seem quite unwarranted. Indeed, these incorrect assumptions may have accounted, in large part, for the history of failure that has characterized almost every innovative effort in education. There has not been an important change in human education for the past 2000 years, except for a steady increase in the student-teacher ratio.

The first assumption made by the bridge-builders is that the psychologist has available in his laboratory cupboard a collection of laws, principles and behavioral techniques which clearly and precisely describe the dynamics of behavior and behavioral change, and the procedures necessary to produce behavioral modification.

A second assumption is that these principles can be applied almost immediately and directly to the specific, daily problems of instruction which the teacher faces.

A third assumption is that teachers learn by exposure, and that the psychologist need only state his findings to the teacher and she will apply them to her work.

A fourth assumption is that the teacher and the classroom represent the basic, and possibly the only, units of instruction.

A brief glance at the literature of psychology makes us question the first assumption. If the psychologist does have an epistemological closet, it resembles Mother Hubbard's cupboard, rather than Amalthea's cornucopia. As psychologists, we can say very little about the basic principles which govern behavior. We have few quantitative laws of the sort that characterize the other sciences. We are not without some laws and principles. Indeed, in recent years major advances have been made in establishing a solid, systematic science of behavior--advances in technology, in generating principles and in reformulating traditional problems. Nevertheless, it is premature to picture psychologists as a shy group who have the answers and are coyly waiting to be asked the questions.

As for the second assumption, those laws or principles that psychology <u>has</u> generated are usually not directly applicable to complex situations, just as the basic principles of physics are of little use to the mechanical engineer. Thus, Thorndike's <u>Law</u> <u>of</u> <u>Effect</u>, or its more recent restatement as the principle of reinforcement, is a powerful, all-pervading principle. It states that the consequences of a bit of behavior affect the future probability of occurence of that behavior. But such a statement is of little use to the teacher. To the extent that she affects students, the teacher cannot violate that principle. If she is to be effective, she must reinforce her students. But how? with what? when? for the principle is very general. Indeed, that may be an important feature of principles. On the other hand, some psychological laws are too specific. Marbe's law, for example, which states that a logarithmic relationship obtains between individual reaction times for free associations and the frequency of occurence of these responses in the population, may fascinate and prove useful to some psychologists, especially psycholinguists. Obviously, the precision of the law and the highly controlled conditions under which it was generated prevent its application by the practitioner in a classroom. The second assumption of the bridge-builders, that the findings of psychologists can be directly applied to instructional problems, also, seems patently false.

The third assumption was that if principles of behavioral modification were available and were applicable, they could be infused into the educational system merely by having someone inform the teacher of their existence. Psychologists, typically, give talks to teachers, publish articles for general dissemination, and carry out research projects. The assumption is that exposure to information not only brings about behavioral modification (in the teacher), but that such changes in the teacher will automatically be maintained in her daily routines. I indicated earlier that, while we psychologists do not know much about behavior, we are not completely ignorant. The principles that we have established, like the principle of reinforcement and the observations which led to those principles, strongly suggest that mere exposure never has, and never will, teach anyone anything. Harlan L. Lane, in a paper called "Models of Learning and Methods of Teaching", has described the misconception this way:

> The basic tenet of (this) sunburn model is learn-
> ing by exposure. The teacher, the prime source of
> knowledge and light (and occasionally heat)
> 'exposes' the students to the material. The
> brighter students 'soak it up' and eventually
> 'see the light'. Dull students, who fail to
> learn, are not sensitive or receptive.

There simply is no evidence that an exact application of
the sunburn theory by the teacher will lead, analogously, to
mental tanning. Psychologists are the first to point this
out. But, usually, they do so by talking to teachers,
i.e., by exposing them to information (applying the sunburn
theory of learning).

Despite the derogatory student comment to the contrary, we teachers act like other humans, and learn in the
same way. Attempts at innovating in education, which use
as the major innovative procedure exposure of the teacher,
administrator, parent or student to the new information,
seem likely to fail, no matter how beneficial the innovation might be. In short, if the psychologist does have
something of value which can be applied by the teacher, he
will fail if he tries to produce changes in her behavior
by using the very methods of teaching he is attempting to
get her to discard.

The last assumption concerned the basic unit of
education. Innovative efforts, almost without exception,
have been contained by the limits of the teacher and the
classroom. As we begin to find out more about human
learning, as we face a multitude of increasing pressures,
ranging from the pupil population explosion to the information explosion, and as we view the history of failure
of attempts to improve the existing educational system, we
must consider innovations which involve, if not the development of new systems, at least drastic modifications of
the old. Educational innovators have been like men who,
when faced with the problem of developing a better means
of transporting people from New York to Los Angeles, breed
faster race horses, rather than invent jet airplanes.
Self-instructional materials involving only one active
human participant are demonstrating their effectiveness
in replacing the student-teacher dyad. Computer-assisted
instruction, such as the SAID (Speech Automatic Instruction

Device) system, which was developed at the Center for Research on Language and Language Behavior (CRLLB), or Dr. A. K. Moore's talking typewriter, are proving to be beneficially inhuman, in the sense of being super-human tutors. Truly innovative efforts in language teaching and elsewhere in education must at least pay heed to the development of new instructional systems.

The staggeringly complex task of producing a major behavioral change in a student (e.g., teaching him to speak a second language) most likely requires at least effective management of the whole learning environment and, very possibly, development of a new environment for learning.

The consequence of incorrectly assuming that psychology has a complete, precise and systematic set of laws and principles of behavior, that these laws and principles are directly applicable to the problems in applied areas such as education, that all that needs to be done is to communicate the basic principles uncovered in the laboratory to the teacher in order to modify the teacher's behaviors and, finally, that all innovation must be limited to retreading the present instructional system, has, of course, been the repeated failure of innovative efforts in education. Unhappily accompanying this cumulative record of failure has been, I think, the disillusionment on the part of each member of the dyad. The teacher has become suspicious of just how much the psychologist can do for her, and the psychologist has often concluded that when he does try to do something, his effort is not accepted, or certainly not maintained by the educational system.

However, I think that rapport _can_ be established and successful innovation _can_ be brought about. But a new set of assumptions are required and new strategies are called for.

Let us assume, for example, that psychologists, engaged in basic research, have not generated all of the answers to the problems faced by the instructional engineer. Let us assume further that almost nothing the psychologist does discover or invent can be applied immediately and directly to behavioral engineering problems. Let us assume not the need for a bridge, between the laboratory and the classroom, connecting two discrete groups of people, but rather a fine-grained continuun stretching from the laboratory to the pupil. This continuum would include basic researchers studying problems of learning, applied researchers working on typical instructional problems but in carefully controlled environments, applied researchers in the field, instructional systems designers, instructional materials designers, innovative agents, who would guide on-site innovation, and, finally, behavioral engineers who would deal directly with the student. Picture a T with a spectrum of research and development experts ranging along the stem of the T, reaching from basic research to the student. The cross bar represents another spectrum at the instructional site: a group of applied experts involved in the practical problems of student diagnosis and placement, guidance, evaluation, tutoring, content specialists, and the like.

Let me point out that this picture is quite unlike the present structure of instructional research: the stem of the T is missing and the cross-bar is represented only in outline--at present a shadow no bigger than the special education teacher's or guidance counselor's hand.

Every technology in the past has at least been accompanied by (and in some cases preceded by) the proliferation of specialists. Instruction, on the other hand, has traditionally involved primarily one person: the teacher. In former times we conceived of medicine as involving one person--the general practicioner, i.e., the family doctor who diagnosed, or attempted to diagnose, everything; who set bones and rolled pills; who provided primitive psycho-therapy; and who dabbled in surgery. Today, we would be appalled at such a Renaissance medicine man. Similarly, it seems that rapidly-increasing role specialization is developing in instruction. There is no reason to think that teaching someone to speak Spanish should require less of a team and less of a sophisticated effort than curing him of a cough.

Now, concerning a different third assumption, let us assume that the teacher, parent and administrator all learn according to the basic principles of behavior that apply to the acquisition of behavior by the student. We would then suppose that innovative efforts, if they are to be accepted and, importantly, maintained, by the school, they must be accompanied by sophisticated planning for innovation.

Finally, a different fourth assumption: the basic unit of instruction consists of the student and <u>some</u> instructional system, only one of which is the teacher. The ineffectiveness of the teacher in a classroom as an instructional system surely need not be belabored with an audience interested in language learning and aware of its present sad state. But even if the teacher-classroom system was effective, being so temporarily and geographically constrained, it simply is not able effectively to deal with such problems as continuing education and instruction of specific skills at the time the student really needs those skills, and continuing adjustment of curriculum to changing social needs.

Recently, CRLLB became allied with the Michigan secondary public school system in a project called FLICS (Foreign Language Innovative Curricula Studies). This Office of Education-sponsored project, directed by James McClafferty, could have been another of the many efforts devoted to developing methods of instructional materials external to the school system, and there seeking, however subtly, to impose the new materials and systems on the school. We, the staff of FLICS, have taken another tack, one which is congruent with the new set of assumptions outlined above.

Although the project has several parts, I shall describe only the one in which I direct staff training.

We have interpreted our task as an opportunity to design one of the many new instructional roles I mentioned before. We are attempting to develop a curriculum for the training of what has been variously labelled by members of our group as "educational managers" "innovative agents", or, more colorfully, "midwives of change". Regardless of the name of the job, its many characteristics are interesting and demanding.

First, we see this person located in, or very close to, the school. We see the need for an on-the-spot, full-time innovative agent in second-language learning. We place him there for several reasons: some have to do with the greater ease in guiding externally-developed innovations; some have to do with the generation of and evaluation of local innovations; and some have to do with the generation of specific research problems which can be fed back to centers, such as CRLLB.

93

The innovative agent will have several important skills and tasks. First, he will be sophisticated about specifying instructional goals. He will spend time probing teachers and administrators, students and parents, and, importantly, the final consumers of education--the people who hire our students--to determine realistic goals for second-language teaching. This may well result in major curriculum changes. Clearly, part of the problem of unsuccessful instruction lies not merely in the methods used to teach but in the uselessness of what is being taught. This lack of correspondance between what is being taught and what the student will need, once he is released from his academic confinement, is all too clear to almost everyone but the teacher. The development of new methods which more successfully teach old curricula may often be inane and even socially irresponsible. The innovative agent is in a unique position to spend time considering the usefulness of the school's product.

A second role will be that of evaluator. Education has known almost continuing change, but it has remained whimsical and ephemeral. The educational system can make change cumulative and can turn change into progress only when it incorporates adequate evaluation schemes. "Our man in the schools" should be skilled in evaluation of goals, i.e., long-term evaluation (the psychologist's word might be <u>validation</u>). He should be equally skilled in short-term evaluation, i.e., in evaluating particular innovations in terms of whether they do, indeed, produce the behavioral changes they were designed to produce or laid claim to producing. He will be the evaluative super-ego in second-language learning. The positive side of this critical facility will be helping to construct tests, stretching the instructor's imagination to new and more adequate means of measurement, and reminding the system continually of its primary committment to evaluation. Though he may be labelled an innovative agent I would predict more of his time will be spent shooting down suggested innovations than putting a data-based seal of approval upon them. Like a good doctor, he will most often prescribe restraint from medication until that medication is proved effective and applicable.

A third skill our agent should have is that of a designer of instructional systems. I believe that this phrase is descriptive but perhaps too elegant for many of the rather menial activities we have in mind. A system might consist of nothing more than a certain sequencing of assignments in the text, recitations, and the like. He can help produce a variety of such designs, and then, putting on his evaluator hat, compare the effectiveness of the different arrangements. Of course, a system can also be something as complex and original as Dr. O. K. Moore's autotelic environment, involving programmed interventions of a variety of sub-systems, including the teacher and the computer.

The agent may help develop such sub-systems and aid in the production of the teaching materials. As such, he assumes a fourth role of instructional materials designer. He will be able to at least produce models for the teacher of a great variety of materials; perhaps, he will encourage her to become an author of self-instructional materials or to co-author text materials with another teacher of a different language.

Still another role we hope to prepare him for is that of behavioral engineer. Some of the jobs I have described might be called, correctly, behavioral engineering. But we have in mind a more limited use of the phrase to denote pupil management, an almost exclusive concern with the means of modification, the particular processes involved in behavioral change. Dr. Donald E. P. Smith, of CRLLB, and his staff have devoted themselves for years to examining more effective means of classroom management. (His report on some of that work is part of these Proceedings.) As a behavioral engineer, our innovative agent would study classroom and learning problems which are commonly classified as disciplinary, motivational, and the like.

In addition, this agent will be a disseminator--a source of information about materials, methods, and research for the school system. He will also be a source of information about researchable problems to the applied and even to the basic researcher. The school system has traditionally taken from research, regardless of the worth these products may have. But we see our innovative agent supplying to research people, who are removed from the instructional environment, descriptions of real-world constraints and needs, fueling, we hope, the furnaces of applied research.

The man I have described in some ways resembles the curriculum coordinator in some schools. But there are major differences. One is that he does not take the traditional classroom unit as a limit for innovative efforts. Another is that he does not merely suggest: he works on innovations directly. Still another difference is that we have purposely planned a man with split allegiances. Hopefully, not a man without a country, but one who garners reinforcers from two communities. He will spend time in, be in communication with, and be respected by research people at centers like CRLLB. He will be accepted by the teacher and principal, and listened to.

In discussing the FLICS proposal recently with a group of teachers, one asked: "Where do you see this all ending." Being a teacher, I gave a long and unnecessarily complicated answer. I think the correct answer should have been: if we are successful, our innovation, unlike so many others, will not end. Indeed, that is the point of the system we propose--the beginning of an innovative system that is self-maintaining and continually evolving.

Footnotes

[1]This report is based on research supported by a contract with the Office of Education, U. S. Department of Health, Education, & Welfare, under provisions of P. L. 83-531, Cooperative Research, and Title VI, P. L. 85-864, as amended.

[2]The author is a member of the research staff of the CRLLB, and also of the University of Michigan Psychology Department faculty.

Discrimination Auditive et Apprentissage Des Langues[1]

Emmanuel Companys[2]

Nous allons nous efforcer de présenter notre hypothèse de travail sur la discrimination auditive, assez rapidement pour pouvoir nous étendre un peu plus sur quelques exemples entéressant l'apprentissage des langues.

Cette hypothèse part de théories linguistiques généralement admises par les linguistes et les psychologues, et que nous allons supposer connues. Il s'agit d'une part de la <u>théorie phonémique</u>: les phonèmes, les variantes combinatoires, les traits pertinents, les neutralisations et les archi-phonèmes, etc.[3], d'autre part la <u>théorie des niveaux paradigmatiques</u> ou, si l'on préfère, <u>des strates</u>: forme, substance, expression et contenu chez Hjemslev et la Glossématique, où les différents niveaux de la linguistique stratificationnelle, décrits par S. Lamb aux Etats Unis: sons, phonèmes, morphèmes, lexèmes, sémèmes. Tous les linguistes ne donnent pas le même sens à des mots tels que <u>morphème</u>. Le tableau LES STRATES (hors texte 1)--tiré de notre cours de linguistique en préparation--résume ces notions et aidera le lecteur à s'y retrouver dans notre terminologie.[4]

Notre hypothèse comprend:

a) des points généralement admis par les linguistes et/ou les psychologues,

b) des points que l'observation confirme, sans que l'on puisse d'ailleurs dire toujours dans quelle mesure elle les confirme, et

c) des points qui semblent rendre compte des faits observables, mais ne sont pas nécessairement prouvés par eux.

B. E. L. ET
UNIVERSITE DE
POITIERS

COURS DE LINGUISTIQUE GENERALE
par E. Companys

Hors
Texte
No. 1

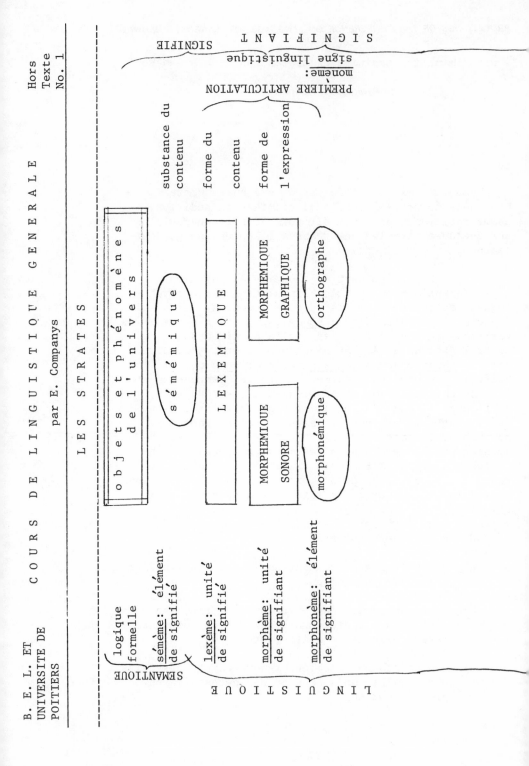

LES STRATES

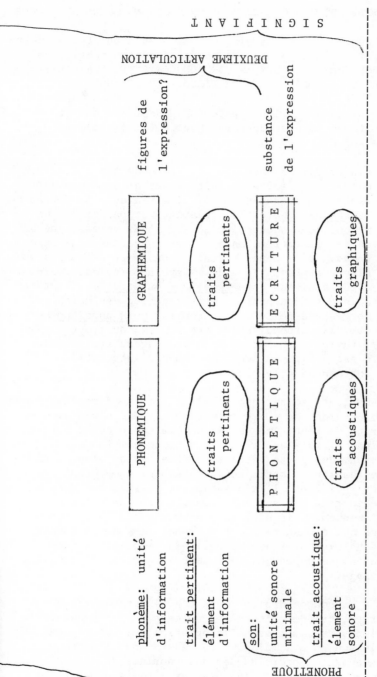

SIGNIFIANT

DEUXIEME ARTICULATION

figures de l'expression?

substance de l'expression

PHONEMIQUE

GRAPHEMIQUE

traits pertinents

traits pertinents

PHONETIQUE

ECRITURE

traits acoustiques

traits graphiques

phonème: unité d'information

trait pertinent: élément d'information

son: unité sonore minimale

trait acoustique: élément sonore

PHONETIQUE

LINGUISTIQUE

REMARQUE: Etude provisoire sujette à modifications éventuelles.

REFERENCES: Classement et terminologie très largement inspirés de LAMB et HALLIDAY. Autres sources importantes: MARTINET, HJEMSLEV et l'école danoise, POTTIER, CHOMSKI et l'école transformationaliste, SAUSSURE.

B. E. L. e c 1539   15.11.65

Pour faciliter la discussion, nous présenterons notre
théorie en douze points regroupés en quatre rubriques:
DECODAGE IMMEDIAT, UTILISATION DU CONTEXTE, CAS PARTI-
CULIERS DE DECODAGE, CAS DE L'AUDITEUR ETRANGER.

Nous avons intitulé DECODAGE NORMAL les quatre
propositions de base de notre hypothèse, que allons
maintenant étudier.

1. <u>Linéarité</u>: Le message est perçu de façon linéaire,
   mais la linéarité décroît au fur et à mesure que
   l'on atteint des strates, plus élevés. Au niveau de
   la <u>chaine sonore</u>, la linéarité est parfaite. On
   perçoit une succession de <u>sons</u>, qui ne sont pas des
   unités discrètes, mais qui se succèdent dans le
   temps. Les phonèmes sont probablement entendus au
   niveau <u>syntagmatique</u> de la syllabe (ne pas confondre
   avec le niveau <u>paradigmatique</u> ou <u>strate</u>). Le temps
   d'intégration pour l'identification des morphèmes
   correspond de la même façon aux <u>mots phoniques</u> et
   pour la reconnaissance des lexèmes au <u>groupe
   rythmique</u>. Quand on en arrive au strate sémémique,
   c'est à dire au sens, le temps d'intégration
   correspond à la prase.

Au strate <u>sémantique</u> celui qui influe directement sur
le comportement de notre interlocuteur, il n'y a plus de
linéarité du tout: non seulement le cadre de la phrase
est dépassé, mais encore il faut tenir compte de la
situation, des gestes et des expressions du visage, ainsi
que des habitudes socio-culturelles qui complètent, et
souvent modifient, l'information linguistique. Nous ne
nous étendrons pas sur ces questions qui sont extra-
linguistiques, puisqu'elles concernent non la langue mais
l'usage qui en est fait, et relèvent donc de la compétence
du psychologue plus que de celle du linguiste. Nous
reconnaissons cependant leur importance pour l'intelligence
du message.

Le schéma de droite de la Fig. 1 représente la
linéarité, qui décroît du son au sens. Cl est naturellement l'inverse du temps d'intégration qui est minimal
pour le son et maximal pour le sens. Nous l'avons
disposée dans l'ordre du décodage normal, du son vers
le sémème, si bien que les niveaux paradigmatiques les
plus elevés se trouvent vers le bas. D'autre part, nous
utilisons le mot <u>monème</u>, employé par Martinet, pour

100

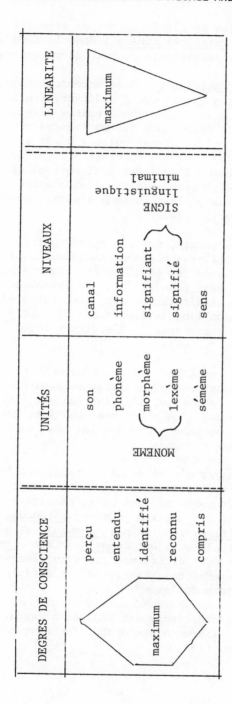

Fig. 1. Decodage aux différents niveaux paradigmatiques: degrés de conscience et de linéarité.

désigner la réunion du signifiant et du signifié, c'est à
dire le <u>signe linguistique minimal</u>, dont le décodage
constitue l'étape essentielle de tout le processus.

2. <u>Niveau de conscience</u>. Nous entendons par là le
degré de conscience que l'auditeur, (ou le sujet
parlant) a des differentes unités linguistiques.
Ce degré de conscience est maximum au niveau du
monème, et c'est normal puisque c'est le signe
linguistique. Grosso modo, cela signifie que le
locuteur comme l'auditeur sont surtout conscients
des mots utilisés. Dès que l'on s'éloigne du
monème, dans un sens ou dans l'autre, cela devient
beaucoup moins clair.

Un espagnol est très surpris quand on lui montre que
dans le mot <u>dado</u> il prononce deux consonnes différentes
[daδo], les deux sons [d] et [δ] n'étant que deux variantes
combinatoires du même phonème /d/. Ne jouant aucun rôle
dans sa langue pour distinguer des mots, cette différence
n'a qu'une fonction linguistique secondaire et échape
normalement à la conscience de l'auditeur comme à celle
de l'auditeur.

Le degré de conscience baisse également quand on
atteint des niveaux psycholinguistiques plus élevés. La
difficulté que l'on éprouve à définir un mot à brûle-
pourpoint montre que l'on n'est pas conscient des sémèmes
qui sont le contenu sémantique des lexèmes dans le
système d'une langue donnée.

On peut essayer d'utiliser le vocabulaire français
pour indiquer une sorte de gradation dans le processus de
décodage des différents niveaux paradigmatiques. On dira
que les sons sont <u>perçus</u>, les phonèmes <u>entendus</u>, les
morphèmes <u>identifiés</u>, les lexèmes <u>reconnus</u>, et qu'au
niveau du sémène, le sens est <u>compris</u>. Cette <u>comprehen-</u>
<u>sion</u> ne concerne pas les sémèmes individuellement, mais
l'ensemble de sémèmes qui constituent la définition
logico-linguistique du lexème.

Le degré de conscience est indiqué à gauche de la
figure 1 par un diagramme accompagné des cinq mots qui
expriment la gradation.

3. <u>Identification par éliminations successives</u>. On
procède par élimination à tous les niveaux. Pour
la comodité du langage nous emploierons désormais
<u>identification</u> dans tous les cas comme terme
générique englobant perception, reconnaissance,
compréhension etc. Nous allons donner un exemple
pour les phonèmes en français, dont la description
est donnée par le tableau de la Fig. 2.

On entend un son et on se demande: "voyelle ou
consonne?" On élimine consonne. On prend le premier
paramètre des voyelles, le plus important: le point
d'articulation, et on se pose la question du degré. Après
avoir éliminé, par exemple, <u>antérieur</u>, <u>médial</u>, <u>mi-postér-</u>
<u>ieur</u> et <u>postérieur</u>, il nous reste <u>mi-antérieur</u>. On a donc
le choix entre /e/, /ɛ/, /ɛ̃/, /ø/, /œ/, /œ̃/. Les trois
param tres qui nous restent peuvent être représentés sur
trois dimensions sur la Fig. 3: la labialité en profondeur,
la nasalité latéralement, et le timbre verticalement.
Chaqun des six plans du cube represente un degré d'un
paramètre: en bas fermé, en haut ouvert; à gauche nasal,
à droite oral; devant, non labial, derrière labial.
Chacune des six voyelles qui nous restent se trouve ainsi
à l'intersection de trois plans, représentant leurs traits
pertinents. On prend le deuxième paramètre et on se dit
"ce n'est pas labial" ce qui élimine le plan arrière de la
figure: il ne nous reste plus que /e/, /ɛ/, /ɛ̃/. De même
le plan de gauche peut être éliminé par le réponse "ce n'est
pas nasal" à la question du degré du troisième paramètre,
ne laissant que /ɛ/ et /e/. Enfin "ce n'est pas fermé"
éliminera le plan supérieur quand on pasera au paramètre de
timbre, et /ɛ/ se trouvera identifié, par1 élimination
de /e/.

La façon dont on entend et dont on imite un accent
étranger, confirme la théorie des éliminations successives.

4. <u>Importance primordiale des phénomènes suprasegmen-</u>
<u>taux</u>. L'arrangement séquentiel des unités linguis-
tiques ainsi que les variations du ton et de
l'amplitude en fonction du temps qui constituent
l'intonation (rythme, débit, contour mélodique, etc)
ont une importance primordiale pour le décodage. Ce
sont ces éléments qui sont pris les premiers en
considération, dans la mesure où le permet leur
nature qui exige naturellement un temps d'intégration assez long. L'information qu'ils apportent

PARAMÈTRES	DEGRÉS	antérieur	mi-antérieur	médial	mi-postérieur	postérieur
POINT D'ARTICULATION		/i/, /y/	/e/, /ɛ/, /ɛ̃/, /ø/, /œ/, /œ̃/	/a/, /ɑ/, /ɑ̃/	/o/, /ɔ/, /ɔ̃/	/u/
LABIALITE	labial /y/, /ø/, /œ/, /œ̃/ /u/, /o/, /ɔ/, /ɔ̃/ non-labial /i/, /e/, /ɛ/, /ɛ̃/, /a/, /ɑ/, /ɑ̃/			Le respect des oppositions relevant des deux premiers paramètres est indispensable à la compréhension dans toutes les variétés de français, sauf pour /œ̃/.		
NASALITE	nasal /ɛ̃/, /œ̃/, /ɑ̃/, /ɔ̃/ non-nasal /i/, /e/, /ɛ/, /a/, /y/, /ø/, /œ/, /ɑ/, /u/, /o/, /ɔ/			Ce paramètre n'existe pas en tant que tel dans le français du Midi: la nasalité y est remplacée par un archiphonème nasal consonantique.		
TIMBRE	ouvert /ɛ/, /œ/, /a/, /ɔ/ ferme /i/, /y/, /u/, /e/, /ø/, /ɑ/, /o/, /ɛ̃/, /œ̃/, /ɑ̃/, /ɔ̃/			Ce paramètre n'existe pas dans le français du Midi, et son rendement est très faible dans le français parisien. On peut s'en passer complètement en tant que trait pertinent.		

REMARQUES:

1. Les noms que nous donnons ici aux paramètres sont impropres parce que d'origine articulatoire, mais ils ont l'avantage d'être couramment utilisés.

2. Le "point d'articulation" est sans doute identifié à son tour par les paramètres "diffusion" et "gravité", mais au niveau du système phonémique on a un seul paramètre avec cinq degrés équivalents.

3. Phonémiquement /a/ se comporte comme les voyelles ouvertes et /ɑ/ comme les voyelles fermées, bien que, phonétiquement [a] soit plus ferme que [ɑ]; les nasales se comportent comme des fermées.

4. On n'a pas tenu compte ici du [ə] dont le statut phonémique est très discuté. /e/ est probablement à interpréter comme une médiale labiale.

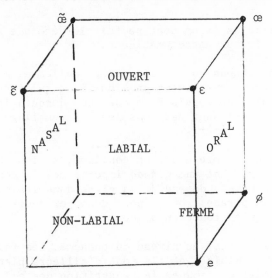

Fig. 3: VOYELLES MI-ANTERIEURES DU FRANÇAIS: Les deux
places vides correspondent aux sons [ẽ] et [ø̃]
qui n'existent pas en français.

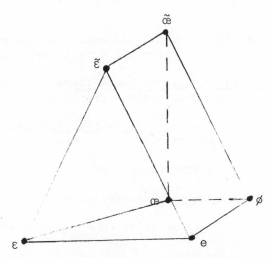

Fig. 4: VOYELLES MI-ANTERIEURES DU FRANÇAIS: En haut:
nasales; en bas: orales; devant: non-labiales;
derrière: labiales à gauche: ouvertes; à
droite: fermées. La disposition de la figure
montre que le contraste ouvert ˜ fermé est
neutralisé par la nasalité.

modifie la façon dont se fait le décodage à tous les niveaux paradigmatiques.

Cela n'est pas surprenant parce que les éléments suprasegmentaux constituent un signifiant qui intervient à tous les niveaux depuis la phonétique jusqu'à la sémantique, en passant par tous les strates linguistiques, du son jusqu'au sémème.

La chaine sonore étant un continum, et les phénomènes d'articulation ayant une grande importance, le contenu acoustique d'un son dépend de sa place dans les courbes du contour de la phrase: on ne peut donc percevoir correctement un son qu'en fonction de ces courbes.

Si nous passons au niveau du phonème, les faits sont encore plus sensibles, et ils sont d'ailleurs bien connus. Dans la plupart de langues la repartition des allophones dépend en grande partie de la place par rapport à l'accent. Or celui-ci n'est pas perçu directement mais combiné avec les variations de fréquence, d'amplitude et de rythme. De plus, beaucoup de morphonèmes sont réalisés uniquement par des moyens suprasegmentaux, par exemple les jonctions.

C'est ainsi que seuls les éléments suprasegmentaux permettent de distinguer entre les deux phrases espagnoles:

Señor, muerto está; tarde hemos llegado (Seigneur, il est mort; nous sommes arrivés trop tard)

Señor muerto, esta tarde hemos llegado (Monsieur le mort, nous sommes arrivés cette après midi);

ou selon l'exemple du Professeur Faure:

Jean Laval, ma soeur (présentation de deux personnes)

Jean l'avale, ma soeur (mise en garde en s'adressant à une réligieuse)

Jean Laval, masseur (présentation d'une personne).

Il s'ensuit que l'intonation conditionne l'identification des morphèmes en contribuant à leur segmentation. Mais de plus, certains morphèmes ne sont constitués que par des éléments suprasegmentaux. C'est souvent le cas de la marque de l'interrogation:

<u>Il vient</u>   <u>Il vient</u>?

mais parfois aussi d'autres marques.

Plus souvent, c'est seulement l'identification du lexème qui dépend de l'intonation: <u>señor</u> seigneur ou monsieur, <u>soeur</u> lien de parenté ou réligieuse, le morphème restant le même.

Enfin, au niveau sémantique, l'intonation constitué l'expressivité qui peut changer totalement le sens d'un phrase (parler par antiphrase). Selon la façon dont on prononce

<u>Il est gentil, ce garçon</u>,

la jeune fille à qui l'on s'adresse rougit ou non: "il te plaît bien!", "c'est un grossier personnage", "il n'est pas très fort" et même, tout simplement "je trouve que ce garçon est gentil".

Nous renvoyons le lecteur à notre petite étude <u>Notes de Phonétique suprasegmentale</u>[5] et nous signalons que Mademoiselle Monique Callamand est en train de travailler sur la question[6] avec nous, et qu'elle doit poursuivre ses recherches au CRLLB.[7]

Passons maintenant aux deux propositions concernant l'UTILISATION DU CONTEXTE.

5. <u>Utilisation du contexte à tous les niveaux paradig-matiques</u>: L'information obtenue à tous les niveaux paradigmatiques est utilisée pour le décodage des éléments environants. Le contexte connu modifie d'une façon plus ou moins considérable le processus de décodage, transformant l'ordre dans lequel sont normalement posées certaines questions, et surtout en supprimant d'autres. Cela concerne non seulement les paramètres des différents niveaux, mais l'ordre d'identification des strates lui-même. Par exemple il arrive dans certains cas qu'un lexème est deviné par le contexte, le morphème correspondant m'étant même pas entendu, quitte à effectuer après coup une verification pour s'assurer que le morphème en question est bien là. Cette influence du contexte n'est pas obligatoirement <u>progressive</u>: ce n'est pas nécessairement sur la façon dont nous décoderons ce

107

qui va suivre qu'influent les informations déjà
acquises. L'information contextuelle agit aussi
regressivement, sur ce qui précède, soit que
l'identification d'éléments précédents ait été
laissée totalement ou partiellement en suspens,
soit qu'elle soit rectifiée après coup par
l'identification de ce qui suit.

Voyons d'abord la modification dans l'ordre des
questions concernant les paramètres, et leur suppression
éventuelle. Si l'on se rapporte à la Fig. 3 on remarque
qu'il n'y a rien au bas à gauche du cube: les phonèmes
/ø̃/ et /ẽ/ n'existent pas en français. Le trait de
nasalité neutralise l'opposition de timbre, autrement dit,
sur cette figure la place qu'occupent /œ̃/ et /ɛ/ sur les
arêtes de droite n'est pas pertinente. Une meilleure
représentation est donnée par la figure 4, qui rend compte
de cette neutralisation. Cela montre qu'il est plus
économique de poser d'abord la question de nasalité: si
la réponse est "ce n'est pas non-nasal", le paramètre de
timbre se trouve du même coup éliminé ainsi que les dégrés
antérieur et postérieur du paramètre de point d'articulation, et les questions correspondantes n'ont plus besoin
d'être posées. Par contre, si l'on commence par le point
d'articulation, le degré antérieur élimine le timbre et la
nasalité, le degré postérieur, le timbre, la nasalité et
la labialité, le degré médial, la labialité. L'ordre
indiqué par la figure 2 est basé sur l'importance
statistique des contrastes. Mais l'ordre utilisé
effectivement par l'auditeur natif est certainement
modifié à chaque instant par l'information déjà obtenue,
le moyen le plus économique étant déterminé par ce que
l'on croit avoir le plus de chances d'apparaître en
fonction du contexte.

Le mot enfantin "dodo" était entendu /tutu/ par une
bonne andalouse. Après une voyelle le phonème /d/ est
réalisé en espagnol par la fricative [ð], donc pour cette
personne, la réponse était "ce n'est pas un /d/." La
seule dentale mate possible était donc obligatoirement
/t/ et la question concernant l'opposition lenis-fortis
qui aurait permis de rectifier l'erreur n'était même pas
posée. L'exemple est intéressant, parce qu'il prouve que,
dans ce cas, on a posé très tôt la question d'occlusivité,
trait qui n'est pas pertinent en espagnol et qui normalement n'intervient éventuellement que pour apporter un
supplément d'information. C'est le contexte immédiat, le
fait que le phonème précédent était déjà identifié comme

108

une voyelle, qui a provoqué ce bouleversement dans l'ordre des questions. C'est un exemple d'influence <u>progressive</u>.[8]

Dans la chanson "Lili Marlene", célèbre pendant la guerre, le mot allemand [marle n] était entendu /marlɛn/ parce que la présence de la consonne finale neutralisant le timbre dans le cas de l'archiphonème /E/, la question correspondante n'était pas posée, et la variante combinatoire normale dans cette position en français, était automatiquement supplée par le contexte.

6. <u>L'utilisation du contexte est normale</u> On ne recourt pas seulement au contexte quand l'information est insuffisante, ce qui est souvent le cas. Le contexte intervient toujours pour commander le processus de décodage et le rendre plus économique. Comme on l'a vu, cette recherche de l'économie conduit à ne plus poser de questions une fois que l'on croit avoir obtenu suffisamment d'information. Et cette "optimalisation" peut conduire à des erreurs à tous les niveaux quand un événement jugé peu probable vient à se réaliser.

En effet on n'<u>entend</u> pas plus tous les phonèmes de la chaîne parlée qu'on ne <u>lit</u> toutes les lettres de la chaîne écrite. Le contexte peut nous faire deviner partiellement ou totalement un morphème, affectant la façon dont sont identifiés tous les phonèmes qui les rendent. Cela est également vrai pour les strates morphémique, lexémique et sémémique, bien qu'à un moindre degré. Les erreurs des dactylos tapant des textes scientifiques portent souvent sur des mots connus mais qu'elles n'attendent pas dans le contexte.

L'intonation, comme on peut s'y attendre, agit surtout contextuellement et souvent elle permet de lever des ambiguités que l'environement segmental (quel que soit le strate) ne permet pas de résoudre.

Les six points que nous venons d'exposer concernent le décodage immédiat et médiat dans les conditions normales: réception dans des conditions acoustiques satisfaisantes, la communication s'effectuant entre deux adultes normaux s'exprimant dans leur langue maternelle. Avant de passer au cas de l'AUDITEUR ETRANGER, nous allons exposer les deux points qui concernent les CAS PARTICULIERS DE DECODAGE, valables également pour des adultes natifs.

7. <u>Transmission mauvaise</u> Quand le canal détériore le
    signal en supprimant de l'information, en la
    distordant ou en ajoutant du bruit, le processus de
    décodage est modifié en conséquence. L'information
    jugée moins sûre est utilisé, et l'on se rabat sur
    l'information plus claire, dont on fait un plus
    large usage. Naturellement, l'information
    contextuelle prend de ce fait une importance encore
    plus grande que dans les conditions normales.

Cette utilisation forcée de l'information bien reçue
au détriment du reste, conduit souvent à bouleverser la
hiérarchie des paramètres, et par conséquent, l'ordre du
décodage. Il n'est pas rare, par exemple, que des traits
secondaires, ou même redondants, se substituent complètement aux traits pertinents si leur contenu acoustique se
trouve déformé par une distorsion électronique (téléphone)
ou acoustique (hall d'un gare), masqué par du bruit, ou, à
plus forte raison, fortement atténué ou même supprimé.

C'est ainsi que la bande passante du téléphone se
situant en dessous des fréquences nécessaires pour la
distinction entre les consonnes normales et palatalisées
du russe (<u>dures</u> et <u>molles</u> selon la terminologie grammati-
cale traditionnelle, becarres et dièzes selon la
terminologie de la phonétique acoustique), l'auditeur
concentre son attention sur le timbre de la voyelle
adjacente, dont la variante combinatoire est souvent
conditionnée par la nature de la consonne. Par exemple
devant consonne palatalisée /e/ est réalisé [e] et non [ɛ];
après consonne palatalisée /i/ est réalisé [i] et non [ɨ].[9]
Cette opposition de timbre vocalique qui n'est pas normalement pertinente pour l'identification des <u>voyelles</u>--les
russes ne remarquent même pas la nuance dans bien des
cas--devient l'élément déterminent pour l'identification
de la <u>consonne</u> qui les précède ou les suit. Nous avons
là un exemple du bouleversement de la hiérarchie des
paramètres en même temps que de l'influence progressive
et regressive du contexte dans le cas d'une transmission
défectueuse.

8. <u>Au moment de l'émission</u> La discrimination auditive
    intervient aussi au moment de la production de la
    parole. L'auto-audition immédiate constitue le
    feedback ajustant à chaque instant l'articulation
    pour nous permettee de parler correctement.

Cette retroaction implique un décodage plus complexe que la perception normale parce que tout se passe comme si le signal passait à travers une sorte de filtre correcteur compensant la distorsion introduite par la conduction interne (directement des organes phonateurs à la membrane basilaire à travers les muscles et les os). Or ce filtre semble bien être _sélectif_, c'est à dire qu'il agit en fonction de l'importance fonctionnelle du signal et _individuel_, c'est à dire qu'ils est adapté à la structure anatomique et aux habitudes articulatoires du sujet.

Tout le processus d'autoaudition dépend donc à la fois du système phonologique de la langue _et_ des caractéristiques personnelles du locuteur. Nous n'avons pas la possibilité de nous étendre ici sur cette question fort complexe où beaucoup de travail reste à faire. Nous avons essayer de clarifier le problème en vue de recherches ultérieures dans une récente étude à laquelle nous renvoyons le lecteur[10].

Ce probleme a évidemment une importance énorme pour l'enseignement des langues comme nous allons le voir à propos de la discrimination auditive chez L'AUDITEUR ETRANGER, rubrique qui groupe les quatre derniers points de notre hypothèse de travail, et que nous allons aborder maintenant.

9. _Le processus de décodage utilisé_ L'auditeur étranger utilise le processus de décodage de sa langue maternelle qui est le seul qu'11 possède en abordant l'etude de la seconde langue. Or ce processus n'est pas fait pour la langue cible. Il ne prévoit, pour le décodage, ni les mêmes catégories ni la même hiérarchie fonctionnelle. L'étudiant ne peut donc pas poser les bonnes questions, ni les poser dans le bon ordre. Il n'entend pas ce qu'il faut entendre, et attribue une importance excessive dont il tire des conclusions erronées à des informations qui parfois ne sont meme pas prises en considération par le natif. L'auditeur étranger peut être considéré comme un malentendant.

Nous avons déjà donné des exemples mettant en jeu l'audition d'une langue étrangère: /e/, allemands attendu /ɛ/ par des français; /d/, /o/ français entendus respectivement /t/, /u/ par des espagnols; etc. De même

/i/ et /ɪ/ anglais sont confondus par les personnes
parlant une langue romane; /y/ français est confondu avec
/i/ par les hispanophones, avec /u/ par les anglophones;
les consonnes arabes vélaires et post-vélaires sont
largement confondues entre elles par la plupart des
occidentaux. Certains phonèmes ne sont pas entendus du
tout, par exemples le /h/ des langues germaniques ou le
/ʔ/ (stød du danois, hamsa de l'arabe) ne sont pas
entendus par les français.

Il en est de même des éléments prosodiques, qu'ils
soient segmentaux ou suprasegmentaux. On sait la
difficulté qu'éprouvent les occidentaux à entendre
correctement les tons du chinois ou du vietnamien.

Pour des raisons analogues les français n'entendent
pas l'accent d'intensité des expagnols qui en renvanche
substituent un brutal accroissement de l'intensité à
l'accent en grande partie tonal de l'italien, ou en grande
partie quantitatif (longueur) et qualitatif (netteté du
timbre de la voyelle) du portugais ou du russe.

Par des comparaisons phonetiques, le linguiste peut
prévoir les erreurs de discrimination (et par conséquent
de production de l'étranger). Quand ses prédictions se
trouvent infirmées par les faits, c'est généralement que
son analyse a été trop superficielle. Le plus souvent ces
"comparaisons" se bornent à mettre face à face des listes
de phonèmes avec leur réalisations principales. L'analyse
en traits pertinents et secondaires manque le plus souvent,
et quand elle est faite, il est rare que la hiérarchie
fonctionnelle pour les différents environnements soit prise
en considération. Il est encore plus rare que l'on tienne
compte des variations dialectales de la langue source; et
la notion de diasystème, pourtant essentielle pour la
perception de la parole, manque dans la plupart de ces
études.11

Cependant la meilleure de ces comparaisons phonologiques ne saurait tout prévoir sans erreur, précisément
parce qu'elle ne peut être qu'une comparaison phonologique
alors que le décodage implique un incessant va-et-vient
entre l'information obtenue aux différents niveaux comme
on l'a vue au point 5. Or nous allons voir dans les
trois derniers points que ce processus ne peut pas se
dérouler de la même façon chez l'auditeur étranger.

10. <u>Les conditions de l'enseignement</u> font que l'étranger se trouve le plus souvent dans une situation artificielle en ce qui concerne la linéarité et les niveaux de conscience. Cette situation dépend de la méthode d'enseignement utilisée, et elle change constamment au fur et à mesure que les études avancent. Le plus souvent l'image du signifiant écrit (orthographe) vient interférer avec la perception orale, rendant le processus plus complexe. Les temps d'intégration sont plus courts que chez le natif et les niveaux de conscience plus élevés aux strates phonétique et lexémique.

Dans la plupart des cas, l'influence du signifiant écrit constitue l'élément le plus important. La segmentation en unités linguistiques, et par conséquent les temps d'intégration aux différents niveaux paradigmatiques tend à se mouler sur les divisions de l'orthographe. Le niveau de conscience maximal correspond au signifiant du mot écrit plutôt qu'au monème.

L'étranger est plus conscient que le natif aux strates phonémique et surtout phonétique parce que les exercices de prononciation attirent constamment son attention sur ces points. Il s'ensuit que le mot phonétique est plus conscient que le mot morphémique; or ce dernier bénéficie chez le natif du niveau de conscience maximal, immédiatement après le monème.

D'autre part l'étudiant ne maîtrise pas suffisamment les différentes structures syntaxiques servant de cadre pour des suites relativement longues et permettant ainsi au natif de les identifier partiellement en bloc, c'est à dire en mettant en jeu des temps d'intégration plus longs. Enfin, le plus souvent le rythme utilisé en classe--et parfois même au laboratoire de langues, quand il existe--est nettement plus lent que dans la conversation normale: l'étudiant est habitué à un rythme de perception plus lent, ce qui tend à raccourcir les temps d'intégration, le contexte étant moins disponible à un instant donné, et la mémoire véhiculaire devant embrasser une plus grande période de temps pour une même longueur de signifiant linguistique.

11. <u>Le contexte</u> ne peut pas jouer le même rôle chez l'étranger que chez le natif pour les raisons que l'on vient d'exposer pour le point 9, notamment en

ce qui concerne le temps d'intégration. Mais la
raison la plus importante, c'est que le contexte lui
apporte beaucoup moins d'information parce qu'il ne
connaît pas les règles d'accord entre les différentes unités linguistiques d'un même strate, et
surtout que certains monèmes peuvent être inconnus
de lui.

Ne maitrissant pas le système phonémique de la langue
étrangère, l'étudiant ne tient pas compte des incompatibi-
lités séquentielles et accepte la possibilité de suites de
phonèmes interdites par les règles phonologiques. Il se
prive ainsi de l'information contextuelle qui simplifie le
processus de discrimination du natif en restreignant le
nombre de traits pertinents à un instant donné. Quand le
contexte est utilisé pour modifier le processus d'audition,
c'est presque toujours en accord avec les règles phonologiques de la langue maternelle (point 8). Au lieu d'une
optimalisation nous avons alors plutot le remplacement de
certaines erreurs par d'autres. Par exemple le /ʕ/ arabe
est entendu par les français /ʀ/ dans /ʕin/, /a/ dans
/lʕwina/, et n'est pas entendu du tout dans /ʕali/, mots
du dialecte tunisien signifiant respectivement source,
petite source (El Aouina: nom de l'aéroport de Tunis) et
Ali.

La même méconnaissance des règles séquentielles
intervient aussi aux autres strates. Mais il arrive plus
fréquemment que le contexte ne puisse pas apporter
d'information tout simplement parce que des unités
linguistiques sont inconnues ou mal connues de l'élève:
on n'identifie pas un morphème parce que l'on ne l'a
jamais entendu ou parce qu'il n'a pas été mémorisé. On
ne reconnaît pas un lexème parce que--comme on dit--on a
oublié le sens de ce mot, etc. Ces "trous' seront peut
être comblés grace au contexte mais il n'en reste pas
moins, que même dans ce cas, le contexte ne fera
qu'apporter une information essentielle, alors qu'il
apporte au natif une redondance qui facilite considérablement le processus de décodage.

La méconnaissance des règles de phonémique suprasegmentale gêne aussi considérablement l'étudiant dans
son utilisation du contexte. Ce handicap se manifeste
surtout au niveau sémantique (expressivité) et au niveau
morphémique. Bien souvent des morphèmes connus ne sont
pas identifiés parce qu'une connaissance insuffisante
des règles de phonémique suprasegmentale fait que les

contours de fréquence et d'amplitude soient mal interprétés et conduisent à une segmentation erronée: "les mots sont mal coupés".

12. Difficultés d'ordre socio-culturel Les habitudes socio-culturelles de l'étudiant interviennent au niveau du signifié et notamment aux strates sémémique et sémantique. La compréhension et l'interprétation du message s'en trouvent gênées et parfois distordues. De plus, par le jeudes connotations dans la langue maternelle, et des ressemblances morphémiques entre celle-ci et la langue cible, des associations d'idées pouvant étendre ces difficultés aux strates du signifiant sont également susceptibles de se produire.

La substance du contenu, c'est à dire le sémantème, est souvent mal comprise à cause de ces différences socio-culturelles. Le mot pain ne signifie pas, pour un français, la même chose que le mot bread, pour un américain. Il en est de même de mots comme café, bar, pharmacie, et coffee, bar, drug store. La difficulté est de deux ordres: d'une part la catégorie d'objets et différente (one cup of coffee ne contient pas la même boisson qu'une tasse de café); d'autre part le champ de l'utilisation de ces objets est également différent: on boit du coffee pendant le repas, on boit du café après le repas.

La différence de champ d'utilisation se manifeste surtout par le contexte. S'il vient d'être question de coffee, un mot comme chili survenant dans la phrase suivante risque d'être compris comme désignant une liqueur et non une soupe de haricots. Il en est de même de la confiture que l'on sert avec les oeufs sur le plat, du fromage que l'on sert comme apéritif, des frites que l'on trempe dans la sauce tomate, ou des biscuits que l'on trempe dans le fromage. Dans ce dernier cas la difficulté de champ d'utilisation se combine avec la différence de catégorie d'objets: le fromage en question est en realité une sorte de crème.

On nous excusera d'avoir limité ici nos exemples à ces questions gastronomiques qui avaient l'avantage d'être plus frappantes. Il est évident que les différences socio-culturelles peuvent se retrouver partout. Dans la plupart des situations on peut rencontrer de triades de mots qui comme biscuit, tremper et fromage s'excluent

115

réciproquement dans l'esprit de l'auditeur étranger, rendant plus difficile l'identification du morphème et la reconnaissance du lexème.

Notre hypothèse de travail s'achève avec cette étude concernant l'AUDITEUR ETRANGER adulte. Nous n'avons pas abordé l'enfant étranger pas plus que l'enfant décodant sa langue maternelle.

Tout au cours de notre exposé nous avons souligné l'importance des associations d'idées sur l'axe syntagmatique—entre unités consécutives d'un même strate—comme sur l'axe paradigmatique—entre différents strates. Association d'idées, connotations, contexte, éléments suprasegmentaux, situation, nous conduisent à l'appréhension du message plus qu'à sa compréhension. En définitive le strate le plus important est le strate sémantique, qui est extra-linguistique. Plus que la langue, c'est l'usage qui en est fait qui importe pour la communication. Le point de vue du psychologue est donc aussi important que celui du linguiste.

La psycholinguistique, cette jeune science au domaine et aux objectifs encore mal définis, vient à point nommé pour jeter un pont entre le linguiste et le psychologue "purs", dont la coopération nous paraît indispensable pour comprendre le langage et la pensée en général et les problèmes que pose la discrimination auditive en particuller. C'est pourquoi des centres de recherche tels que le CRLLB, des publications telles que le LLBA, rassemblant 22 domaines de recherche relatifs au Langage et au Comportement Linguistique, nous paraissent riches de promesses pour le developpement des Sciences de l'Homme.[12]

Appendix A[13]

UNE HYPOTHESE DE TRAVAIL:

Nous partons de théories linguistiques généralement admises et que nous supposons connues:

a) Théorie phonémique: phonèmes, traits pertinents, neutrallsations, etc.

b) Théorie des niveaux paradygmatiques: forms et substance, expression et contenu chez Hjemsiev et la glossématique; strates chez Lamb et la linguistique stratificationnelle: sons, phonèmes, morphèmes, lexèmes, sémèmes.

Notre hypothèse comprend:

a) des points généralement admis par les linguistes et/ou les psychologues.
b) des points confirmés par l'observation.
c) des points rendant compte des phénomènes observables mais pas nécessairement prouvés par eux.

LE DECODAGE IMMEDIAT:

1. <u>Linéarité</u>: le message est perçu d'une façon linéaire, mais la linéarité décroît au fur et à mesure que l'on atteint des niveaux plus élevés (de plus en plus bas sur la figure 1, qui indique l'ordre de décodage).

2. <u>Niveau de conscience</u>: maximum au niveau du monème et décroissant des qu'on s'on éloigne (Fig. 1).

3. <u>Identification par éliminations successives</u>: tout se passe comme si les phonèmes étalent identifés par élimination en commençant par les traits les plus importants. Exemple das voyelles françaises (Fig. 2).

4. <u>Importance primordiale des phénomènes suprasegmen-taux</u> qui appartiennent à tous les niveaux. Voir <u>Motes de phonétique suprasegmentale</u>, E. Companys, polycopié au BEL, Paris 1965.

L'UTILISATION DU CONTEXTE:

5. <u>Information obtenue à tous les niveaux paradygma-tiques</u>: modifie l'ordre d'élimination en restreignant les possibilités d'apparition.

6. <u>Cette utilisation est normale</u>: les natifs font des erreurs de discrimination quand lis sont privés du contexte.

CAS PARTICULIERS DU DECODAGE:

7. <u>Transmission mauvaise</u>: processus de discrimination modifié: par exemple des traits secondaires deviennent pertinent (téléphone).

8. <u>Au moment de l'émission</u>: la discrimination auditive fournit le feedback à travers un système de correction compensant les distorsions de la conduction interne et qui est fonction de la langue et de l'individu.

L'AUDITEUR ETRANGER:

9. <u>Le processus de décodage</u> utilisé est celul de la langue maternelle.

10. <u>Les conditions de l'enseignement</u> font qu'll n'a ni la même linéarité ni les mêmes niveaux de conscience que le natif.

11. <u>Le contexte</u> ne paut pas être utilisé comme chez le natif.

12. <u>Difficultés d'ordre socio-culturel</u> s'adjoutant aux difficultés linguistiques à tous les niveaux paradygmatiques. L'étranger a encore moins le temps d'utiliser le raisonnement que le natif.

Appendix B [12]
(English version of Appendix A)

A WORKING HYPOTHESIS:

We begin with generally accepted linguistic theories that we take to be known.

(a) Phonemic theory: phonemes, distinctive features, neutralizations, etc.
(b) Theory of paradigmatic levels: form and substance expression and content according to Hjelmslev and glossematics; strata according to Lamb and stratificational linguistics: sounds, phonemes, morphemes, lexemes, sememes.

Our hypothesis includes:

(a) points generally accepted by linguists and/or psychologists.
(b) points confirmed by observation.
(c) points accounting for observable phenomena but not necessarily proved by them.

IMMEDIATE DECODING:

1. <u>Linearity</u>: The message is perceived linearly, but linearity decreases proportionately as higher levels are reached (progressively lower in Fig. 1, which indicates the order of decoding).

2. <u>Level of consciousness</u>: maximal at the level of the moneme and decreasing according to distance away from it (Fig. 1).

3. <u>Identification by successive eliminations</u>: everything happens as if phonemes were identified by elimination beginning with most important features. Example of French vowels (Fig. 2).

4. <u>Primary importance of suprasegmental phenomena</u> which belong to all levels. See E. Companys, <u>Notes de phonétique suprasegmentale</u>. Paris: BELC, 1965.

UTILIZATION OF CONTEXT:

5. <u>Information obtained at all paradigmatic levels</u>: modifies the order of elimination by limiting the possibilities of appearance.

6. <u>This utilization is normal</u>: native speakers make errors of discrimination when they are deprived of context.

SPECIAL CASES OF DECODING:

7. <u>Poor transmission</u>: process of discrimination is modified; for example, secondary features become distinctive (telephone).

8. <u>At the moment of production</u>: auditory information provides feedback through a correction system which is a function of the language and of the individual and which compensates for the distortions of internal conduction.

THE FOREIGN LISTENER:

9. <u>The process of decoding</u> used is that of native language.

10. The conditions of teaching are such that he has neither the same linearity nor the same levels of consciousness as the native speaker.

11. The context cannot be utilized as by the native speaker.

12. Difficulties of the socio-cultural level add to the linguistic difficulties at all paradigmatic levels. The foreigner has still less time to use reasoning than the native speaker.

Footnotes

[1] This report is based partially on research supported by a contract with the Office of Education, U. S. Department of Health, Education & Welfare, P. L. 83-531, Cooperative Research, and Title VI, P. L. 85-564, as amended.

[2] The author is a member of the research staff at the Center for Research on Language and Language Behavior, and formerly a member of the Bureau pour l'Enseignement de la Langue et de la Civilisation Francaise à l'Etranger (BELC), Paris, France.

[3] Pour la phonétique et la phonémique voir les ouvrages suivants:

Kaiser, L. Manual of Phonetics. Amsterdam: North-Holland publ. Co., 1957.

*Malmberg, Bertil. La Phonétique. Paris, Presses Universitaires de France, 1960.

Malmberg, Bertil. Phonetics. New York: Dover Publications Inc., 1963.

Martinet, André. Phonology as Functional Phonetics. Oxford: Blackwell, 1955.

Troubetzkoy, N. S. Principes de phonologie. Paris: Klincksieck, 1957.

*Jakobson, Roman, et al. Preliminaries to speech analysis, the distinctive features and their correlates Cambridge, Mass.: M. I. T. Press, 1966.

Vachek, Josef. <u>A Prague school reader in linguistics</u>, Bloomington, London: Indiana University Press, 1966.

Pike, Kenneth L. <u>Phonemics</u>, a technique for reducing languages to writing. Ann Arbor: University of Michigan Press, 1964.

*Martinet, André. <u>Eléments de linguistique générale</u>. Paris: Collection Armand Collin, 1960.

Martinet, André. <u>La linguistique synchronique, études et recherches</u>. Paris: Presses Universitaire s de France.

*[<u>Remarque</u>: Dans la sélection ci-dessus nous avons marqué d'un astérisque les ouvrages dont la lecture nous paraît la plus importante au début. En outre, le manuel de KAISER constitue un livre de base pour la phonétique et la phonologie, et l'ouvrage de PIKE est le meilleur manuel de phonémique appliquée que nous connaissions.]

⁴Pour plus de détails voir:

Companys, Emmanuel. <u>Signifiant et signifié</u>. Paris: B.E.L.C., 1966.

⁵Companys, Emmanuel. <u>Notes de phonétique suprasegmentale</u>. Paris: BEL, 1965.

⁶Callamand, Monique. <u>Etude des composantes de l'accent en français</u>. Ann Arbor: Center for Research on Language and Language Behavior (CRLLB) University of Michigan, 1967 (in <u>Progress Report V</u>).

Companys, Emmanuel. <u>French suprasegmentals</u>, (rapport sur une recherche en cours) in <u>Progress Report V</u>, Ann Arbor: Center for Research on Language and Language Behavior, University of Michigan, 1967.

⁷Le CRLLB est particulièrement bien équipé pour des recherches sur l'intonation, grâce notamment à un ordinateur PDP. 4 et au SAID, appareil construit au centre qui compare automatiquement deux phrases en termes de fréquence, amplitude et durées relatives. Sur le SAID voir:

Buiten, R. L. et Lane, H. L. <u>A self-instructional device for conditioning accurate prosody</u> (a) tiré àpart

CRLLB, University of Michigan, (b) in Int. Rev. Appl.
Ling. 1965, 3, 205-219, (c) in Valdman, A. (Ed.).
Trends in language teaching: New York: McGraw-Hill,
1966.

Lane, H. L. et Brethower, D. M. Reconditioning vocal
rhythm with an auto-instructional device, Proceedings
XIII Int. Cong. on Logopedics and Phoniatrics, 1965,
325-327.

Rammuny, R. An analysis of the differences in the
prosodies of General American English and Colloquial
Jordanian Arabic and their effect on second-language
acquisition. Ann Arbor: CRLLB, The University of
Michigan, 1966.

[8]Nous avons également ici un bon exemple de
l'identification des phonèmes par élimination: le [o]
fermé français est pris pour un /u/ bien que sa réalisatio
phonétique [o] soit plus proche de [ǫ] (timbre moyen du
/o/ espagnol) que de [u].

[9]Voir un exemple analogue cité dans Preliminaries to
speech analysis ouvrage cité: 1.2 pa. 8. Il concerne la
paire minimale russe [sir'ejut] (deviennent humides) et
[şir'ejut] (deviennent gris).

[10]Problèmes psychopédagogiques des laboratoires des
langues, section III: Le système audio-actif. Ann Arbor:
Center for Research on Language and Language Behavior,
The University of Michigan, 1967.

[11]Nous nous sommes efforcés de ne pas mériter ces
critiques dans notre petit livre à l'usage des professeurs
de français: Phonétique française pour hispanophones,
Collection "Le Français dans le Monde-BELC" Paris,
Hachette-Larousse, 1966. Voir aussi les brochures
polycopiées au BELC suivantes, établis sous notre
direction et qui seront publiées dans la même collection:

Companys et Gallison: Phonétique française pour
italophones (deuxième édition en préparation).

Companys et Harvey: Comparaison phonologique entre le
français et l'arabe dialectal de Syrie et de Tunisie.

Hermann: Phonétique française pour germanophones.

Harvey: Phonétique française pour anglophones.

122

[12]The author has included a summary of his paper (in French) which is included here for the benefit of readers. The English version (translated by F. Phillip) was also included for non-French readers.

PROGRAMMED MATERIALS FOR TEACHING ARABIC SCRIPT[1]

Ernest McCarus and Raji M. Rammuny[2]

The teaching of Arabic has undergone a revolution in this country since World War II, with several revisions and adjustments. A basic principle would be enunciated, put into practical terms, then revised on the basis of experience and hindsight. For example, fifteen years ago, it was felt that the teaching of Arabic should be "natural," that is, it should reflect what the Arab himself does in learning Arabic. Today, the feeling is gaining ground that Arabic should be taught in such a way as to satisfy the probable needs of American students. I would like to describe here a particular set of teaching problems that Dr. Raji Rammuny and I are working on, and our progress to date in resolving them.

First, permit me to make a few remarks concerning what is often loosely called "the Arabic language." The Arab of today is born into a situation called "diglossia," the use of two quite different forms of a language to satisfy one's linguistic needs. That is, every Arab speaks the local Arabic dialect of the community in which he is born and brought up, using this colloquial dialect for all his usual day-to-day oral communications. These dialects vary from one community to the next throughout the Arab world, and a person's precise origin can be determined from his speech. On the other hand, there is a literary Arabic which is used for practically all written communication, as well as for formal speeches or discussions. This literary Arabic is uniform throughout the world, so that newspapers or books published in Damascus, Tunis or New York will be in essentially the same literary idiom. This literary Arabic must be learned through many years of schooling and cannot be picked up from the environment, as a dialect is. Thus, for example, if this conference today were being given in Arabic, I would be delivering this talk in literary Arabic. Then, if I were to make arrangements for lunch with somebody, I would probably do so using my local dialect. Romance scholars will be reminded of medieval Europe, where

literary Latin was the medium of communication for all
serious discourse and written communication, whereas the
vernacular--French, Italian or Spanish, etc.--was used for
day-to-day activities.

The traditional way of teaching Arabic is to give
the students a medieval literary Arabic text and a
reference grammar and then start translating this into
English. Today, most Arabists agree that it is desirable
to teach both modern literary Arabic and some colloquial
dialect; it really does not matter too much which colloquial dialect is chosen. One of the controversies in the
teaching of Arabic today is which should come first, the
colloquial or the literary. At first the consensus was
for teaching the colloquial first and then the literary,
since this is what the Arab does. On the other hand, the
Arab has no choice--he has to follow this sequence--whereas
the American student might be better off following a
different order. At any rate, the trend in American
colleges in recent years has been to start with the
literary, later on adding a colloquial. Furthermore, the
consensus has come to favor instruction based on an audio-
lingual, or some sort of oral, approach. Aside from the
advantages usually adduced for the audio-lingual approach
in foreign language teaching from a pedagogical point of
view, the fact that a dialect should eventually be
attacked is also, I think, an important argument for
devoting a great deal of attention to the pronunciation
of literary Arabic from the beginning.

Arabic has its share of difficult consonants, such
as χ, ɣ, ʕ, ħ, and q. The fact that phoneticians love to
talk about the "emphatic" consonants of Arabic, its
pharyngeals, and other unusual sounds is little consola-
tion for the student who merely wants to learn to read
Arabic. But the problems of double language--diglossia--
and of a difficult phonology are not the extent of the
student's tribulations. There is still the Arabic writing
system. The 28 letters of the alphabet are used to
represent the 29 consonants, plus the three long vowels.
The three short vowels are represented by diacritic marks
added above or below a given letter; when these are
written, Arabic script is fully phonemic (or, rather,
morphophonemic). For example, this is the letter د d;
دا daa is د d plus the long vowel ا aa; and دَ da
is د d plus the short vowel ◌َ a. The three short
vowels are illustrated in دَب dab, دُب dub and دِب dib.

125

Normally, however, these diacritic marks are not used
(they usually are found in the Koran and elementary
textbooks); thus you might see on the page the combination
دب which could be pronounced <u>dab</u>, <u>dub</u> or <u>dib</u>, depending
on which one best fits the context. That is, Arabic is
written for those who know Arabic, not for the beginning
foreign student who has yet to master the vocabulary.

The writing system is further complicated by a
multiplicity of shapes for each letter, depending on its
position in the word. For example, the letter for <u>b</u> is
ب in its independent form, but ب when joined to a
following letter, ب when joined to preceding and following letters, and ب when joined only to a preceding
letter. ب written three times appears as ببب .

Although the Arabic writing system is simple in the
ideal, in practice it is a bit complicated. Since mastering the language itself--the phonology, morphology, syntax
and especially lexicon--is quite a burden for Americans,
the favored approach just after the War was to postpone
the writing system in order to tackle as few complicated
problems at a time as possible. Psychologically, however,
most students feel achievement when they attack the
writing system. This exotic script symbolizes for them
the real language; controlling it gives them a feeling of
progress and accomplishment. At the same time, in an
oral approach, a phonemic transcription often amounts
to not much more than a mnemonic device for remembering
texts, and the ones who do master the phonemic system as
such are usually those who never feel quite at home when
they transfer to the Arabic script itself. Accordingly,
we have introduced the Arabic script earlier and earlier
each succeeding year, and now our attempt is to bypass
phonemic transcription altogether.

We believe that the audio-lingual approach tackles
many of the problems mentioned above. Its immediate
concentration on oral work permits mastery of the phonolog
from the beginning of language study, and, at the same
time, anticipates the eventual study of a dialect;
structural drills permit the controlled introduction and
assimilation of new vocabulary, a serious problem, since
English and Arabic are not cognate languages. As for
the writing system, Dr. Rammuny and I are currently
engaged, under the auspices of the CRLLB, in the preparation of what will ultimately be a programmed,

self-instructional course on the Arabic writing system,
with emphasis on the relationship between the sound and
its written symbol. We are also preparing handwriting
exercises coordinated with the reading drills.

In May and June of this year Dr. Rammuny tested
twelve American students whose study of Arabic had ranged
from one semester to several years. The first part of the
test involved the recording of their oral reading of a
text in Arabic from Arabic script; the second part was a
test of their aural perception of Arabic phonemes played
to them from a tape. The errors were listed and classified as pronunciation errors--for example, failure to
pharyngalize a given sequence of phonemes; or reading
errors for example, misreading ﺩ d for ﺫ th, the
difference in these two being a dot in the Arabic writing
system. These were compared with our collective empirical
experience and a list of problem areas was drawn up; for
example, these included long consonants and long vowels as
opposed to short ones, and pharyngeal and velarized
consonants.

Another preparatory step was to analyze Arabic script
in terms of basic recurrent elements common to groups of
letters. Thus, the letters ﺱ s, ﺵ sh, ﺹ ṣ, and
ﺽ ḍ are based on the letter ﻥ n. By grouping these
together with ﻝ as the basic component element some
economy is obtained. In this analysis we had recourse to
selected samples of handwriting and penmanship manuals
from the Arab world. We also used the electro-writer of
the Center, an instrument which isolates and records on
strip charts the direction of the movements of the hand,
helping identify the basic recurrent elements of letters.
The letters were then grouped according to similarities of
component elements and ordered by groups according to
general applicability of those basic elements.

A separate study was conducted to choose the most
useful vocabulary. We went through ten basic textbooks
of modern literary Arabic in use in this country and
extracted their vocabulary, sorting this out on a sorting
machine in terms of words which were used in all ten books,
those in all nine books, and so on. This gives us, of
course, not necessarily words of high frequency in the
language as a whole, but high-frequency "textbook Arabic."
We chose first those items of greatest frequency in order
to permit the widest possible use of these materials. We

were obliged in many cases, however, to use low-frequency
words in order to exemplify all combinations of letters.

On the basis of these preparations the following sets
of materials were made:

(1) reading exercises to introduce the letters of
     the alphabet (see Figure 2);

(2) pronunciation drills to precede the reading
     exercises, to help link up the aural and visual
     symbols (see Fig. 1);

(3) writing exercises, to develop proper handwriting
     from the outset (Fig. 3);

(4) a series of three taped tests for each reading-
     and-writing unit, measuring aural perception,
     recognition of written symbols, and ability to
     write in response to oral cues (Fig. 4).

Figs. 1-4 represent a typical sequence in instruction.
These materials are now being used in class, and are being
constantly modified in accordance with student response.
This unit introduces and drills the letters ع ʕ and
 غ ɤ. Fig. 1 is a pronunciation drill that presents
the consonants in question. The instructor first describes
the consonants in phonetic terms, contrasting them with
each other, with other Arabic consonants as pertinent, and
with English. Non-technical hints on production are given,
as "to produce غ ɤ, gargle without water." Then the
conventional repetition, perception and production drills
are done. During all of this the student does not see
the paper. Later on, when all the forms of this letter
have been introduced, this sheet can be given to the
student as a review reading drill.

Fig. 2 is a reading drill which introduces the two
new letters (see [A]; Arabic script reads from right to
left, as the reader may well know); this is the "independent form" of the letter. This is followed by the letters
of the alphabet [B] that have been taught so far, in
conventional order; the two new letters are boxed.
Examples in words, showing the relative size, height,
etc. of the letter are given after C. Section D gives
additional examples, using a variety of non-connecting
vowels and consonants. These examples are, as far as

128

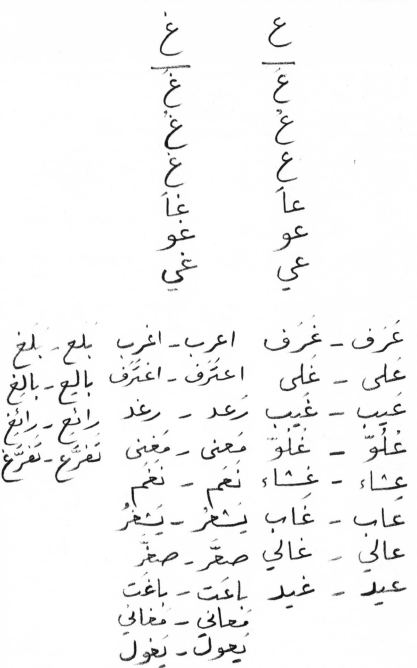

Fig. 1. Pronunciation Exercise.

129

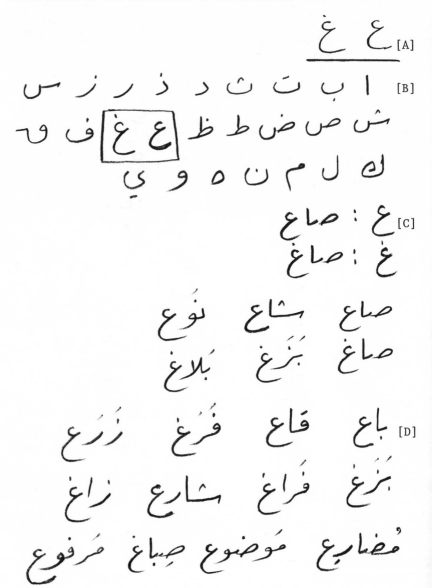

Fig. 2.   Reading Exercise.

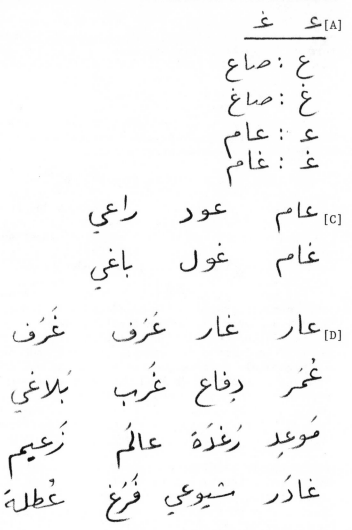

Fig. 2.   Reading Exercise (cont'd.)

possible, vocabulary that the class has studied or will be likely to come across. Fig. 2 (cont'd.) presents the form of these letters when joined to a following letter, usually called the "initial form" of the letter.

Next comes a writing drill (Fig. 3). Line A shows the order and direction of writing, and the relationship of the letter to the line. Tracing over dotted letters, completing partial forms, and unguided writing are some of the drill types illustrated here.

Finally come the tests (Fig. 4) which are done in the language laboratory. Part I, Pronunciation, tests the student's perception of the phonemes involved. In the Reading Test (Part II), the student must associate the word he hears on the tape with the proper spelling on the paper. The dictation drill (Part III) is an active test of perception, spelling and handwriting.

It may be of interest to note that these materials observe the approved sequence of listening, speaking, reading and writing, but vertically, rather than horizontally. Rather than concentrating on listening and speaking for the first five lessons, say, then adding reading and ultimately writing, we begin drilling all four skills from the beginning. We find that each of these activities complements and reinforces the others. Further, they give more of the individuals in the class an area in which to excel; thus we cater to a greater range of personalities.[4]

I should clarify the nature of the pronunciation drills described here. In previous years we have used pronunciation drills designed to treat pronunciation difficulties encountered by American students, and ordered by minimal pairs; we have always found them quite effective. This year, however, in order to tie together the spoken and written symbols, we presented the pronunciation drills in the same order as the corresponding letters. This necessitated the postponement of certain of the more difficult consonants, and the class' pronunciation was inferior to that of previous years. Consequently, we are reinstating the former phonologically-based pronunciation drills, and we now use both sets concurrently.

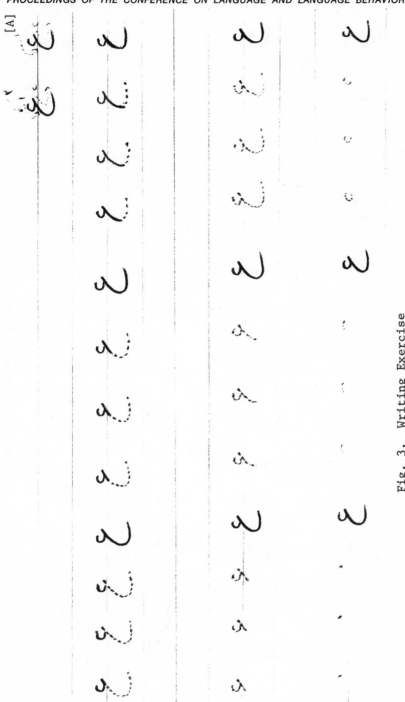

Fig. 3. Writing Exercise

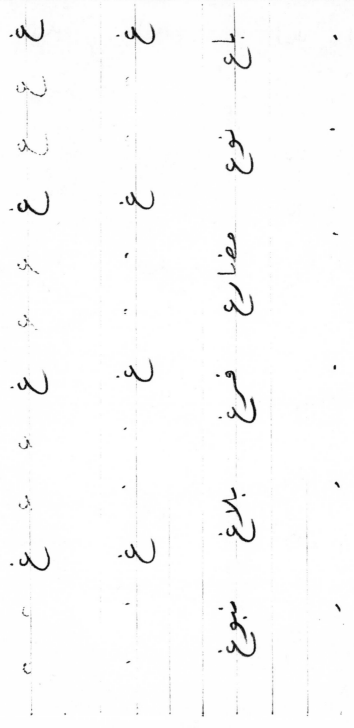

Fig. 3. Writing Exercise (cont'd.).

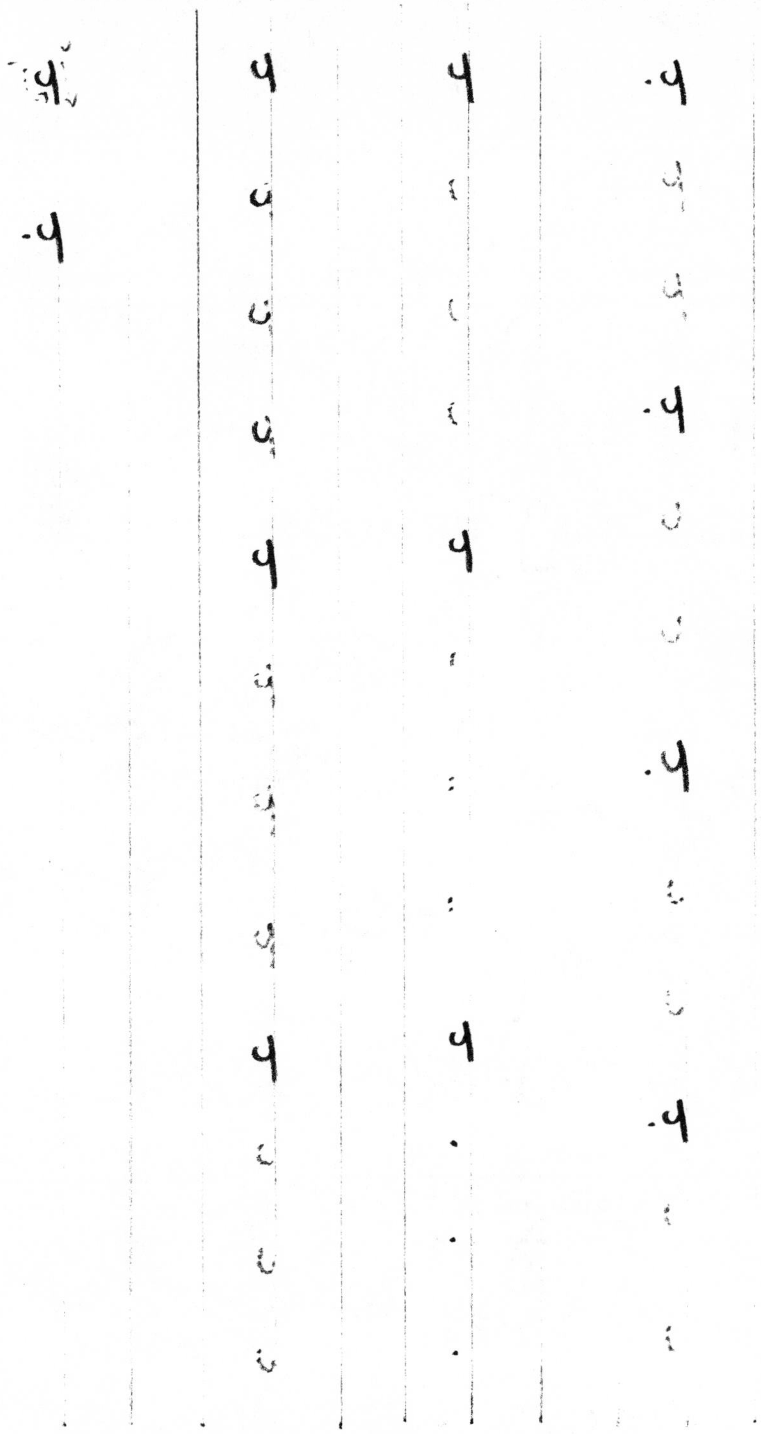

Fig. 3. Writing Exercise (cont'd.).

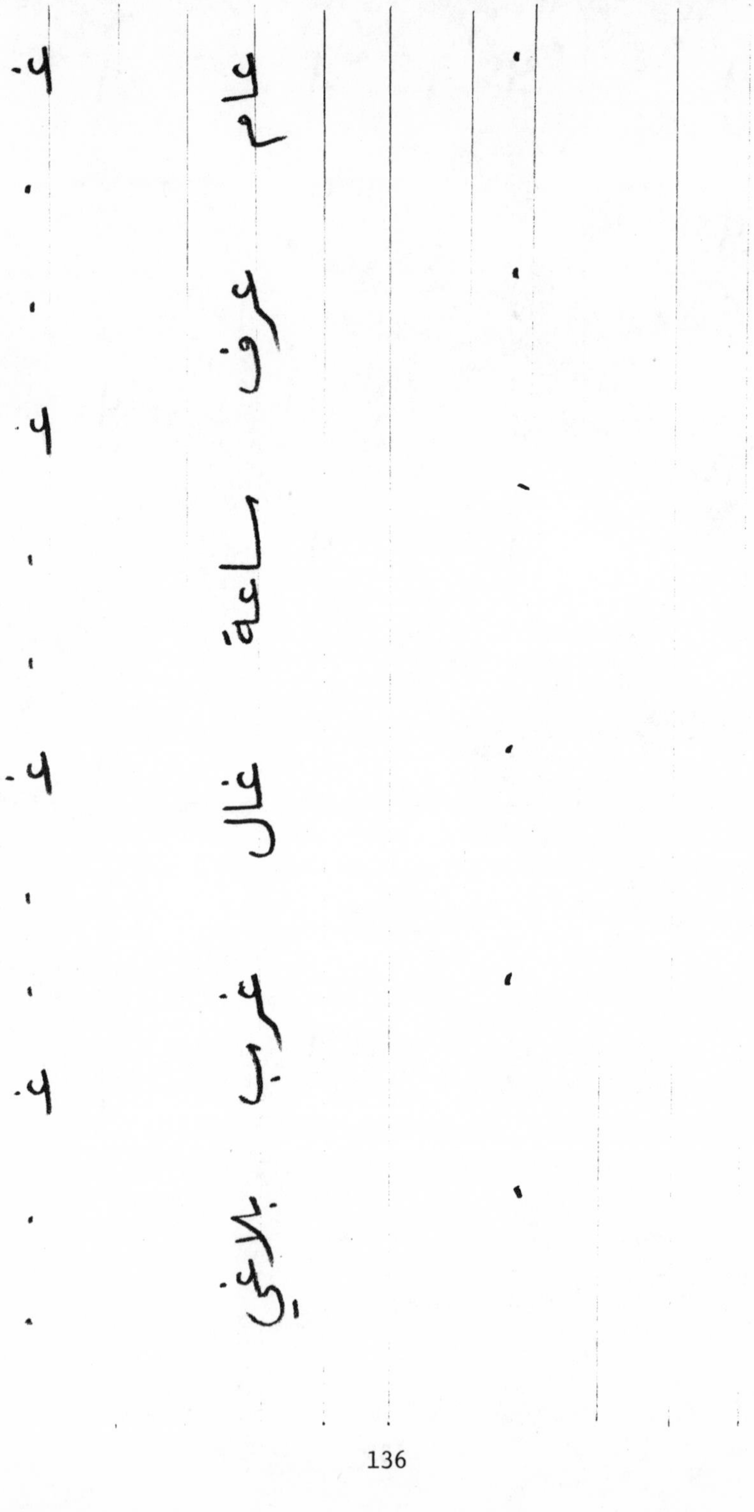

علم

حرف

سلامـ

قال

عرب

الخير

Fig. 3. Writing Exercise (cont'd.).

Part I Pronunciation

Fifteen words will be read, each one twice. Each word will contain a ع or غ sound. Place a check in the appropriate column.

غ	ع	
		١
		٢
		٣
		٤
		٥
		٦
		٧
		٨
		٩
		١٠
		١١
		١٢
		١٣
		١٤
		١٥

Fig. 4. Tests.

137

Part II Reading

Ten words will be read, each one twice. For each word two choices are given below. Circle the letter of the correct choice:

(١ (أ) بَاع (ب) بَاغ	(٦ (أ) عَدَد (ب) دَعَد
(٢ (أ) فارع (ب) فارغ	(٧ (أ) عَرَض (ب) غَرَض
(٣ (أ) شارع (ب) شاعر	(٨ (أ) راغِب (ب) غارِب
(٤ (أ) زاغ (ب) غاز	(٩ (أ) بارع (ب) عابِر
(٥ (أ) غاري (ب) راغي	(١٠ (أ) عَرَب (ب) غَرَب

Part III Writing

Ten words will be dictated, each one will be read twice. Please listen carefully to each word and then write it in the space below:

Fig. 4. Tests (cont'd.).

I would like to conclude with some observations on the contrastive approach in foreign language teaching. Experience in teaching Arabic has shown that the writing system must be included if the analysis is to be complete. To illustrate: both English and Arabic have a voiced interdental flat fricative phoneme (th in this) and the corresponding voiceless phoneme (th in think). Theoretically, Americans should have no trouble reading the Arabic letters ﺫ (voiced th) and ﺙ (voiceless th); but they do, apparently, because conventional English orthography does not distinguish between the two English phonemes. The native speaker's visualization of his language is greatly influenced by its orthographic representation; the affect of this colored conception on foreign language learning is worthy of research.

Until the theory of the contrastive approach and its application are perfected, it will always have to be tempered with experience. For example, Arabic ﻉ ʕ is usually described as a "voiced pharyngeal fricative," and English r as a "voiced retroflexed rounded midcentral vocoid." There is no interference here. And yet, periodically, we get a student who hears r for ʕ, e.g., hearing ﻣﻮﺭﺩ mawrid 'source' for ﻣﻮﻋﺪ mawʕid 'appointment'. However, when the consonant ﻉ is (correctly) labeled a "faucalized voiced midcentral vocoid" the phonetic overlap with r becomes apparent. Thus, a contrastive approach is only as effective as it is accurate and thorough.

A distinctive feature of the materials described here is that they follow the principles of programmed learning, and will eventually be made into a programmed, self-instructional course for use by the individual student, one which ties phonology and script together, with drills to develop acceptable handwriting. There is need for such a course in view of the rapidly growing trend in this country to use audio-lingual techniques in Arabic language instruction, and the increasing number of advanced students of Arabic who go abroad to pursue their studies in the Arab world itself.

Footnotes

[1]This report is based on research supported by a contract with the Office of Education, U. S. Department of Health, Education & Welfare, P. L. 83-531, Cooperative Research, and Title VI, P. L. 85-564, as amended.

[2]This is a slightly-revised version of the paper presented by the first-named author at the Conference. Both authors are members of the Department of Near East Language and Literature, University of Michigan, and of the CRLLB.

[3]See Charles A. Ferguson, "Diglossia," Word, Vol. 15 (1959), pp. 325-340.

[4]For a report of a similar approach applied to Spanish see Juan Estarellas and Timothy F. Regan, Jr., "Effects of Teaching Sounds as Letters Simultaneously at the Very Beginning of a Basic Foreign Language Course," Language Learning, Vol. 16 (1966), Nos. 3 and 4, pp. 173-182.

REMARQUES SUR LA VALEUR PREDICTIVE DE
L'ANALYSE DIFFERENTIELLE EN PHONOLOGIE[1]

Guy C. Capelle[2]

En 1965 paraissait, dans la série des études
différentielles dirigée par Ch. Ferguson, un ouvrage
intitulé "The Sounds of English and Spanish". Deux
excellents linguistes, R. P. Stockwell et J. D. Bowen
y consacrent, entre autres, un chapitre à l'établissement d'une hiérarchie de difficultés fondée sur une
analyse de l'anglais et de l'espagnol et sur leur
expérience en matière d'enseignement de l'espagnol à
des Américains.[3]

Les auteurs voient, dans la comparaison des types
de choix qui "existent à un point donné de la chaîne
parlée dans les deux langues" le moyen de tourner les
problèmes rencontrés jusqu'alors dans la détermination
des types de transfert. Pour cela, ils distinguent trois
types de choix: le choix "facultatif" qui est celui des
phonèmes, le choix "obligatoire" qu'impose au locuteur
les variantes conditionnées et les restrictions dans la
distribution des phonèmes, et le choix "zéro" dont nous
parlerons plus loin.

Huit cas hiérarchisés nous sont présentés. Nous
laisserons de côté les deux cas de parallèlisme
susceptibles de provoquer des transferts positifs
(no 7 et 8) et les deux cas où un choix "obligatoire"
dans une des deux langues peut être mis en parallèle
avec un choix "facultatif" dans l'autre langue (n° 3 et
4) pour nous attacher aux quatre cas restant (n° 1, 2,
5 et 6) qui font apparaître un choix "zéro" (ou ϕ) dans
une des deux langues. Les auteurs définissent de deux
manières ce choix "zéro": un phonème de la langue cible
(Lc) n'a pas de correspondant dans la langue source (Ls)
(par exemple /y/ en français - ϕ en anglais) ou bien un
choix obligatoire dans la Lc qui n'a pas de correspondant
dans la Ls (par exemple l'obligation d'utiliser la

variante conditionnée [ɫ] en position finale en anglais,
sans contrepartie en français, ou la possibilité
d'utiliser un /ʒ/ initial de mot en français alors que
la distribution du phonème correspondant en anglais
interdit ce choix).

Nous voudrions présenter quelques remarques critiques
sur ce point de vue en nous appuyant sur une analyse
différentielle de l'anglais et du français. Dans la
pratique, en effet, la hiérarchie proposée semble
n'avoir qu'une portée très limitée, tout au moins en ce
qui concerne ces deux dernières langues. Si nous
considérons le cas d'anglophones apprenant le français,
le deuxième niveau de difficulté (ɸ dans Ls, choix
"facultatif" dans Lc) regrouperait, sans faire de
distinctions entre eux, des problèmes aussi divers que
l'acquisition des phonèmes français /ɲ, r, y, ø, œ, ɛ̃,
œ̃, ɑ̃, ɔ̃/. L'expérience nous force à penser que l'étudiant
n'est pas également démuni dans tous les cas et à reposer,
en termes plus précis, le cas du ɸ.

Nous savons que, dans les débuts de l'apprentissage,
l'étudiant ne dispose pas de toutes les clés qui nous
permettent de décoder. Il n'a à sa disposition ni la
connaissance des structures grammaticales et de leurs
relations dans le système, ni la possibilité d'anticiper
le sens d'une unité avant de l'avoir entendue en entier.
Il dépend en grande partie de la forme phonique des
énoncés et ses interprétations reposent largement au
premier stade sur les composantes phoniques des unités
perçues. Nous croyons savoir également que l'étudiant,
dans son effort de communication en langue étrangère, ne
peut laisser subsister de trous dans la chaîne parlée
qu'il perçoit ou qu'il produit. Un francophone produit
un [θ] anglais soit comme [z], soit comme [d] et nous en
concluons qu'il les entend ainsi par analogie avec des
unités de son propre système. En fait, nous ne savons
pas exactement ce qu'il perçoit; nous savons seulement
qu'il perçoit quelque chose et que le choix "zéro" reste
théorique.[4]

Dans nos observations qui ont porté sur l'apprentissage de l'anglais par des francophones et du français par
des anglophones, le cas d'un choix ɸ dans la Ls empêchant
l'étudiant de percevoir et de produire un son de la Lc
n'a été relevé qu'une fois chez un nombre suffisant de
sujets pour que cette catégorie de difficulté soit

retenue dans notre liste comme le cas de différence le
plus marqué--mais pas nécessairement le plus difficile
pour l'étudiant. Il s'agit de la perception et de la
production du /h/ de l'anglais par les francophones. Le
/h/ n'est pas un phonème du français (mais on trouve
quelques réalisations, assez rares, de [h] dans des
énoncés exclamatifs). Dans le système du français, il
n'existe aucun trait permettant de le composer, ni
aucune unité proche (possédant au moins un trait commun
ou un trait contigu). Le plus souvent l'étudiant francophone n'entend rien et ne produit rien.[5]

En descendant dans l'échelle des difficultés, nous
situerions au niveau suivant le cas de /œ̃/. Non seulement
le phonème n'existe pas en anglais, mais il fait
intervenir un trait, la nasalité, qui n'existe pas comme
trait pertinent dans le système des voyelles de la langue
des élèves. Si les trois autres traits, labialité,
antériorité et timbre existent en anglais, ces traits
n'ont pas le même rôle dans le système et surtout ils ne
se combinent jamais ainsi.

Une troisième catégorie regrouperait /ø/, /œ/ et
/y/ qui illustrent un cas semblable au précédent, mais
plus simple dans la mesure où n'intervient pas le trait,
nouveau pour les anglophones, de nasalité. (On constate
cependant dans la pratique que le /y/ s'acquiert plus
facilement: le problème est compliqué pour les deux
autres phonèmes par des règles de distribution
particulière).

Dans un quatrième groupe, on pourrait faire entrer
/ɑ̃/, /õ/ et /ɛ̃/, voyelles nasales qui n'ont pas de
contrepartie en anglais. Mais les traits composants
existent en anglais et, qui plus est, ils se combinent
de la même manière. Le trait de nasalité est nouveau et
sa perception peut être difficile pour l'étudiant
américain habitué à ne pas tenir compte phonologiquement
de la nasalisation des voyelles précédant une consonne
nasale.

Le niveau suivant peut être illustré par le cas du
/r/ français lorsque l'étudiant anglophone parle une
variété d'anglais "r-less". Une correspondance est
établie entre les phonèmes "r" des deux langues mais les
traits composants sont complètement différents de même
que la distribution. Les anglophones doivent acquérir
une vibrante vélaire.[6]

Un sixième groupe est constitué par les quatre phonème vocaliques /o/, /ɔ/, /e/ et /ɛ/ (ou, selon la variété de français considérée, par les deux archiphonèmes /O/ et /E/ et leurs variantes combinatoires [o, ɔ, e et ɛ]). Ces phonèmes ont des correspondants en anglais mais leur distribution est très différente. De là proviennent des fautes qui ne compromettent que rarement la compréhension mais qui résistent aux meilleurs conditionnements. Par exemple le français n'a que [ɔ] en syllabe fermée finale alors que [o] peut être soit en syllabe finale ouverte (ex.: lot = [lo]) ou en syllabe finale fermée (ex.: saute = [sot]).⁷ L'anglais, au contraire, admet "low" et "law", "load" et "lawn".

Le cas de [t] initial en français pose un nouveau type de problème. Le son de [t] initial est utilisé par l'anglophone dans une autre position, après [s] dans la syllabe et avant le noyau vocalique. Il convient de transplanter cette variante dans une autre position et d'éteindre une habitude. (Le cas où l'étudiant doit suprimer un trait phonique redondant, l'aspiration par exemple, semble plus difficile que celui où il doit en ajouter un.)

La huitième catégorie peut se définir comme l'inhibition d'une des variantes conditionnées d'un phonème de la Ls. C'est le cas pour la prononciation du [l] final en français par un anglophone qui doit remplacer sa variante [ɫ] par celle qu'il produit normalement à l'initiale. Il s'agit d'une substitution de variante.

La catégorie suivante est illustrée par le cas du /ʒ/. Le phonème existe dans la Ls avec une forme phonique très proche, mais il est exclu de la position initiale de mot. Il suffit d'étendre son utilisation à cette position (on peut essayer de réduire le [d] du complexe [dʒ] qui constitue l'habitude antérieure).

Le dixième cas peut se décrire ainsi: /w/ est un phonème consonantique en anglais et sa réalisation [w] est phoniquement très proche de celle d'une des variantes du phonème vocalique /u/ en français, variante dont la distribution est très strictement limitée à la position prévocalique dans la syllabe. Cette distribution comparable à celle de certaines consonnes ne fait aucun obstacle au transfert positif de l'anglais en français. Le Ø n'en est plus un, bien au contraire.

Enfin, un onzième et dernier cas est celui où un phonème de la Lc peut être réalisé par une suite de phonèmes de la Ls. C'est le cas du /ɲ/ français qui est souvent réalisé comme /n+j/ par les anglophones. Ici encore le ɸ sur le plan du système n'est plus un obstacle dans le transfert.

Pour simplifier et résumer, il est possible de regrouper ces onze cas en quatre catégories définissables en termes de traits distinctifs, de types de combinaison de ces traits, et de types de distribution des phonèmes:

A) Le ɸ en Ls s'accompagne

dans le cas n° 1 de l'absence totale en Ls des traits qui permettraient de constituer le phonème,

dans le cas n° 2 de la présence de certains de ces traits (sauf la nasalité), mais d'une combinatoire différente,

dans le cas n° 3 de la présence des traits mais d'une combinatoire différente,

dans le cas n° 4 de la présence de certains traits (tous sauf la nasalité) et d'un certain parallèlisme dans la manière dont ils se combinent.

B) Alors que dans la catégorie A) nous constatons un ɸ en Ls, il existe dans les deux langues des unités que l'on peut considérer comme correspondante, mais

dans le cas n° 5 les traits qui constituent l'unité en Lc n'existent pas en Ls et la distribution des phonèmes est différente,

dans le cas n° 6 les traits existent (bien que présentant des différences sensibles de réalisation) alors que la distribution des phonèmes est différente.

C) Le parallèlisme sur le plan des systèmes est encore plus grand puisqu'il ne s'agit plus que de transplanter, d'ajouter ou d'inhiber des variantes (cas n° 7, 8 et 9).

D) Nous retrouvons de ɸ, mais il existe des possibilités de transfert de la Ls à la Lc.

La classification précédente n'est évidemment pas définitive dans notre esprit: nous n'avons pas envisagé tous les cas et nous ne sommes pas en mesure d'évaluer les difficultés réelles pour l'étudiant avec précision. Fondée sur des considérations linguistiques, cette "hiérarchie" ne peut tenir compte ni des difficultés créées par l'élève lui-même (inhibitions individuelles, fausses analogies internes, hyper-correction), ni des difficultés provenant des conditions dans lesquelles est donné l'enseignement (qualité du modèle fourni en classe, stratégie pédagogique adoptée...), ni des difficultés qui surgissent au fur et à mesure de l'acquisition.

Afin d'améliorer l'efficacité de notre classification précédente dans l'évaluation des difficultés, nous avons defini les deux critères supplémentaires suivants:

a) la densité des unités nouvelles pour l'étudiant dans une zone articulatoire donnée de la Lc. Il est certainement difficile pour un anglophone d'acquérir les distinctions entre /ø, ə, et œ/ dans une zone où il n'est pas entrainé à discriminer en Ls.

b) la proximité phonétique de certaines réalisations d'unités nouvelles de la Lc et de certaines variantes conditionnées de la Ls (voir la remarque de W. Moulton rapportée dans la note 4, page 5).

Bien que nous n'accordions à cette classification dans laquelle nous avons essayé d'introduire une hiérarchie qu'une valeur prédictive assez limitée, nous la croyons utile. Elle peut servir d'hypothèse pour les expériences du psycholinguiste, aider l'auteur de méthode à estimer le coût de l'enseignement, qui en tiendra compte dans l'établissement de la progression et du rythme de présentation des difficultés nouvelles. Elle doit permettre également la mise au point de la stratégie pédagogique en facilitant la recherche des points d'appui et des itinéraires les plus satisfaisants. Elle a enfin le mérite d'éclairer le professeur qui doit assurer ses diagnostics et trouver les procédes de correction.

Footnotes

[1] This report is a slightly edited version of the paper presented at the Conference on Language and Language Behavior.

[2] The author is a visiting professor of French, Department of Romance Languages, University of Michigan, and a senior research associate at the Center for Research on Language and Language Behavior.

[3] Voir chapitre 2, "Sound systems in conflict: a hierarchy of difficulty," et plus spécialement le tableau de la page 16.

[4] E. Brière a montré qu'on pouvait fort bien produire sans "entendre" en termes de système. "Percevoir" s'applique ici seulement à l'audition d'un son.

[5] Il semble que dans ce cas la meilleure stratégie pédagogique consiste à essayer de faire prononcer le son avant de le faire entendre. Le /h/ continue de poser des problèmes même après des années d'étude, mais la communication n'en est pas vraiment gênée à cause de son rendement fonctionnel relativement faible.

[6] Dans son article "Toward a Classification of Pronunciation Errors", The Modern Language Journal, March 1962, W. Moulton note que beaucoup d'étudiants finissent par confondre un [r] allemand et un [ɫ] arrière anglais, car ils n'entendent plus que le trait de vélarité et pas le trait vibrant.

[7] Cela n'est valable que pour quelques variétés de français, le français parisien notamment. Les variétés méridionales n'acceptent pas le [o] en syllabe finale fermée.

THE INDICES OF COVERAGE:

A NEW DIMENSION IN LEXICOMETRICS

W. F. Mackey and J. G. Savard[1]

In the selection of items for language teaching, two types of criteria have been used: those based on the usefulness of items and those based on their facility or ease of learning. Since what is easy is not necessarily useful, it is the first type that has the priority in the choice of items for language learning.

Lists of the most useful words for a number of languages have already been compiled. They have been established by applying one or more of the four following internal criteria: (i) on the basis of frequency of occurrence in everyday speech or in writings (e.g., Schonell), (ii) on the range or number of different texts in which the word has been found (e.g., VanderBeke), (iii) on the availability of a word for a given semantic field (e.g., Michéa), and (iv) on coverage, or the capacity of replacing other words (e.g., Ogden).

The first three of these criteria have been quantified. Indices of frequency and range have already been worked out for most of world's chief languages. Indices of availability are now being elaborated (e.g., Michéa, Mackey, et al). Using these figures, it has already been possible to apply techniques for measuring the usefulness of items found in textbooks for language learning.

Up to the present, however, it has been impossible to make use of the fourth criterion in the measurement of usefulness, since no indices of coverage existed. Yet this criterion has often been used to justify modifications made in frequency and range in establishing basic vocabulary lists for purposes of language teaching (e.g., West). In fact, some of the lists have been based exclusively on this criterion (e.g., Ogden). To measure the usefulness of what is taught it is necessary to have indices not only of frequency, range and availability, but of coverage as well. Such indices of coverage are what the research described here has attempted to produce.

Since coverage has to do with the capacity of an item to take the place of others, it was necessary to find out how such replacements took place.[7] The most usual replacements take place by restatement in other words. This is what happens in dictionary definitions. We can say, for example, that <u>a puppy</u> is <u>a young dog</u> and that <u>a kitten</u> is <u>a young cat</u>, so that <u>young</u> covers part of <u>puppy</u> and <u>kitten</u>. <u>Definition</u>, therefore, is obviously one of the constituents of coverage.

A second way of replacing a word is to use another word instead. Instead of <u>conflagration</u>, for example, we can use the word <u>fire</u>. This is the sort of replacement we find in a <u>thesaurus</u> and in certain dictionaries of synonyms. Since one word includes the meaning or part of the meaning of another word, <u>inclusion</u> can be said to be another constituent of coverage.

A third way of replacing a word is to extend the meaning of a simpler word. By extending the meaning of the word <u>body</u>, for example, to include the idea of framework, we can replace the word <u>fuselage</u> when speaking of airplanes; some of the more complete dictionaries have listed such meanings. <u>Extension</u>, therefore, is another constituent of coverage.

A fourth constituent is <u>combination</u>, or combining power. A word which can combine with a large number of items can be used to replace a large number of words. <u>Newspaperman</u> (<u>news</u> + <u>paper</u> + <u>man</u>) replaces <u>journalist</u> and <u>handbook</u> (<u>hand</u> + <u>book</u>) takes care of <u>manual</u>. Most dictionaries list such usual combinations.

Regardless, however, of the number of replacements already recorded, it seemed reasonable to suppose that the power of a word to define, to extend its meaning, to include or to combine with other words could be regarded as a measure of its usefulness. The problem was to establish such a measure.

In order to arrive at the measurement of coverage, it was necessary to begin by obtaining measures for each of its constituents--measures for the capacity of definition, of inclusion, of extension, and of combination.

149

Table 1

Number of Occurrences in Dictionary Definitions[2]

LE,L-,LA,Les	3234	ON	935
DE,D-	3135	DES	803
UN	2425	EN	754
QUI	2297	A	715
QUE, QU-	1172	CHOSE	715
ETRE [M.O.]	1081	OU	680
FAIRE	1080	QUELQUE	679
CE,C-,CET,CES	677	DU	424
SE,S-	673	POUR	417
AVOIR [M.O.]	636	CELUI,CELLE,CEUX	386
NE,N-	628	PERSONNE [M.F.]	343
DANS	536	PLUS	298
PAS [M.O.]	535	METTRE	287
ET	475	AVEC	284

M.O. = as function word. M.F. = as content word.

Table 2

Number of Word Replacements

TROMPER	82	RAILLER	38
TUER	61	MONTRER	37
MOURIR	54	MELANGE	35
FATIGUER	52	REMUER	35
PARTIR	48	PRENDRE	34
HOMME	40	SECRET	34
SUITE	39	VOLER	34
BATTRE	33	SOLDAT	31
ENFANT	33	SOT	31
PIECE	33	TOUCHER	31
TRAITER	33	VOLEUR	31
VAINCRE	33	AVARE	30
FAUX	32	EXTRAORDINAIRE	30
OBSCUR	31	PARTIE	30

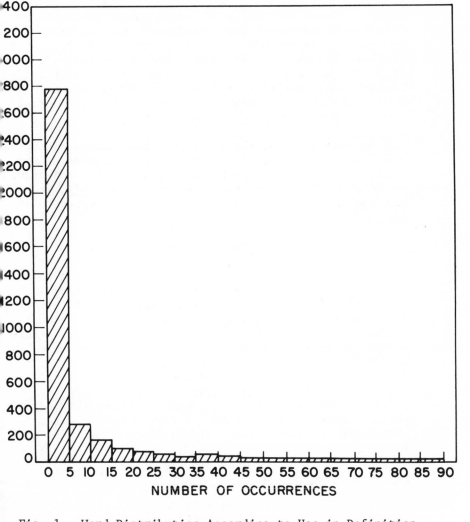

Fig. 1. Word Distribution According to Use in Definition

Omitted at the right of the horizontal axis are 69 words of
very high frequency, with occurrences between 95 and 3, 234.

Measures of Definition

Starting with definition, we postulated that the
extent to which a word was needed to define another word
could be used as a measure of its power of <u>definition</u>.
If a person were given a thousand or so basic words, for
example, and, using only these, were asked to supply
definitions for twenty or thirty thousand others, he
would produce a document which would enable us to determine a word's capacity for definition. Whether or not
they were aware of this possibility, this is in fact what
happened when West, Ogden, and Gougenheim defined all
the words in their respective dictionaries within a self-
imposed basic vocabulary. These, therefore, were the
documents we used in establishing our measures of definition capacity.

We reasoned that the number of times each defining
word had to recur could be taken as an indication of its
capacity for use in definition. The use of the adjective
<u>young</u> in helping define the five words <u>colt</u>, <u>calf</u>, <u>lamb</u>
and <u>puppy</u>, for example, could add five more points to its
definition capacity.

Starting with Gougenheim's dictionary, we thus
totaled the number of times each word was used in the
definitions, obtaining a figure for each different word
(see Table 1). Of the 49,835 running words (tokens) used
in all the definitions, there were only 1,724 different
words belonging to the basic vocabulary, or less than half
the allotted number - 1,904 not being used in the definitions. If to these 1,904 we add the words rarely used in
the dictionary definitions (less than 5 times in the
entire dictionary), we account for 2,790 of the total
basic vocabulary of 3,628 words (see Fig. 1). Of the
1,724 defining words which are used, over one-third occur
not more than twice; of these, 170 are function words,
leaving 900 content words, only 75 of which are used more
than fifty times.

Measures of Inclusion

The second constituent of coverage is that of
<u>inclusion</u>. A word which already includes the meanings of
another word can be used instead of it; some words can
take the place of a large number of other words. Words
differ in their capacity to displace others. If we look

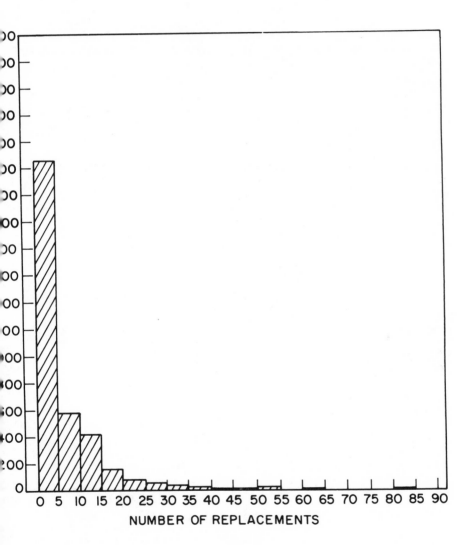

Fig. 2. Word Distribution by Degree of Inclusion

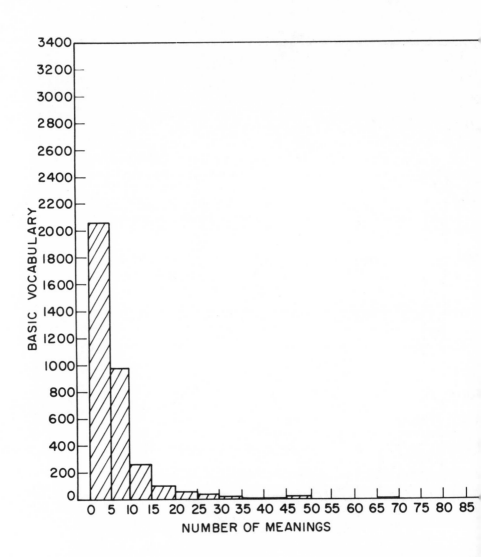

Fig. 3.   Distribution According to Extension of Meaning

up a thesaurus we find that the word seat, for example, replaces more words than does the word chair. (Seat: chair, bench, stool, sofa, post, location, position, place, rear. Chair: seat, professorship.) If we were to base our measures on this listing, we could say that the power of inclusion of the word seat is 9, that of chair is 2.

We postulated that the number of items for which a given word could be used would be an indication of its power of inclusion. As documentation we selected the two most available dictionaries of this type for the French language, those of Bénac and Bailly, and, in each case, taking the higher score, compiled inclusion figures for each word (see Table 2).

This yielded 2,041 word-types, which theoretically replaced 15,963 word-types. This excludes 1,587 words of the basic vocabulary; adding to these the words with a low-inclusion capacity (less than 5), we get a total of 2,437 words (see Fig. 2). Only seven percent (146 words) replace upwards of twenty words; of these, 72 were verbs, 44 nouns, 28 adjectives, and two function words (see Fig. 4).

Measures of Extension

The third constituent of coverage, extension, has to do with the power of a word to multiply its meanings. The verb get, for example, runs into more meanings than receive, and run into more meanings than jump. We postulated that this could be measured by counting the number of different dictionary meanings. Thus, according to the Oxford English Dictionary, jump would have an extension figure of 38, and run of 435.

For French we used the biggest and most contemporary dictionary available, the Robert. It yielded 17,523 extensions of 3,624 words of the vocabulary (see Table 3) selected. Fully a third of this basic vocabulary (1,119 words) had only two extensions of meaning or less (see Fig. 3).

Measures of Combination

The fourth constituent of coverage, combination, represents the power of words to form new lexical items by combining with other words. For example, the fact that the word leg yields fewer combinations that the word foot gives it that much less covering power. (Leg: legless,

Table 3

Number of Dictionary Meanings

FAIRE	65	TENIR	31
PASSER	52	METTRE	30
PRENDRE	52	PERDRE	30
TIRER	40	ALLER	29
ROULER	37	MOURIR	29
QUE, OU-	33	PIQUER	29
SI, S-	31	SUIVRE	29
DONNER	28	COURIR	24
SORTIR	28	LEVER	24
TETE	28	RETIRER	24
LE,L-,LA,LES	26	VOLER	24
PORTER	26	TEL	23
SERRER	26	DE,D-	22
BATTRE	25	FORME	22

Table 4

Number of Word Combinations

DE,D-	772	ETRE M.O.	118
LE,L-,LA,LES	496	AVOIR M.O.	110
A	355	AU	103
SE,S-	300	SON,SA,SES	84
UN	242	DU	74
EN	224	QUE, OU-	73
FAIRE	135	METTRE	65
TOUT M.O.	64	PAR	35
PRENDRE	59	CE,C-,CET,CES	33
SUR M.O.	59	COUP	33
BON	58	TETE	33
NE,N-	58	HOMME	31
DES	51	TEMPS	31
GRAND	35	ET	30

M.O. = as function word.

156

legman, legwork, legging. <u>Foot</u>: football, foothold, footbath, footstep, footnote, foothill, footboard, footwork, footbridge, footing, footman, footworn, under foot, foot-and-mouth disease.) On the bases of this information we could arrive at the following measures of the combining power of these words: <u>leg</u> 4; <u>foot</u> 14.

We postulated that the combining power of an item could be measured by the number of compounds which it actually produced; we included both hyphenated and unhyphenated words, phrasal verbs and syntagmata listed in the dictionaries. Ambiguities were settled by applying the commutation test. For French we were thus able to obtain figures for some fifteen hundred words (see Table 4).

Using the dictionaries of both Gougenheim and Pradez for the French language, we first obtained 8,018 word-tokens, yielding 1,473 of the words found in the basis vocabulary, or less than half. The remaining 2,155 words which do not combine at all, added to those which combine very seldom (less than 5 times), give a total of 3,354, or 92 percent of the basic vocabulary. Only 7 percent (106 words) came up ten or more times. As many as 39 of these (including the first 17 on the list) were function words, 42 nouns, 17 verbs and 8 adjectives.

Validation

We now had four separate lists of words with corresponding figures for the capacity of definition, inclusion, extension, and combination for each word on the list. Before using these to establish indices of coverage, it was necessary to validate its four constituents, determining the degree of correlation, and discovering any overlap which might exist; for it would be a waste of time to measure all constituents if figures for one or two would do the job.

In order to make our raw data for the four constituents mutually comparable, we reduced all our figures to T-scores. By cross tabulating the scores for the four constituents with one another, we found that the highest correlation was only .602. It existed between the figures obtained for the measurement of defining capacity and those of combination. This, we thought, might have been due to the presence of function words in both measures: <u>de</u>, for

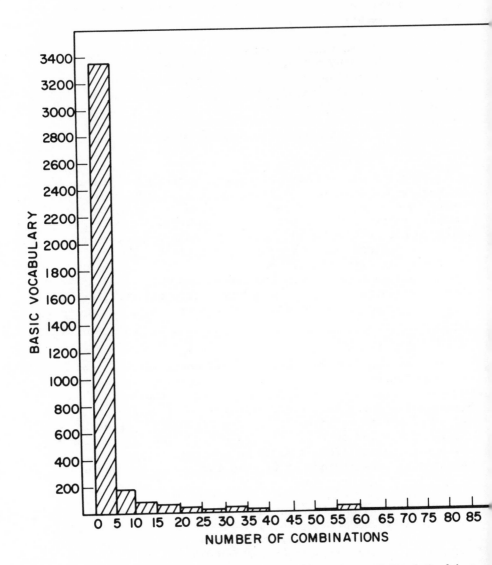

Fig. 4. Distribution According to Number of Word Combinations

[Omitted at the right of the horizontal are data for ten words with combinations ranging from 95 to 772.]

example, une partie de la maison (definition); pomme de terre (combination).

It was now necessary to find out the extent to which each constituent of coverage measured something different. Was it possible to eliminate one or two of these constituents and still have a measure of coverage?

By testing with the Varimax technique of factor rotation, we got some very interesting results (see Table 5).

Table 5

Saturations by Factor Rotation

	1	2	3	4
DEFINITION	.934	.110	.164	.294
INCLUSION	.097	.979	.168	.059
EXTENSION	.161	.186	.945	.213
COMBINATION	.306	.066	.226	.922

From these results we can see that .935 of a certain factor (call it Factor 1) is included in our measure of definition; inclusion is taken care of by .979 of Factor 2; extension by .945 of Factor 3; and combination by .922 of Factor 4. It seemed evident, therefore, that we must retain all four constituents in the measurement of coverage if we were to establish valid indices.

There remained the possibility that coverage measured the same thing as frequency, range and availability. On the face of the evidence accumulated so far, however, this would seem unlikely, since, as we have seen, a good portion of the basic vocabulary, established according to these criteria, did not appear in one or more of the constituents of coverage. And those which did appear did

159

Table 6

Coverage Compared with Frequency

WORD	Coverage Rank	Frequency Rank	WORD	Coverage Rank	Frequency Rank
faire	1	19	venir	23	76
prondre	2	77	terre	27	387
homme	5	253	porter	30	406
passer	5	86	donner	31	105
mourir	7	455	tour	31	454
mettre	8	85	mauvais	35	341
tirer	9	485	perdre	36	247
tête	11	328	savoir	37	45
aller	12	34	tomber	37	304
partir	12	139	tourner	37	374
grand	14	103	voir	37	43
pièce	14	316	entendre	41	208
petit	16	65	manger	41	166
battre	18	919	beau	45	171
maison	18	148	coup	45	236
partie	20	402	gros	45	210
vouloir	22	64	tuer	48	593
dire	23	28	marcher	49	215
parler	23	96	maître	51	811
tenir	23	147	revenir	51	220

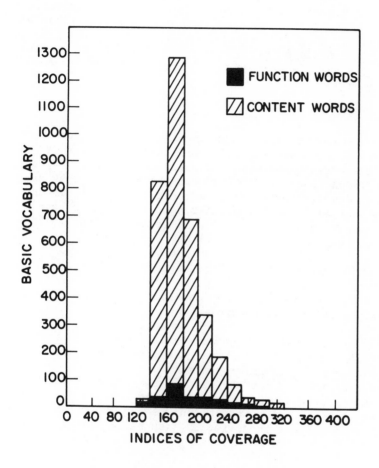

Fig. 5. Distribution According to Degree of Coverage

not seem to have the same importance in coverage as they have in the lists of frequency, range and availability. This we decided to check by comparing frequency rank with coverage rank.

A glance at the ranks of the forty first-words with the greatest coverage, compared with their corresponding frequency rank, as recorded by the count of the français fondamental, seems to indicate that we are quite clearly measuring two different things. (see Table 6).

The Indices of Coverage

It is not without some statistical confidence, therefore, that we are now able to present the coverage indices of the first three thousand words of the French vocabulary. The index of coverage of a word was arrived at by adding the index (T-score) for each constituent (definition + combination + inclusion + extension), since we have no reason at the present time to give more weight to one constituent than to another.

The distribution of the basic vocabulary according to coverage is shown in Fig. 5. As in all other vocabulary studies, we note that the function words play a disproportionately prominent role.

By eliminating function words from the analysis, we are now attempting to obtain distinctiveness among constituents. We have started the task of obtaining coverage indices for the rest of the French vocabulary on a much larger sample of some million tokens. We have made a start to obtain coverage indices for the vocabulary of other languages; those for English become available this year.

Applications

We hope that these indices may be valuable in providing addition measures of the usefulness of what is taught and perhaps in helping improve some of the basic word lists which are now being employed. (See Table 6 for the coverage indices of the first 3,000 words of French.)

References

Schonell, F. J., et al. A Study of the Oral Vocabulary of Adults. London & Brisbane: University of London Press & Queensland U. P., 1956.

Vander Beke, G. E. French Word Book. New York: American and Canadian Committees on Modern Languages, 1929.

Michéa, R. Mots fréquents et mots disponibles: un aspect nouveau de la statistique du langage. Les langues modernes, 47, 338-44.

Ogden, C. K. The System of Basic English. New York: Harcourt, 1934.

Guiraud, P. Bibliographie critique de la statistique linguistique (rev. ed.). Utrecht: Spectrum, 1954.

Mackey, W. F., et al. Le vocabulaire disponible en France et en Acadie. Ouébec & Montréal: Laval & McGill U. P. (in press). 2 Vols.

Mackey, W. F. Language Teaching Analysis. London: Longmans, 1965.

West, M. (Ed.) A General Service List of English Words. London: Longmans, 1953.

West, M. An International Reader's Dictionary (revision of New Method English Dictionary). London: Longmans, 1965.

Gougenheim, G. Dictionnaire fondamental de la langue française. Paris: Didier, 1958.

Bénac, H. Dictionnaire des synonymes. Paris: Hachette, 1956.

Bailly, R. Dictionnaire des synonymes. Paris: Larousse, 1947.

Robert, P. Dictionnaire alphabétique et analogique de la langue francaise. Paris: Nouveau Littré, 1965. (6 vols.)

Pradez, E. Dictionnaire des gallicismes. Paris: Payot, 1938.

Gougenheim, G. Michéa, R. et al. L'élaboration du français fondamental (2nd ed.). Paris: Didier, 1964.

Footnotes

[1]The authors are members of the Department of Linguistics, Lavel University, Quebec, Canada.

[2]The samples in Tables 1-4 were taken from the top of the respective lists.

INDIRECT VS. DIRECT DISCOURSE IN BARIBA[1]

Kenneth L. Pike[2]

In Bariba, the cultural setting, the focus of attention, and the sequence of pronominal reference are heavily interwoven in the structure of direct versus indirect discourse. Jean Soutar provided the data for this study and also collaborated closely in their presentation.

When, in Bariba, should one use <u>direct</u> discourse in a quotation and when <u>indirect</u>? Constraints are imposed by the total discourse situation, by parts of sentence, and by choice of quotation type.

Primary, Secondary, and Tertiary Statement Patterns

We need to be able to refer to statements which contain no quotation—i.e., non-quotation, or <u>primary</u>[3] statements; to those with an included quotation—which for convenience sake may be called <u>secondary</u> statements; and to those statements with a quote within a quote, which may be called <u>tertiary</u>. For our present purposes, a primary statement is viewed as composed of one part; the secondary of two; the tertiary of three.

The primary statement has a non-quotation filling its total area—e.g., 'The man saw the boy', etc.

The secondary statement has an initial <u>quotation indicator</u>, containing a verb of saying, reporting, or the like, and a second part, representing the quotation reported: e.g., He said to the man that the boy would come. This quotation is called a <u>first degree quotation</u>. The quotation indicator has two diagnostic pronominal (or nominal) parts, whether explicit or implicit, which identify the <u>speaker</u> within the quotation indicator (e.g., 'He [said]') and the <u>audience</u> within the indicator ('...to the boy').

The tertiary statement pattern begins with a quotation indicator, as does the secondary statement. It then, however, follows the quotation indicator with a second quotation indicator which serves simultaneously as a first degree quotation.

Following the second quotation indicator, the tertiary statement then has, in its third position, the second degree quotation:

(3) yèyá_1 na_2 na_3 n_4 nun_5 sõ_6 Woru, siba_7 nɛɛ_8
     nɛn_9 dumà_{10} ba_{11} koo_{12} ka_{13} ȳakuru_{14} ko_{15}
     (Words--minus some names--are numbered to key
     into the translation.)

'So_1 I_2 came_3 in order that I_4 tell_6 you_5 Woru,
they [those people]$_7$ said_8 [to me] it is my_9
horse_{10} they_{11} will_{12} make_{15} a sacrifice_{14} with_{13}.'

This plan can now be diagrammed as in Figure I.

FIGURE I:

STRUCTURE OF BARIBA STATEMENTS

SHOWING DEGREES OF QUOTATION

Non-Quotation Primary Statements	Statements with un-restricted predicate and object 'The boy will come'		
Quotation, Secondary Statements	Quotation Indicator 'He said [to you]	First Degree Quotation "I will come"'	
Tertiary Statements	Quotation Indicator 'You said [to me]	Second Quotation Indicator as First Degree Quotation "He said [to you]	Second Degree Quotation I would come"''

167

We turn to the distribution of direct versus indirect speech in quotations, predictable by various criteria.

Indirect Status of Second Degree Quotations

In the third slot, that of the second degree quotation of a tertiary statement, <u>all</u> quotations are <u>indirect</u>.

(When the particle mà 'that' precedes a quote, we know--as in the English translation--that the quotation is indirect. Unfortunately, for the ease of our analysis, the mà is optional, leaving some ambiguity. Various items other than mà occasionally give hints indicating directness or indirectness of discourse.)

Alternative Forms of First Degree Quotation

In the second slot--the quotation--of a secondary statement of Figure I, direct discourse is sometimes used for the quotation, and sometimes indirect.

Off-Stage First Degree Quotation, as Indirect

In a narration, the setting of the scene before the principal action itself begins, may be called "off-stage". Quotations within such introductory off-stage parts of a narration are in <u>indirect</u> discourse.

On-Stage Quotations with Ranking Matrix

The main part of a discourse, including the action parts of a long discourse, are "on-stage," in contrast to the introductory (or concluding) off-stage elements. An on-stage quotation may be direct or indirect. Several factors control the choice of the indirect or direct form of a first degree on-stage quotation. One is its relation to the dramatis personae (DPs) of the quotation indicator (Q.I.) preceding it. In Matrix A, this factor is charted. The character (first, second, third, or fourth [less important], whether singular or plural), chosen by the narrator to be speaker in the quotation indicator, serves as marking one of the rows of the matrix. The character chosen by the narrator, as explicit or implicit audience to the subject of the quotation indicator, serves to label one of the columns. At the intersection of the

168

relevant row and column, the cell is filled either (1) with the symbol I, meaning 'indirect discourse will be used for the first degree quotation, after the quotation indicator'; (2) with D for direct discourse; (3) with I/D for sometimes one and sometimes the other; (4) with A when the forms are expected to be permanently ambiguous; or (5) with question mark when data are lacking.

MATRIX A: OCCURRENCE OF A FIRST DEGREE QUOTATION AS DIRECT OR INDIRECT, IN ACCORDANCE WITH THE DRAMATIS PERSONAE OF THE PRECEDING QUOTATION INDICATOR.

DPs of the Quotation Indicator	Audience in O. I.			
	2	1	3	4
Subject of Q.I.				
2	?	I	I	I
1	I	A	I/D	I/D
3	I	I/D	?	I/D
4	I	I/D	I/D	?

The matrix has several quite unexpected characteristics. Note, first, that the rows and columns have been specially changed (permuted) from the routine order of 1, 2, 3, 4, to the order 2, 1, 3, 4. Only by this permutation is its special characteristic clearly seen--that whenever 2 (singular or plural) is involved at all in the quotation indicator, whether as speaker or audience, the suceeding quotation will be indirect. The presence (the involvement) of 2 overrides the presence of any other person. I call this a 'ranking'[4] structure.

For an illustration of the 3-2 cell, note the following where the Q.I. is 'They would say [to you]' and the quotation is indirect in that cell of Matrix A (i.e., $M.A_{32}$):

bén tii$_1$ vè$_2$ ba$_3$ tunuma$_4$ ba$_5$ k00$_6$ bikia$_7$, amɔna$_8$ mba$_9$
  ka$_{10}$ mba$_{11}$ i$_{12}$ ka$_{13}$ man$_{14}$ sikua$_{15}$
'When$_2$ they$_3$ arrived$_4$ they$_5$ themselves$_1$ would$_5$ ask$_7$
  [you] how$_8$ you$_{12}$ buried$_{15}$ me$_{14}$ and with$_{13}$ what$_{11}$'

On-Stage Quotations in Focus

Leaving now the quotations preceded by an indicator containing 2, we study only those quotes varying from I to D, and where the indicator has only 1, 3, or 4.

The pattern found for general conversation, on-stage, in focus is represented in Matrix B. Off-diagonal cells are all direct. The parentheses indicate infrequent forms; it is rare to have the general conversation in focus when the conversation is between the narrator (1) and people other than 2.

MATRIX B: ON-STAGE GENERAL CONVERSATION IN FOCUS

DPs of the Quotation Indicator	Audience in Q.I.		
	1	3	4
Subject 1	A	(D)	(D)
3	(D)	?	D
4	(D)	D	?

For an illustration note:

kpa$_1$ Woru$_2$ na$_3$ ù$_4$ nɛɛ$_5$, Sabi, sá$_6$ ǹ$_7$ de$_8$ yam$_9$ mí$_{10}$ dɔɔ̀$_{11}$?

'Then$_1$ Woru$_2$ came$_3$ and said$_5$, "Sabi, aren't$_7$ we$_6$ ever$_8$ going$_{11}$ to that$_{10}$ place$_9$?"' (Here the Q. I. is 'Woru said [to Sabi]'; the direct quotation is from cell M.3$_{34}$.)

It is unusual for one character to be in focus when it is neither the narrator (1) nor audience (2). It is usual, however, when one character is the narrator, for the narrator to be in focus (if 2 is not involved) and to speak with direct quotes; and the other to speak to him with indirect quotes. Focus is likely to be placed on a chief, if a chief and another person (3 and 4) are involved in conversation.

In the reported speech of one character to another in
a given on-stage section of a discourse, on the other hand,
one of those quotations (one utterance of that character)
may be in focus, pinpointed within its Indirect context,
and made direct, for example, if it represents a quotation
which became the source of the name of a person or place:

ba_1 nɛɛ$_2$, a$_3$ doo$_4$ a$_5$ n$_6$ dà$_7$ dãáre$_8$ mí$_9$ yéyá$_10$ ya$_{11}$ka$_{12}$
Dáari$_{13}$ mí$_{14}$...wíyá$_{15}$ ba$_{16}$ mɔ̀$_{17}$ Dáari$_{18}$ yeruma$_{19}$
'They$_1$ said$_2$, "(You$_3$) go$_4$ and stay (drop off)$_8$ there$_9$."
So it$_{11}$ was called Danri$_{13}$ there$_{14}$....It-was-he$_{15}$
they$_{16}$ called$_{17}$ Danri's$_{18}$ oldest-son$_{19}$' (Q.I. 'they
said [to him]'; Quotation 3-19: Direct, quotation
in focus)

On-Stage Quotation Out of Focus

Related criteria affect unfocussed quotations on-
stage. When general conversation is out-of-focus, for
example, all quotations are indirect.

An incident from history, where the action is more
important than the conversation, represents this kind of
circumstance:

yè$_1$ Gɛra$_2$ koo$_3$ tabu$_4$ ko$_5$, u$_6$ Sabi N na$_7$ sɔmɔ$_8$ gɔrima$_9$,
wí$_{10}$ koo$_{11}$ tabu$_{12}$ ko$_{13}$, ú$_{14}$ wi$_{15}$ séenu$_{16}$ kɛ̀$_{17}$
'When$_1$ Gera$_2$ was going$_3$ to make$_5$ war$_4$, he$_6$ sent$_9$ a
messenger$_8$ to Sabi Nena$_7$ (saying) that he$_{10}$ was
going$_{11}$ to make$_{13}$ war$_{12}$, so would he$_{14}$ (Sabi Nena)
give$_{17}$ him$_{15}$ arrows$_{16}$' (Q.I.: 'Gera said to Sabi
Nena'; Quotation: 10-16: Indirect, general conversation, out-of focus).

Of several characters--but usually one of a pair--one
may be out-of-focus. The character out-of-focus is quoted
indirectly--whereas the character in-focus would be quoted
directly. In a string of direct quotations, with the
string as a whole considered to be in-focus, however,
extra attention within the larger attention span may be
achieved for one direct quotation by making the <u>preceding</u>

171

quotation indirect. (Much as in an italic--emphasized-- paragraph, one word may be re-set in Roman type for higher emphasis.)

Although the speech of a chief is normally quoted directly, and the reply to him directly, the following illustration reversed this to highlight the source of the place name:

(a) u_1 $n\epsilon\epsilon_2$ $tamaa_4$ u_5 koo_6 $bù_7$ $gura_8$ $ù_9$ ka_{10} $doona_{11}$

(b) $wíń_1$ $tonu_2$ u_3 $n\epsilon\epsilon_4$, $Domma_5$ $á_6$ $ǹ_7$ $dǎ_8$ bu_9 mo_{10}? $yéyá_{11}$ ba_{12} ka_{13} $mɔ̀_{14}$ $More_{15}$

(a) 'He$_1$ said$_2$ he$_3$ thought$_4$ he$_5$ would$_6$ gather$_8$ them$_7$ and$_{11}$ take them away.'

(b) 'One of his$_1$ people$_2$ said$_4$, "When$_5$ did you$_6$ not$_7$ have$_{10}$ them$_9$?" So$_{11}$ they$_{12}$ called$_{14}$ (that place) More$_{15}$.'

(O.I., Sentence 1.: 'He said (to his people)'; Quotation: 3-11: Indirect, on-stage, one quotation out-of-focus, reversal. O.I., Sentence 2: 'One of his people said to him'; Quotation: 5-10, Direct, one quotation in focus).

Footnotes

[1] This conference paper is a slightly edited version of one section of Dr. Pike's Tagmemic and Matrix Linguistics Applied to Selected African Languages, which volume was his final report to the Office of Education, U. S. Department of Health, Education and Welfare, on Contract No. OE-5-14-065. It was published in November, 1966, by the CRLLB.

[2] The author is a member of the CRLLB and a professor in the Department of Linguistics, University of Michigan.

[3]Primary and secondary are used here in reference to relation to statements. This use differs from that of Section 2.1, in reference to clauses in a clause cluster.

[4]First pointed out in matrix form in the submorphemic (or morphemic) "formatives" of a complicated morphological structure. See K. L. Pike and B. Erickson, 'Conflated Field Structures in Potawotomi and in Arabic, IJAL, 1964, 30, 201-12.

Note: Since this analysis was finished (covering text from seven sources, 660 quotations) a second body of text, which included approximately 1,000 quotations, was studied in the light of the hypotheses here. About fifty quotations did not fit the rules. Ten of these were commands. Four were a repeat of a quotation. Five instances of direct form occurred unexpectedly in a second degree quotation; two of these are speeches making up the important point to the story, so that emphasis or focus brought directness into the second degree slot.

Other things being equal, quotations which are written, or are true, are found in indirect form. Quotations which are oral, or fiction, are given in direct form.

THE PSYCHOLOGICAL REALITY OF THE PARAGRAPH[1]

Frank M. Koen, Alton L. Becker, and Richard E. Young[2]

There is currently an increasing overlap between the
concerns of the linguist and of the psychologist who
studies language behavior. In recent psychological literature, several experiments have dealt with various aspects
of supra-word linguistic structure, such as the psychological reality of linguistic segments (Fodor and Bever,
1965), and of phrase structure rules (Johnson, 1965). In
each case, however, the sentence has been implicitly
accepted as the most appropriate maximal structural unit
for study, while the problems of paragraph structure and
of paragraphing behavior have been largely ignored.

Becker (1965, 1966) has recently begun development
of a theory of paragraph structure which invites empirical
confirmation in the laboratory. Basing his approach on
the tagmemic model first proposed by Pike (1954, 1955,
1960), he suggests that the full explication of paragraphs
must be carried out concurrently along several dimensions.
To date, his analysis has lead to the postulation of three
interlocking, simultaneously-operating "systems" in
written material, which he has labeled lexical, grammatical
and rhetorical. In addition, a fourth system (phonological) is expected to operate in spoken language. Furthermore, he has explicitly rejected the sentence as a
necessarily relevant or important unit in the paragraph.

The lexical system consists of overlapping "lexical
equivalence chains", which may, and often do, extend over
several sentences. A chain is usually a group of sentences
all of which make statements dealing with the same content
domain. In doing so, "equivalence" is maintained by the
use of synonymity, metaphor, paraphrasing, and relative
and personal pronouns. For example, in the following pair
of sentences, "John left the office early, complaining of
a severe headache. I hope he will feel better tomorrow."
John and he are links in an equivalence chain.

174

The <u>grammatical</u> system consists of patterns of formal markers, such as the singularity or plurality of subjects and predicates, the tenses of verbs, and the presence and kind of modal auxiliaries. These elements, depending heavily on word endings as signaling devices, often extend beyond the single sentence.

The <u>rhetorical</u> system consists of a sequence of functional slots, each of which may be filled by one or more sentences. Two patterns of slots that seem to appear often in expository prose are those designated T(topic)-- R(restriction)--I(illustration), and P(problem)-- S(solution). In a sense, they are the formal elements, the result of whose interaction is the paragraph, in much the same way that relationships between subject, verb, and object specify the sentence. Formal markers include cue words and phrases, such as <u>for example,</u> <u>in other words,</u> <u>furthermore,</u> <u>however,</u> <u>then,</u> <u>but,</u> <u>and finally.</u> The semantic markers of the lexical equivalence chains also often supply corroborative information indicating the beginning and end of rhetorical structures.

In this experiment, the term "structural element" designates a string of sentences (not necessarily consecutive) which share a common marker, such as having a given verb tense (grammatical system), or sentence subject (lexical system), or extending between rhetorical transition words (rhetorical system). Within and between the three systems, the structural elements can, and often do, vary quite independently of each other. A sentence juncture at which any element begins or ends is here termed a "structural break", regardless of the system in which it occurs.

The theory seeks to explicate the ability of native English speakers to discriminate the structural cues (a significant portion of which are postulated to be formal in nature) which identify paragraphs. If this is to be done, the functional reality of the systems, and of the structural elements and their junctures, must be established. One way of approaching the problem is to perform theoretical analyses of several passages of English prose, specifying the domains of all structural elements and the systems with which they are associated. Then paragraph indentions can be removed, and naive (as regards the theory) English speakers can be instructed to place "¶" at those sentence junctures where they seem "appropriate".

175

Under these conditions, the theory gives rise to four predictions.

1. If paragraphs are conventional but not arbitrary units, Ss should agree with each other in placing paragraph markers, i.e., the distribution of "¶" responses in the passages will be multi-modal and will differ markedly from a chance (rectangular) distribution.

2. If a significant proportion of paragraphing cues are formal in nature, paragraph markers should tend to cluster at the same sentence junctures, regardless of whether the passages are normal English discourse, or derived nonsense passages in which nouns, verbs, adjectives, and adverbs have been replaced by nonsense words of equal syllabic length. That is, there will be a significant and positive correlation between English and derived nonsense passages in the proportions of Ss placing "¶" at the same sentence junctures.

3. Paragraphing behavior at sentence junctures should co-vary with the number of systems in which structural breaks occur at those junctures. However, since there appears to be a considerable area of individual decision in paragraphing, it would not seem to be necessary to account for all such choices, since a small proportion of them can easily be associated with chance vagaries and fluctuations of experimental "set". Therefore, as a first approximation, a sufficiently rigorous test of the model would be an evaluation of its performance at those sentence junctures where the probability of paragraphing was at least 20 per cent. That is, there will be a significant overlap between the distribution of sentence junctures at which 20 per cent or more of the Ss mark "¶", and the distribution of junctures in which three-system breaks occur. Furthermore, this overlap will be proportionally greater than that with junctures which have breaks in only two of the systems.

4. Assuming that the effects of structural breaks in all three systems are equal and additive, the greater the number of such breaks that occur at a given sentence juncture, the greater should be the proportion of Ss who place paragraph markers at that juncture. More specifically, there will be a significant and positive correlation between the total number of structural breaks at sentence junctures and the percentage of Ss placing paragraph markers at those junctures.

176

Method

Materials. Four expository passages of English prose
were chosen by two of the Es as representative of as many
different paragraph structures. All passages began and
ended with a paragraph (per the original author). For the
nonsense passages, all nouns, verbs, adjectives, and
adverbs were replaced with nonsense words (paralogs) of
equal syllabic length. For example, the sentence "Sloths
have no right to be living on the earth today; they would
be fitting inhabitants of Mars, where a year is over six
hundred days long" becomes "Smars have no mirt to be
lewling on the kust reteb; they would be tibbing nonentants
of Ness, where a reet is over nus cantron tels dan." The
number of sentences per passage varied from 16 to 28; the
number of words from 405 to 592. Word endings that play
a grammatical role were retained (e.g., -ed, -ly, -s, ing),
and all paragraph indentions were removed. Two or three
sentences were added to the beginning and end of two of
the passages, and data were collected using both the
"regular" and "extended" versions. Each passage was
printed on a separate page; the lines in which sentence
junctures occurred were numbered in the left-hand margin.
In the nonsense version, a given paralog replaced one and
only one English word, and was repeated at every occurrence
of the latter.

Subjects. The Ss were 48 college undergraduates;
approximately 50 per cent of them were male, although the
sex of the Ss was disregarded in data collection and
analysis. One-half served as part of a class requirement;
one-half were paid volunteers.

Procedure. All Ss responded to one English and to
one nonsense passage (which was derived from a different
English passage); one-half paragraphed a nonsense passage
first, one-half an English passage first. Passages were
randomly assigned to Ss; the number of Ss responding to
each passage ranged from 11 to 13. The data were collected
in four group sessions, with the number in each group
ranging from 6 to 25.

The experimental session was conducted as a series
of tasks, with each S working at his own pace, and with
successive tasks given him only upon completion of the
preceding one. The S was given an English (or nonsense)
passage and a page of printed instructions which:

177

(1) explained the purpose of the experiment ("to find out how and why we use paragraphs"); (2) asked him to read the passage carefully and to place paragraph markers "at the places that seem right to you", without regard to where the author may have put them; (3) pointed out that there were other tasks to be performed; and (4) requested that he raise his hand when he had finished the current one. The instructions were also read aloud, and questions answered. When the S̲ completed the first passage, he was given the second, with an additional instruction page, which explained that he was to perform the same task on different material.

Upon completion of paragraphing the second passage, the S̲ was given a list of seven paragraphing "cues", plus one open category, and an instruction sheet asking him to designate the one or more cues to which he was responding when he placed each "¶" in the two passages, and to write in additional cues wherever he thought they were operative. The cues supplied were: change of subject, change of time, change of location, change of verb, beginning or end of question-answer pattern, beginning or end of topic-illustration pattern, and transition word.

In addition, one-half of the S̲s were asked to paragraph an English and a nonsense "extended" passage. In this case, instructions specifically stated that "the passage may or may not begin with a paragraph". When the S̲s had completed all tasks, they were dismissed.

One of the E̲s (AB) used his theory as a basis for analyzing the four passages and specifying the domains of the structural elements in each of the three systems independently. This analysis supplied an estimate of the number and kind of theoretical "structural breaks" at each sentence juncture. Both the beginnings and the ends of such elements were considered as breaks in the statistical analysis.

Results

It was possible that the order of presentation of the stimuli (i.e., English-nonsense vs. nonsense-English) could produce differences in paragraphing responses. Chi-square was used to compare the distributions of paragraph markers, and of total number of markers associated with the two orders; there were no significant differences. Therefore, all data were pooled for further statistical analysis. An a priori decision was made to consider the placing of a "¶" by 20 per cent or more of the Ss as defining "significant" paragraphing behavior, and to attribute fewer than that proportion to random variability.

It can be seen in Table 1 that the distribution of paragraphing responses for each passage consists of many sentence junctures at which fewer than 20 per cent of the Ss indicated paragraph boundaries, and a few at which substantial amounts of paragraphing occurred. It is interesting to note that the top four categories of the table account for 86 per cent of all paragraph markers placed in all English and nonsense versions combined, despite the fact that they represent fewer than 30 per cent of the total number of sentence junctures. The distributions, though this cannot be discerned from the table, are indeed multi-modal, with the number of modes varying from three to five per passage. It is apparent that Ss agree with each other in their judgments of paragraph boundaries--in both English and nonsense passages. Paragraphing, then, is a reliable phenomenon and the first prediction is supported.

Prediction two stated that if Ss are responding to formal, as well as semantic, cues in paragraphing, there should be a significant correlation between the English and nonsense passages in the proportions of Ss placing "¶" at given sentence junctures, since semantic cues are severely curtailed in the nonsense passages. This prediction was supported by a Pearson r of .82 across all four pairs of English and nonsense passages. This result tempts one to stress the importance of formal cues even more heavily than the theory suggests, especially when further analysis shows that the lexical system was by far the least accurate of the three individual systems in predicting paragraphing by 20 per cent or more of the Ss.

The third prediction was based on the theoretical assertion that paragraph structure can best be explicated in terms of all three systems. This means that the presence at sentence junctures of structural breaks in three systems should more accurately predict "significant" paragraphing than breaks in any smaller number of systems. Figure 1 shows that this is indeed the case.

179

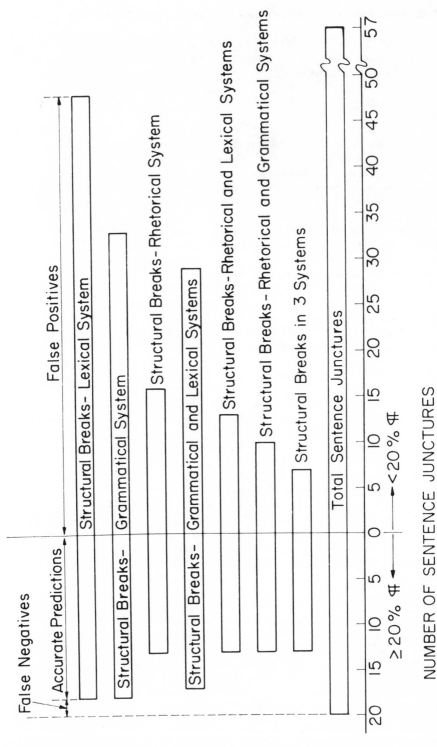

NUMBER OF SENTENCE JUNCTURES

Fig. 1. Relation between sentence junctures in English passages at which ≥ 20
per cent, and < 20 per cent, of Ss marked "¶" and structural breaks in

Table 1

Number of Sentence Junctures at Which Each of

Five Levels of Paragraphing Occurred

Percent Subjects marking " "	1 Eng.	Non.	2 Eng.	Non.	3 Eng.	Non.	4 Eng.	Non.
80-100	1	0	3	0	1	0	0	0
60-80	2	0	0	1	2	3	1	1
40-60	2	5	0	4	1	1	2	4
20-40	0	1	0	2	0	2	5	1
0-20	9	8	24	20	15	13	9	11
Total number of Junctures	14		27		19		17	

Of 20 junctures in the English passages with three-system breaks, 13 of them also exhibit paragraphing by 20 per cent or more of the S̲s. A comparison of this number with the (approximately) five that would be expected if junctures with three-system breaks were evenly distributed among all 77 junctures, yields $\chi^2 = 12.80$ (df = 1, p .001, 2 tails). Fig. 1 shows that distribution overlaps for two-system breaks are proportionally smaller, due mainly to an increasing number of false positives. It should be mentioned, however, that a chi-square test of the overlap between the 20 per cent "¶" distribution, and the "rhetorical-grammatical" break distribution was significant beyond the .01 level ($\chi^2 = 9.83$, df = 1,2 tails). All other overlaps were not significant.

Table 2

Percent Overlap Between Paragraphing Behavior

and Number of Systems in Which Structural Breaks Occur

Systems in which structural breaks occur	Passages	
	English	Nonsense
Three systems	82	75
Rhetorical and grammatical systems	79	71
Rhetorical and lexical systems	75	70
Grammatical and lexical systems	60	64
Rhetorical system	70	66
Grammatical system	55	57
Lexical system	35	48

Table 2 presents the same information in a different form for both English and nonsense passages. Here the statistic used is "per cent overlap between 'significant' degrees of paragraphing behavior and the number of systems in which 'breaks' occur."

It can be seen that the accuracy is greatest (82 per cent for English) with three-system breaks, and decreases as the number of system breaks declines. The Pearson r̲

between system breaks and number of paragraph markers was
.46 for English and .41 for nonsense passages.

The fourth prediction concerned the relation between
the total number of structural breaks occurring at a
sentence juncture and the proportion of $\underline{S}$s placing paragraph markers at that juncture. The Pearson $\underline{r}$ between the
two is .54 for English, and .45 for nonsense passages.
Both of these, of course, are statistically significant
with 76 df, and the prediction is supported, but a large
amount of variance is not yet accounted for.

It will be recalled that two passages were extended
by adding several sentences that were, in the original
work, contiguous with the experimental passage used but
were placed in preceding or succeeding paragraphs by the
author. The question was whether $\underline{S}$s would succeed in
identifying the beginnings and ends of full paragraph
structures, and would recognize less related "dangling"
sentences. The results indicate that they did. In the
two English passages, the proportion of $\underline{S}$s placing "¶" at
the sentence juncture beginning the first full paragraph
(per the original author) were 56 per cent and 71 per cent;
the end of the last paragraph was indicated by 78 per cent
and 28 per cent paragraph markers by $\underline{S}$s.

Of the seven paragraphing cues supplied $\underline{S}$s, "Beginning
or end of topic-illustration pattern" was most often given
for paragraphing (38 per cent of the total number of
reasons for English passages; 30 per cent for nonsense).
"Change of subject" was second most popular, accounting for
29 per cent of the reasons given for paragraphing English
passages, and 23 per cent for nonsense.

Discussion

The $\underline{S}$s in the experiment read and studied the entire
passage before making their paragraph judgments; there
were very few cases in which a paragraph marker was placed
on the first traversal of the material. Post-experimental
interviews disclosed that the $\underline{S}$s were "searching for
patterns", and their substantial agreement with each other
indicates that they must have found very much the same
patterns. Paragraphs, then, appear to be conventional
entities, but they do not represent arbitrary whims on the
part of their authors.

It appears that formal, rather than semantic, cues are dominant--at least in the task of recognizing paragraph structure. This conclusion is supported by three kinds of evidence. First, the high positive correlation between English and nonsense versions cannot be accounted for in terms of thematic or associative relations between content words. Second, the least accurate predictions of paragraphing were associated with the lexical system, either alone or paired with other systems. Both rhetorical and grammatical systems were more accurate in both English and nonsense versions. Third, multiple correlations with the number of structural breaks in each of the three systems as independent variables and percent paragraphing as the dependent variable consistently showed the lowest beta weights attached to the lexical breaks. In a way this is a surprising finding because, if we are to consider the paragraph a semantic unit, we must take account of the formal structural markers of the rhetorical and grammatical systems. They apparently play functional roles in relating the meaningful elements within the paragraph to each other, in a rough analogy to the grammatical structure of sentences.

It was originally expected that the numbers of structural elements which continued without interruption <u>across</u> sentence junctures would show a negative correlation with paragraphing, just as the number of breaks was positively related. However, although structural breaks and these structural "continuants" were negatively correlated (Pearson $\underline{r}$ = -.66), the latter showed only a weak relation to paragraphing. A low incidence of paragraphing, then, is related to the absence of structural breaks, but not to any concentration of continuing elements. One may speculate that this is another instance of the familiar psychological phenomenon of greater sensitivity to changes in stimulation than to steady states.

The current experiment represents only the first step in a continuing investigation. Future studies will involve removing specific markers associated with each of the systems and testing for subsequent changes in paragraphing behavior by <u>Ss</u>. A second area of study will call for <u>Ss</u> to indicate paragraph junctures in orally presented material in order to explore the cues and structure of the phonological system. A third problem area is that of cross-linguistic comparison of paragraph structures and cues; a fourth, developmental changes in paragraphing ability.

The results of this experiment carry implications for the classroom teaching of writing in both first and second languages. The identification of at least some of the cues which are associated with the recognition of paragraph structure should lead to the development in students of greater control and precision in their own paragraphing. Previously vague rhetorical notions of paragraph "unity" and "coherence" may now be functionally defined in terms of the domains and structural breaks of the several systems. Unity may, for example, be interpreted as a significant absence of breaks in one or more systems. Furthermore, comparisons of paragraph systems in different languages may reveal previously unspecified problems in language pedagogy. For example, English requires the use of tense markers; continuity in tense may well be an important structural cue in paragraphing. On the other hand, in languages like Thai and Burmese tense markers are not obligatory, but English-speaking students of these languages tend to use tense markers as a structural device in producing discourse in those languages. In doing so, they fail to exploit the proper systems for marking sequence, with a resultant stilted effect.

It is possible that paragraphs represent our capacity to "chunk" information for greater ease of storage and subsequent use. To date, the recall of continuous discourse cast in paragraph form has been shown to be influenced by such things as internal determinants expressed in "selective" memory (Bartlett, 1932; Levine & Murphy, 1943) and of more public variables such as the degree of associative connections between content words (Rosenberg, 1966). It appears that the structure of the paragraph may well be another parameter relevant to understanding and recall. After some of the more important paragraphing cues have been more precisely identified, it may be possible to affect the accuracy of recall of paragraphs, for example, by systematically manipulating these cues.

What is the nature of paragraphing ability? It appears to be a phenomenon somewhat different from the kind of competence usually associated with the generation or recognition of sentences. The argument that a speaker can and will recognize and correct his "errors" in

performance is often used to support the generative
grammarians' distinction between competence and performance. The implication is that everyone will recognize the
same "errors" and will correct them in substantially the
same way (though this has not been unambiguously demonstrated). It would appear that the Ss' responses in this
experiment represent, in large measure, their competence,
since there was no imposed time limit and they were invited
to rely on their own knowledge of linguistic structures in
making their decisions. Under these conditions there seems
to be very little "error" in paragraphing (as the term is
used with regard to sentence generation); "disagreement"
seems to be a better term for what happens. However,
these disagreements are usually quite readily resolved.
Ss who have placed paragraph markers at different points
in a passage can often give reasons for their decisions
which are mutually acceptable, "if one chooses to look at
it in that way". One explanation that suggests itself is
the multi-systemic nature of paragraphs which lends itself
to differential weighting of the systems by different
speakers. Inducing a set to concentrate on any one system
may well result in greater conformity of response than was
found here.

At any rate, paragraphing rules seem to be more
flexible than are those associated with the generation of
sentences. Perhaps, there are sets of rules, and users
of a language shift from one set to another in response
to cues which have not yet been identified, but which may
well extend beyond the paragraph.

References

Becker, A. L. A tagmemic approach to paragraph analysis.
Coll. Comp. Comm., 1965, 16, 237-242.

Becker, A. L. Symposium on the paragraph. Coll. Comp.
Comm., 1966, 17, 67-72.

Bartlett, F. C. Remembering: A study in experimental and
social psychology. London: Cambridge University
Press, 1932.

Fodor, J. A., & Bever, T. G. The psychological reality of
linguistic segments. J. verb. Learn. verb. Behav.,
1965, 4, 414-420.

Johnson, N. F.   The psychological reality of phrase-
    structure rules.   J. verb. Learn. verb. Behav., 1965,
    4, 469–475.

Levine, J. M., & Murphy, G.   The learning and forgetting
    of controversial material.   J. abnorm. soc. Psychol.,
    1943, 38, 507–517.

Pike, K. L.   Language in relation to a unified theory of
    the structure of human behavior.   Glendale: Summer
    Institute of Linguistics, Part I, 1954; Part II,
    1955; Part III, 1960.

Rosenberg, S.   Associative factors in the recall of
    connected discourse.   Psychonom. Sci., 1966, 4, 53–54.

Footnotes

[1]This report is based on research supported by a
contract with the Office of Education, U. S. Department of
Health, Education, & Welfare, under provisions of P. L.
83–531, Cooperative Research, and Title VI, P. L. 85–864,
as amended.

[2]The authors are members of the research staff at
the CRLLB.

MENTALISM IN THE STUDY OF LITERARY LANGUAGE

Richard Ohmann[1]

Linguistics is the study of languages, and hence of that part of the human mind which is given over to languages and their use.[2] Literary criticism is the interpretation of literary works. Since literary works are in language, plainly there is some kind of connection between the two disciplines. At the very least, the critic deploys a linguistic theory (customarily without conscious knowledge) when he gives a reading to a poem; but since the same can be said of any reader or hearer in any situation, the claim is so far unilluminating. In this paper I wish to consider, somewhat more exactly, the intersection of linguistics and literary criticism. My intent is to clarify issues, especially the question of what role the concept of mind should play in critical theory.

I want to begin with an important concept of psycholinguistics that helpfully applies--in part, and with some stretching--to the business of literary criticism: that is, the idea of intuition, or sprachgefühl. A speaker's linguistic intuition is his knowledge of his language, his ability, among other things, to tell which strings are of that language and which are not. This is mainly a piece of "tacit knowledge," to use Michael Polanyi's phrase. That is, a speaker with no grammatical sophistication cannot in any satisfying way say why "I doubt that he went, nor George either" is English, and "I regret that he went, nor George either" is not. The appropriate rules, which a grammarian might discover,[3] model his tacit knowledge, and thus explain his particular intuitions about grammaticality, relationship, ambiguity, paraphrase, and so on.

I want to suggest that the author of a literary work has a further intuition that is in some ways similar to his sprachgefühl. He knows how he wants the work to go, or sound, or feel--it is hard to be more precise about this matter--and presumably he knows when it is going, or sounding, or feeling right. He knows what strings of words are a proper part of the work, and what ones are not. Like the fluent speaker, he may have very little communicable knowledge about why a certain phrase or sentence belongs in the work, or through what mechanisms it realizes his intuition; yet he chooses his words, tests them against some standard, and frequently replaces them (in revision) with "better" ones. Especially in writing poetry, but in writing prose fiction and non-fiction as well, he frames his discourse according to rules that go beyond those of the language he is writing in. It is not helpful or accurate to suppose that his intuition (or his words) follows simply from what he "wants to say," unless "say" is construed so broadly as to eradicate the distinction between discursive content and artistic form, and hence between literature and random sequences of well-formed sentences.[4]

Almost by definition, literature is discourse with more than ordinary form, with more regularities than those of the language it is written in. A few linguists have attempted to specify these regularities, at least for poetry. Roman Jakobson, for instance, describes "the indispensable feature inherent in any piece of poetry" as follows:

> The poetic function projects the principle of equivalence from the axis of selection into the axis of combination. Equivalence is promoted to the constitutive device of the sequence. In poetry one syllable is equalized with any other syllable of the same sequence; word stress is assumed to equal word stress, as unstress equals unstress; prosodic long is matched with long, and short with short; word boundary equals word boundary, no boundary equals no boundary; syntactic pause equals syntactic pause, no pause equals no pause. Syllables are converted into units of measure, and so are morae or stresses.[5]

Samuel R. Levin extends this idea: characteristic of poetry, he argues, are structures he calls "couplings," in which "naturally equivalent forms (i.e., equivalent as to sound or meaning, or both)" occur "in equivalent positions."[6]

These claims--more precise than the claim that literature has regularities beyond those of the language it is
written in--are at the same time more confining and looser
than what I am suggesting: more confining, because they
isolate just one class of regularity as peculiar to poetry,
and looser, because they do not speak of the unique systems
of regularities that constitute single works of literature.
One might translate the kind of thing Jakobson and Levin
say into the terms I am proposing, roughly as follows:
"when a man composes poetry, he follows an intuition of
poetic form (presumably learned), which dictates that
equivalent linguistic elements will succeed one another
with considerable regularity [Jakobson] and frequency
[Levin]." This may be so, but such an intuition would be
an extremely vague one, and could only operate through
more exact intuitions of form. For instance, an intuition
of meter: Morris Halle and Samuel Jay Keyser have
recently shown that Chaucer's metric is economically
describable by a set of rules that Chaucer himself could
hardly have articulated;[7] yet something like these rules
must have been part of his "metrical intuition"; otherwise
it is difficult to explain why nearly every line in the
canon is regular according to these rules, and not according to some other set. Halle and Keyser suggest that the
rules for Chaucer's iambic pentameter would serve, with
minor adjustments, to generate most iambic pentameter in
English. If so, this strongly implies that a skilled
English poet writing in this verse form follows a learned
intuition, and a rather more complex one than Jakobson and
Levin seem to have in mind.

Evidently there are other literary intuitions of this
same kind: those that govern oral epic; those that govern
rhyme; and so on. In the reservoir of culturally available forms there are still others that may be founded in
intuition, though much more nebulously. I am thinking of
narrative patterns, or "mythoi,"[8] such as comedy, romance,
and tragedy, motifs such as the descent into the under-
world, creation myths, etc. These probably do constitute
a form of tacit knowledge, but they have relatively little
to do with language. Again, there are literary conven-
tions, such as those of the pastoral elegy or the aubade,
some of which are linguistic, but all of which are perhaps
relatively conscious, explicitly known. In any event,
meter, myth, and convention are to a great extent provided
by culture; and whatever their contribution to the
writer's sense of his work, there is a residue of literary

intuition--a larger or smaller residue, depending on how conventional the work is--whose source is not in culture, but in the writer himself. It is with this residue that I am primarily concerned.

Even here it is necessary to distinguish. The decisions that a certain character will be a valetudinarian, and that in chapter 13 the heroine will narrowly escape death are no doubt largely conscious. But there is also a substratum of semi-conscious or unconscious choice that proceeds according to literary intuition. Style is probably the best example of what I mean.[9] The choices that result in a style may or may not strike the writer <u>as</u> choices while he is making them. If he is aware of choosing, his awareness probably extends no farther than the particular passage at hand. Certainly he does not choose an entire style in full consciousness of every structural subtlety it entails. Rather, I imagine, he has an intuition as to how it should sound, what view of things it should reflect, and he writes accordingly.

A few sentences from Chapter 15 of Gibbon's <u>Decline and Fall of the Roman Empire</u> should help me to be clear about this:

> The expulsion of the demons from the bodies of those unhappy persons whom they had been permitted to torment was considered as a signal though ordinary triumph of religion, and is repeatedly alleged by the apologists as the most convincing evidence of the truth of Christianity. The awful ceremony was usually performed in a public manner, and in the presence of a great number of spectators; the patient was relieved by the power or the skill of the exorcist, and the vanquished demon was heard to confess that he was one of the fabled gods of antiquity who had impiously usurped the adoration of mankind. But the miraculous cure of diseases of the most inveterate or even preternatural kind can no longer occasion any surprise when we recollect that in the days of Irenaeus, about the end of the second century, the resurrection of the dead was very far from being esteemed an uncommon event; that the miracle was frequently performed on necessary occasions by great fasting and the joint supplication of the Church of the place; and that the persons thus restored to their prayers had lived afterwards among them many years.

Gibbon likes the passive voice; in the first two sentences
alone he uses it six times. Now, the standard form for
the passive of "The power or the skill of the exorcist
relieved the patient" is the transform that appears in
sentence two of the passage: "The patient was relieved by
the power or the skill of the exorcist." But this is the
only one of the six that appears in standard form--that
is, without having undergone further transformation. In
all the rest but one, Gibbon has deleted the logical
subject (By + NP). The exception--"is repeatedly alleged
by the apologists. . ."--has had its <u>grammatical</u> subject
deleted, to allow conjunction with "was considered. . ."
In addition, one of the passives is embedded in a relative
clause ("whom they had been permitted to torment"); likewise, the one passive verb in the third sentence occurs
within an adverbial clause. These deformations and
embeddings vary the surface structures, and make the
seven passives relatively unobtrusive, so much so that it
seems at least doubtful that Gibbon used them in conscious
awareness of their similarity in structure.

But for <u>seven</u> we must read <u>fourteen</u>, because that is
the number of times the passive transformation has in fact
applied in the derivation of these three sentences. The
phrase "being esteemed an uncommon event" in sentence three
is a transform of "the resurrection of the dead was
esteemed an uncommon event (by someone)." Both subject
and direct object have disappeared, and the underlying
sentence has become a nominal, object of the preposition
"from." Still more altered is "restored to their prayers"
(sentence 3), which has passed through the relative
transformation, and then, through deletion of Rel + Tense
+ Be, been reduced to an adjectival. It is similar to the
past participles in "vanquished demon" and "fabled gods,"
which also have their origins in the passive, but have
gone through one further change. An abbreviated view of
their history will suggest how later transformations
conceal the effects of early ones:

(Someone) vanquished the demon

The demon was vanquished (by someone)   Passive

The demon was vanquished   Agent deletion

(The demon) who was vanquished   Relative

```
(The demon) vanquished        Post-nominal adj.

(the) vanquished (demon)      Pre-nominalization
```

The one word "vanquished" in the surface structure represents an entire sentence in the deep, and indicates, furthermore, that the sentence has been through the passive transformation.

The other three crypto-passives figure in the surface structure as nominals: "The expulsion of the demons" (sentence 1), "the miraculous cure of diseases" (sentence 3), and "the resurrection of the dead" (sentence 3). That these are passives is shown by the possibility of providing them with logical subjects in the characteristic form, By + NP (e.g., "The expulsion of the demons by the exorcist"). But they bear little physical resemblance to the passives of standard form, to which they are nearly identical in underlying structure ("the demons were expelled (by someone)"). Thus it seems reasonable to suppose that neither they nor the adjectivals just discussed are there because Gibbon consciously chose them as passives. Yet he did choose them, presumably under the guidance of a particular stylistic intuition.

Can this intuition be modeled by grammatical rules that supplement the rules of English? Or is it realized statistically, simply by a high frequency of passives? Let us consider the verbs that do not appear in the passive form: a few--"triumph," "fast," and "live"--are intransitive, and hence have no passives. The rest share no grammatical feature that I can discern, but they do (all but one) have a common ground in the reference of their logical subjects: none of these subjects refers to the early Christians.[10] By contrast, of the verbs in the passive, all but three have subjects in the underlying structure that refer to one or more of the Christians.[11] Thus one might write a simple--though admittedly inelegant--rule for the main stylistic feature of this passage: "for every transitive verb the passive transformation is obligatory if the subject of the verb refers to one or more of the early Christians, unless the verb undergoes a transformation that blocks the passive transformation." It seems likely, given the evidence at hand, that this rule sums up Gibbon's intuition of the form the passage was to take; certainly the particular distribution of passives and actives here seems a matter of more than

193

chance, though it could hardly have been the consequence of <u>conscious</u> planning.

To what impulse may we attribute this practice? The passive assigns a secondary role to the logical subject by relegating it to a prepositional phrase, and, once in this position, the logical subject commonly drops out altogether by another transformation. Clearly the semantic tendency is toward throwing emphasis on the direct object and reducing emphasis on the subject. In the passage from Gibbon (and in Chapter 15 generally) the noun so deprived of importance or specificity often refers to the early Christians, as we have seen. By suppressing their active roles and their individuality, Gibbon places their actions and beliefs behind a screen of generality, which, to me, suggests law-like and predictable, conventional happenings, everything in order: "the vanquished demon was heard to confess. . . ." Compare "The congregation heard the demon that Marcus had vanquished confess. . . ." Gibbon's version seems to confer on the event a greater plausibility. But of course the reader will test this implicit claim of plausibility against the exotic quality of the event itself; moreover, he knows that the deep structure contains the banished logical subjects. Hence a tension between impersonality (surface structure) and personal involvement (deep structure) combines with a conflict between implied ordinariness and actual strangeness.

Here, I believe, is one general source of Gibbon's irony, which typically sets off the extravagance of human conduct by pretending to accommodate it within a knowing, imperturbable rationality. More generally still, the passive answers well to a preference for objectivity and distance. By allowing human agency to recede into an obscure limbo, Gibbon locates the events of Roman history in a neutral framework of plain fact, mere occurrence, and absolves himself from a potentially sentimental attachment to the participants. "Just representations of general nature": the neo-classical slogan is Johnson's, but the goal informs the passage at hand, and Gibbon's history at large, even more pervasively than it does Johnson's work. The passive voice implements it here in a rather concrete way.

To return to the main theme: I am suggesting that Gibbon knew, and could have said, in what way he regarded the marvelous doings of the early Christians, and knew the

general effect he wished to achieve in his writing, but
that the intricate embedding of passives was an unwilled
accomplishment of his stylistic intuition. To get at such
intuitions is part of the critic's business; they are what,
ultimately, he is describing when he describes the style
of a literary work.

Stylistic intuitions put the language to use in very
different ways, and it will be instructive to examine a
contrasting example. On a quick count, it may appear that
this very different passage hangs by the same syntactic
thread as does Gibbon's:

> The afternoon was ending, and in the widening area
> of demolition was a fire, fed by the wreckage.
> Moses heard the air, softly pulled toward the
> flames, felt the heat. The workmen, heaping the
> bonfire with wood, threw strips of molding like
> javelins. Paint and varnish smoked like incense.
> The old flooring burned gracefully--the funeral
> of exhausted objects. Scaffolds walled with
> pink, white, green doors quivered as the six-
> wheeled trucks carried off fallen brick. The
> sun, now leaving for New Jersey and the west, was
> surrounded by a dazzling broth of atmospheric
> gases. (Saul Bellow, *Herzog*, p. 175)

One full passive, six past participles acting as adjectives.
Two of these, however, have no passive transformation in
their derivational history: "six-wheeled trucks" comes
from "the trucks had six wheels," and "fallen brick" comes
from "the brick had fallen," rather than the impossible
"[someone] fell the brick." In Bellow's style, the passive
itself counts for little. Far more characteristic is the
way in which some of his passives enter their matrix
sentences:

> a fire, fed by the wreckage

> the air, softly pulled toward the flames

> Scaffolds walled with pink, white, green doors

The underlying relative clauses (two of them non-
restrictive, one restrictive) have gone through the transformation that deletes Rel + Tense + Be, and places the
remainder of the clause directly after the noun it
modifies.

195

Notice now that two other nouns in the passage have similar modifiers:

The workmen, heaping the bonfire with wood

The sun, now leaving for New Jersey and the west,

and that there is another construction at least rhythmically similar:

The old flooring burned gracefully--the funeral of exhausted objects.

The intuitive similarity of these locutions has a foundation in grammar, as it happens, for the deletion of Rel + Be (and sometimes NP + Be) is a highly general operation, which may apply to almost any clause, no matter what follows the verb "Be," or what previous history the clause has. Not only do passive clauses fall in the domain of the transformation, but active clauses in the progressive tense, as well (the workmen, who were heaping the bonfire ⟹ the workmen, heaping the bonfire). Moreover, it applies to structures in which "Be" is not an auxiliary at all, but a copula:

The man, who was old and tired ⟹ the man, old and tired

The man who was on the platform ⟹ the man on the platform

The man, who was a deputy ⟹ the man, a deputy, etc.

The last example shows how appositives derive from relative clauses, and accounts indirectly for Bellow's "the funeral of exhausted objects," which seems to be an oblique form of "an event which was the funeral of exhausted objects."[12]

In discussing the excerpt from Gibbon's history, I pointed out that after the deletion of Rel + Tense + Be, post-nominal passives may be moved ahead of the noun, in fact, must be, if the remainder of the passive contains only one word. The provenance of pre-nominal adjectives and participles is the same. Hence, in addition to the phrases already mentioned, there are several others in the passage from Herzog that result indirectly from the deletion of Rel + Be: "the widening area," "the old

flooring," "exhausted objects," "pink, white, green doors,"
"a dazzling broth," "atmospheric gases." The underlying
structure of the passage is pretty well dominated by this
sequence of transformations; conjunction is the only other
one that figures significantly in the makeup of the
passage. Pre-nominal modifiers are common enough in most
narrative prose, it should be noted, and they alone would
not suffice to identify Bellow's style. But together
with post-nominal modifiers--which, recall, have exactly
the same derivation except for one obligatory transforma-
tion--they make a distinct contribution. The post-nominal
modifiers themselves stand out rather sharply, moreover,
sometimes to the point of idiosyncrasy:

> Moses, *a collector of pictures*, had kept a photograph
> *of Madeleine, aged twelve, in riding habit*. She
> was posed with the horse, *about to mount, a stocky
> long-haired girl with fat wrists and desperate
> dark shadows under her eyes, premature signs of
> suffering and of a craving for revenge*.
> (Herzog, p. 126; my italics)

Here ten post-nominals, some with pre-nominals embedded,
crowd into two sentences, and account for virtually all of
the transformational structure; and this concentration is
only a little out of the ordinary.

> In the morning, *eating gelatin pie for breakfast*,[13]
> he saw Idwal, *ruddy and small, with steel spectacles,
> in his bedroom swinging indian clubs, doing knee-
> bends in his long underwear*. (Herzog, p. 127;
> my italics)

Constructions of every provenance find their way into the
preferred form.

It is worth while to look more closely at this fact,
for it distinguishes, rather sharply, Bellow's reliance on
post-nominals from Gibbon's on the passive, and points to
a tentative generalization about the working of syntax in
style. The relative transformation can apply, tolerantly,
to almost any underlying structure that contains "Be,"
whether previously transformed or not. Whenever the
result contains the sequence Rel + Tense + Be, that
sequence may drop out, as we have seen. But the structures
that are alike in containing it have quite diverse origins--
some in structures that contain the copula to start with:

197

1) NP + Be + Adj: The gases were atmospheric $\Longrightarrow$ the gases that were atmospheric $\Longrightarrow$ *the gases atmospheric $\Longrightarrow$ the atmospheric gases

2) NP + Be + NP: Moses was a collector of pictures $\Longrightarrow$ Moses, who was a collector of pictures $\Longrightarrow$ Moses, a collector of pictures

3) NP + Be + Loc: Idwal was in his bedroom   Idwal, who was in his bedroom   Idwal,. . . in his bedroom

and some not:

4) NP + be + V + ing + X: The sun was now leaving for the west   The sun, which was now leaving for the west   the sun, now leaving for the west

5) NP + Have + NP: the girl had fat wrists   *the girl was with fat wrists   *(a girl) who was with fat wrists   (a girl) with fat wrists

6) NP + V + NP: The wreckage fed the fire   the fire was fed by the wreckage   (a fire), which was fed by the wreckage   (a fire), fed by the wreckage

Notice that the underlying sentences in (5) and (6) undergo one transformation each before the relative; so does (2), for "collector of pictures" is a transform of "Moses collects pictures." For that matter, most of Bellow's post-nominals have in their histories at least one transformation before the relative, commonly either conjunction, passivization, nominalization, or additional relativization.

A simple fact of English syntax explains the miscellaneous ancestry of these constructions: the deletion of Rel + Tense + Be, like sentence conjunction, has a low priority in the ordered application of transformational rules. It operates on (and of course alters) structures that have already undergone transformations of higher priority. By contrast, the passive transformation, so prominent in Gibbon's syntax, does its work relatively early in the cycle. It transforms structures of the shape NP + Aux + V_t + NP, and no others. By the same logic, it is apparent that passive transforms may be further altered by application of subsequent rules, whereas the constructions that result from deletion of

Rel + Tense + Be remain as they are (except for position-
ing). It is fairly easy to see the effect of this contrast
on the superficial impressions that the two styles make:
Gibbon's passives recede behind later structural changes
and make a smaller claim on the reader's notice than their
frequency would suggest, while in some parts of <u>Herzog</u>
the concentration of post-nominals is immediately apparent,
compelling attention as both the rhythmic and the structural principle of Bellow's prose. And this is precisely
the difference to be expected between the stylistic
imprints of a transformation whose operation may be buried
in deep structure and of one whose application is
uniformly represented in surface structure.

The conceptual impulses behind such a contrast in
stylistic intuitions are more difficult to understand, and
any explanation must be tentative. Consider, for a start,
what unchosen alternatives the two transformations imply.
In the grammar, the alternative to applying the passive
transformation is leaving unchanged a sentence that is in
standard form; in doing one or the other, a writer selects
a way of framing a basic proposition in English, and
hence a way of conceptualizing an element of experience or
thought (the terms are loose, but they will have to do).
By the time the deletion of Rel + Tense + Be applies, all
such choices have been made, and the writer is merely
choosing a way to incorporate an element of experience in
a larger structure--i.e., he chooses the post-nominal
modifier rather than the relative clause. Let us say,
then (still speaking loosely), that in Gibbon's passage
the style proceeds in large part from a tendency to
formulate the basic structures of discourse in a certain
manner, whereas Bellow consistently chooses a way of
assembling and relating structures of various origins.
In other words, in comparing the use of an early-applying
transformation to the use of a late-applying transformation, I have been setting a preferred <u>formulation</u> of
elemental meanings beside a preferred <u>arrangement</u> of
meanings.

Something more specific remains to be said of
Bellow's procedure. Among the choices that govern style--
though they are not stylistic choices, properly speaking--
are choices of what to say. Bellow tends to accumulate
information about, and attitudes toward, a single subject,
to surround a semantic nucleus with separate radii, like
spokes that attach to the center but not to each other.

Grammatically speaking, this means that a Bellow sentence is likely to have in its deep structure clusters of sentences with the same noun as subject:

Herzog saw Idwal in the morning

Herzog was eating gelatin pie for breakfast.

Idwal was ruddy

Idwal was small

Idwal had steel spectacles

Idwal was in his bedroom

Idwal was swinging indian clubs

Idwal was doing knee-bends

Idwal was in his long underwear

Given these elements of content, and given the stylistic choice, moreover, of placing them all in the same sentence, a certain amount of post-nominalization is nearly inevitable. Relative clauses—"Idwal, who was ruddy and small, who had steel spectacles, who was in his bedroom, who was swinging indian clubs, etc."—are a clumsy alternative. No less so, prenominal modifiers. Post-nominals, by contrast, represent a compact and efficient form within which to house incidental or supplementary information. And doing so suits Bellow, at least in the novels beginning with The Adventures of Augie March. He seems impelled to admit a generous quota of contingent circumstances, as if in wry acquiescence to their plenitude and oddity, to the way things are.[14] As Augie says, at the beginning of his "free style" account, he "will make the record in my own way: first to knock, first admitted." Thus, the stylistic intuition under scrutiny here answers not only to what I have called a "preferred arrangement of meanings," but to a preferred selection of meanings as well. We may expect the same to be true, in one degree or another, of many traits of style. For evidently a stylistic intuition proceeds from, and evokes, a way of experiencing, and literary styles are closely allied to styles of perception and styles of cognition.

The same sense of the mind behind the work may be quite vivid even when the style and the attitudes it embodies are considerably more complex than those I have been examining. The syntax of the following could hardly have been mapped out with full conscious intent, yet it presents a coherent, if subtle, view of the experiences it reports:

> Charleston early in the morning, on my driving from the station, was, it had to be admitted, no very finished picture, but at least, already, it was different--ever so different in aspect and "feeling," and above all for intimation and suggestion, from any passage of the American scene as yet deciphered; . . . (Henry James, "Charleston," in The American Scene)

This passage is typical of James in its convolution and interruptions, which give the feeling that experience is being oddly complicated, that the focus is not quite what it appears to be, and that this is a peculiarly inward form of description. Syntax is largely responsible for these groping apprehensions.

Notice, first, that in the surface structure "Charleston" is the subject, but that in the deep structure the entire clause is embedded in the matrix, "it had to be admitted." But this does not take us to the bottom of deep structure. "It had to be admitted" is itself the result of the passive transformation, from "(someone) had to admit (something)." Hence the logical subject of the sentence is neither "Charleston" nor "it," but an indefinite human noun. We know it is human because "admit", in the sense required, takes only human subjects.

Nor is this the only suppressed element of the human. Buried in the embedded temporal phrase "on my driving from the station" is the word "my," an adjective in the surface structure. But of course this phrase is derived by transformation from "I drove from the station," which also reveals a concealed human subject. Next, consider the adjectival phrase, "as yet deciphered." It comes, by a process I have already described, from "(neg) (someone) had deciphered (Det) passage." The concealed logical subject is a pronoun that stands in for a human noun.

201

The process of suppressing the human shows also in three of James' nominals. The word "feeling" is the surface representation of "(someone) felt (something)." And the abstract nouns "intimation" and "suggestion" are the tokens of underlying sentences with human indirect objects: "(something) intimated (something) (to someone)" "(something) suggested (something) (to someone)."

To press the analysis one step farther, consider the sentence modifiers "at least" and "above all." Such modifiers as a class carry a semantic feature something like this: "way of regarding the proposition expressed by the nucleus of the sentence." That is, they represent an implied comment on or qualification of the sentence's content, by the speaker or writer--in short, by a human mind.

In all these ways, the deep structure of the sentence bulges with human agents or observers or receivers of impressions, who play virtually no role in the surface structure. The suppressed relations are, I believe, accountable for the sense of double-focus that the passage gives rise to--for the feeling that we are getting more of the narrator than we are of Charleston, the ostensible subject of the passage, and for our awareness that we are in the presence of mind playing over experience in an exceedingly fastidious way--qualifying, commenting, setting in the proper light, and so on.

This might well have been how James thought of it. But it seems to me highly unlikely that he set about his task by determining to delete as many human nouns as possible before they reached surface structure. Surely we are again confronted with a firm but delicate stylistic intuition at work. And in general, I think that when a critic describes and analyzes a style, he is trying to describe that intuition, trying to make explicit the constraints that the writer imposes on himself, in large part unconsciously, in order to present his vision of things. If so, the critic is to that extent a crypto-psycho-linguist, or possibly a psycho-crypto-linguist.

It may appear that the position I am maintaining runs afoul of the familiar distinction between competence and performance. It does. The work of literature is, to be sure, a single, unique performance; that is one of the reasons we value it. And yet I have been speaking as if

202

certain aspects of its form--its meter, its style, perhaps others--reflect the kind of intuition that one usually associates with linguistic <u>competence</u>. I want to suggest that the intuition I speak of occupies a middle ground between competence and performance, that it is a nonce-intuition, an intuition temporarily adopted, which reflects the <u>special</u> competence of the writer to tell what does and what does not belong in his work. Such an intuition supplements, and may even contradict, his ordinary linguistic intuition; it is what lies behind regularities in the work's linguistic form; and it is what the critic is studying when he studies that form.

Up to this point, I have been considering the literary work as related to the real or imagined person who is its source. On the receiving side is the reader, and in him is another intersection of linguistic and literary studies. But "the" reader is an elusive personage, and caution is necessary. I do not propose to study actual "responses" to literature, a procedure which--whatever its usefulness to pedagogy--is not likely to yield much insight into literature or language, at least not at present. It seems profitable, rather, to postulate a model reader, one fully versed in his language, wealthy in experience, and alive to possibilities. In short, the reader one tries to become. The relevant question to ask about him in this context is, what does his knowledge of his language contribute to his understanding of the literary work? Elsewhere, I have attempted some answers to this question, with particular attention to literary structure, metaphor, and other common critical notions.[15] Here, for exemplary purposes, I wish to choose a less likely candidate--the <u>image</u>. I shall contend that the image, far from being a kind of literary prime or element, is itself structurally complex, that it makes delicate use of linguistic resources, and, surprisingly, that its sensory content, for the reader, depends largely on his knowledge of syntax.

The word "image" implies a fully articulated sensory pattern, but how can a few words in a poem determine anything of the sort? Is the "dead tree" in the Waste Land an ash or a ginkgo, massive or scrawny, with "yellow leaves, or few, or none" (to use Shakespeare's agreeably indeterminate phrase)? And if these questions are impertinent, as I take it they are, what ghostly paradigm of things must the mind contain in order to comprehend even the most detailed image?

Let me simplify matters by declining part of the psychological challenge, both as beyond my competence, and as irrelevant. Readers of poetry do no doubt construct full-blooded mental images, in which dead trees, if present, look like something rather than like nothing. A mental image of treeness is a contradiction. But your mental tree differs from mine, and both of them differ from Eliot's. The private images that so variously take shape in readers' minds are not a proper subject for criticism because criticism occupies itself with the part of a poem's meaning that is in the public domain, the part that is available to readers by virtue of their knowing the appropriate language. I wish to carry the inquiry as far as language takes it: that is, to consider the image as a structure of linguistically-determined meaning.

In particular, how do we comprehend anything so subtle as an image, given the bare text? Literary handbooks, if they bother at all, say that images derive from words with sensory content. This will not suffice. A reader who knew only the <u>words</u> of English could not construe even the phrase, "dead tree," for he could not amalgamate the meanings of the two words, would not know that the tree was what was dead. The syntax of the phrase, so transparent that it seems non-existent, is nonetheless as essential to the image as the sensory words themselves. I venture this truism because it is easy to forget, and because its moment becomes less negligible as we apply it to more complex images.

Consider now the following sensory morphemes: "dance," "bright," "sway," "glance," "music," "body." They probably seem vague individually (not young girl or aging athlete, but "body"; not gavotte or minuet, but "dance"), and muddled as a group. Yet these are the only sensory words in an image which nonetheless is both memorable and remembered: the closing image of Yeats' "Among School Children":

O body swayed to music, O brightening glance,
How can we know the dancer from the dance?

Now it is possible to tell what goes with what, and how, but the mere <u>relational</u> force of syntax seems inadequate here to account for poetic meaning. The image is justly famous as Yeats' emblem for annihilation of the striving self. Whence does it derive its character, if not from the sensory words? Let me suggest some partial explanations.

204

Most importantly, in the surface structure there is only one verb--the non-sensory verb "know." But in the deep structure there are five: "sway," "brighten," "glance," and "dance" twice. They appear on the surface as adjectives and nouns, but the verbal force lingers beneath. It is diverted into forms that half-deny it, subdue it, put it in a lower key. Energy and action are balanced with stasis and control, just as the formal art of the dance holds the dancer's personality in check, and allows her to represent so fittingly the perfection of being.

Another syntactic configuration supports this one: the verb "sway" originates in deep structure as an active verb with an indefinite subject, but after going through the passive transformation it has had its subject deleted. Thus an unnamed agent moves the dancer's body (to music-- music is not the agent, but the accompaniment); through syntax we receive the notion both of a mysterious force and of the dancer's loss of will, subordination of self. There are two more obvious roles that syntax plays in the image: first, Yeats uses a question and two apostrophes, so that nothing is asserted. Even the degree of intellec- tual mastery implied by statement is absent from this climactic image. And second, Yeats uses two inanimate nouns--"body" and "glance"--in a form--direct address-- that normally requires animate nouns, thereby reinforcing the tension between the human and the non-human, and the peculiar hypnotic quality of the image. The dancer is out of herself; her mind and will are dormant. In all these ways, syntax creates a kinesthetic feeling barely sug- gested by the words themselves, and conceptualizes the dancer's motions in a form that richly supports the theme of the poem. The reader's knowledge of syntax is what makes it possible for him to resolve the image in anything like the way it deserves.

For the sake of comparison, and to bolster my point, let me examine another complex image, equally familiar, that shares one structure with Yeats':

> But here there is no light,
> Save what from heaven is with the breezes blown
> Through verdurous glooms and winding mossy ways.
> (Keats, "Ode to a Nightingale")

The second line of the image rests on the deep structure, "(something) blows (some) light from heaven with the breezes"; it has passed through the passive transformation, then lost its logical subject, in the same sequence that we have seen at work in Yeats and Gibbon. Here, though, the sense we get is of the light's obscure and distant origins, for the setting is different. "Light," needless to say, is inanimate, and we would not expect it to be exercising will or control. More to the point, the whole structure has been embedded in the main clause by a transformation that relegates it to a prepositional phrase ("save what. . ."). That phrase, and the entire last two lines of the image, have the function of qualifying "no light." The image begins boldly and negatively, and everything that follows--namely the image of light--is by way of exception, afterthought. Furthermore, the phrase "some light" in the underlying structure has become "what light" and then simply the indefinite and abstract "what," in a further denial of light.

There is another interesting collaboration of deep and surface structures in the last line. The deep structure contains two concrete mass nouns, "verdure" and "moss," both of which appear in the surface structure as adjectives, so that their concreteness is diffused, distributed broadly. A third mass noun--"gloom"--is converted by the poet's grammatical licence into a count noun through pluralization. "Gloom" has no boundaries, but Keats gives a shape to it, and multiplies it, thus rounding off the curious interaction here of the spatially definite and the spatially indefinite.

Finally, and more obviously, the last two lines of the image are developed through a series of four prepositional phrases (five, in the deep structure), mainly adverbial phrases of spatial relationship. To me the construction suggests attenuated motion, a series of further removes. Syntax, in short, does something in this image that the sensory words cannot do: it creates an almost physical sense of diffusion, removal from the source, distancing, and attenuation.

Not only the structure of an image, but the syntactic framework that contains that structure can count for much. A striking example is the final image in Yeats' "The Tower":

           the clouds of the sky
    When the horizon fades;
    Or a bird's sleep cry
    Among the deepening shades.

In itself the image is rather ordinary, in context quite
extraordinary:

    Now shall I make my soul,
    Compelling it to study
    In a learned school
    Till the wreck of body,
    Slow decay of blood,
    Testy delirium
    Or dull decrepitude,
    Or what worse evil come--
    The death of friends, or death
    Of every brilliant eye
    That made a catch in the breath--
    Seem but the clouds of the sky
    When the horizon fades;
    Or a bird's sleepy cry
    Among the deepening shades.

There are several reasons for the striking effect of
context, but I wish to mention only a syntactic one that
may escape notice.

     A simple structure can of course be embedded in
another that is in turn embedded in another, and so on.
Thus a given structure may be embedded more or less deeply.
Yeats begins his longish sentence with the structure in
which all that follows is embedded. The adverbial,
"compelling it," is at depth 2, if I may be allowed to
use a simple notation. With the complement structure,
"to study in a learned school," he moves to depth 3, then
to depth 4 with an adverbial of time: a steady progression
into syntactic depth and away from the resolve of the
first line. Here the descent halts, and a five-fold
coordinate structure begins, delaying the verb. After
"what worse evil come," the sentence moves to depth 5
with an appositive structure, then to depth 6 with the
relative clause, "that made a catch in the breath." Only
after this syntactic figure of descent, pause, and further
descent, is the structure of depth 4 completed by the
final image. I want to suggest that the syntactic figure
sustains the thematic movement of the poem in two ways.

First, as the poet is leaving his pride behind, relinquishing the active life of "young upstanding men climbing the mountainside," in favor of a "mirror-resembling dream," so the sentence moves farther and farther from its surface, into syntactic recesses.[16] Second, the image in which the poem comes to rest is offered as an equivalent (predicate noun) for no less than seven noun phrases, counting those introduced by the appositive. This multiplicity--and notice the disheartening content of the seven phrases-- this multiplicity of evils is resolved into the single image, as if to bind up all loose ends, all refractory and dissonant experiences.

My first two examples displayed the image as grammar, my third the image in grammar. But of course many poetic images occur more or less in defiance of grammar. For an example, take the first stanza from Richard Wilbur's poem "Beasts":

> Beasts in their major freedom
> Slumber in peace tonight. The gull on his ledge
> Dreams in the guts of himself the moon-plucked waves
> below,
> And the sunfish leans on a stone, slept
> By the lyric water. . .

There are some departures from English syntax here, not spectacular ones of the sort common with Dylan Thomas and E. E. Cummings, but distinct nonetheless. Let me simply record them, first. The verb "dream" is not ordinarily transitive, except with an abstract object--usually a "that" clause. Here it has as object the noun "waves." Second, the phrase "moon-plucked waves" rests on the deep structure, "the moon plucked the waves," which makes its oddity plain: "pluck" needs an animate subject. Finally, beneath "slept by the lyric water" is the deep structure "the water slept the sunfish," which is deviant in both these ways: "sleep" is an intransitive verb, and it also needs an animate subject, rather than a noun like "water."

The question I should like to ask about Wilbur's language is this: How do we interpret structures such as these, which will not be directly given a reading by the grammar of English? Briefly: by assimilating the word out of place to a nearby class that would make the sentence grammatical. "Water" becomes, for the nonce, an animate noun, as does "moon." Syntax forces us, by this extension, to conceive of the water and the moon as

vibrant, capable of actively working upon the fish and the
waves. Similarly, we read "dream" as if it were transitive, and the private inner activity of dreaming becomes
capable of playing upon and altering the physical world.
By the same logic, the syntax invites us to conceive
sleeping as an exchange between water and fish.

In the first two stanzas of this poem, Wilbur pictures
a condition of perfect harmony and communion in the king-
dom of the beasts; he erases the boundaries that ordinarily
isolate living creatures within themselves, and those that
separate mental phenomena from physical. Things participate wholly in each other, without dissonance. The
syntactic liberties that Wilbur takes are far from insignificant in placing the physical scene under the conceptual
rubric of concordance, and in doing so they control the
way the reader perceives the image. He will not, of
course, notice how syntax is working on his comprehension,
but it is doing so nonetheless.

To grasp even the barest image is to perceive
grammatical relations, and to understand how they shape
lexical content. A literary image is by no means simply
a collection of sensory words that refer us to, or remind
us of, the physical world. On the contrary, it shapes the
reader's comprehension in intricate ways, and may draw
heavily on his grammatical competence. Correspondingly,
the critic who treats of imagery--and a fortiori the one
who treats of metaphor, style, structure, etc.--inevitably
engages in psycholinguistic interpretation, covertly if
not openly. He makes judgments about the way the literary
work impinges on the mind of the reader.

I am now in a position to put my concluding point.
For a long time now it has been common for critics and
critical theorists to say that the only legitimate focus
for literary study is the work itself, and to mean by that
the text: the self-contained structure made of words.
That was, and perhaps still is, a salutary doctrine, as
against the always present tendency of criticism to drift
off into biography on one side or into a solipsism of the
sensitive reader on the other. But whatever its strategic
virtues, the position is strictly speaking untenable. The
text in itself, without the background system of the
language, is simply marks on a page, or noises. And the
locus of a language is the minds of its speakers. Quite
literally, the structures and forms in a literary work can

only be forms--be realized as forms--in some mind. It
follows that literary criticism is the study of mental
structures, and that the sense of objectivity one may get
from insisting on the "real" work, out there, the work-in-
itself, is illusory, in the same way that the comfort of
an objective corpus was illusory in linguistics.

An ecumenical spirit is leading many linguists to
think of their subject as a part of psychology. Literary
criticism would profit from a similar accommodation, both
with linguistics and with psychology.

Footnotes

[1]The author is professor of English at Wesleyan
University in Connecticut.[Editor's footnote]

[2]It will be evident that I am writing against a
background of recent work in generative grammar, and I
shall not trace in detail the linguistic genesis of the
positions I take or assume. But they derive especially
from Noam Chomsky, Aspects of the Theory of Syntax (New
York, 1965) and Jerrold J. Katz and Paul Postal, An
Integrated Theory of Linguistic Descriptions (Cambridge,
Mass., 1964). On "mentalism," see also Jerrold J. Katz,
"Mentalism in Linguistics," Language, 1964, 40, 124-137.

[3]See Edward S. Klima, "Negation in English," in
Jerry A. Fodor and Jerrold J. Katz, ed., The Structure of
Language (Englewood Cliffs, N. J., 1964).

[4]This latter, of course, is a distinction that some
wish to deny. One thinks of William Burroughs, who has
introduced techniques of randomness into his writing,
even more than John Cage in music. But it is possible to
maintain an open mind toward randomness without calling
it literature, or at least without denying the difference
between specially formed and specially unformed discourse.

[5]"Closing Statement: Linguistics and Poetics," in
Thomas A. Sebeok, ed., Style in Language (Cambridge, Mass.,
and New York, 1960), p. 358.

[6] *Linguistic Structures in Poetry* (The Hague, 1962), p. 33.

[7] "Chaucer and the Study of Prosody," *College English*, 1966, *28*, 423-39.

[8] See Northrop Frye, *The Anatomy of Criticism* (Princeton, 1957).

[9] For general discussions of the view of style I am here taking, see my "Prolegomena to the Analysis of Prose Style," in Harold C. Martin, ed., *Style in Prose Fiction* (New York, 1959), and "Generative Grammars and the Concept of Literary Style," *Word*, 1964, *20*, 423-39.

[10] The exception is "supplicate," and given the nominalization Gibbon chose, the passive is impossible: that is, "*the* joint supplication *by* the Church" is not English.

[11] The exceptions are "permit," "relieve," and "fable." Of these, the first presumably has "God" for its subject, and although God was not an early Christian, he did have a considerable affinity with the group. The subject of "permit" is "the power or the skill of the exorcist," and the exorcist was, certainly, a Christian, although his skill and power were not.

[12] One might wish to add the phrase, "threw strips of molding like javelins," which is a transform of "threw strips of molding which were like javelins." But the former construction is also a transform of "three strips of molding in a manner which is like the manner in which one throws javelins," and this second reading is almost certainly what the context calls for.

[13] After deletion of Rel + Tense + Be, pre-nominalization is obligatory if the noun phrase is a pronoun; i.e., "he, eating gelatin pie for breakfast, saw Idwal" is ungrammatical. But the stylistic impulse is the same here as with post-nominals.

[14] For a critical study that comes at the same conclusion in a different way, see Marcus Klein, <u>After Alienation</u> (Cleveland, 1964).

[15] "Literature as Sentences," <u>College English</u>, 1966, <u>27</u>, 261-267.

[16] It is worth noticing that the verbs are at the same time becoming less vigorous: from "make" to "compel" to "study" to "seem" is a steady progression away from activeness.

WORD-FREQUENCY STUDIES AND THE LOGNORMAL DISTRIBUTION[1]

John B. Carroll[2]

My interest in word-frequency distributions was first inspired when I was a student of B. F. Skinner at the University of Minnesota around 1938 and 1939. At that time Skinner considered that a person's vocabulary represented a sort of reservoir of operant responses, with different probabilities, from which the individual drew as he spoke or wrote. In fact, with Stuart Cook, who was then also a graduate student at Minnesota, Skinner published a paper (Cook and Skinner, 1939) on the frequency distribution of words elicited in free-association tasks. Several years previously, Zipf had published his book The Psychobiology of Language (1935) in which he had announced his harmonic series "law" of the rank-frequency function, a law which had already been discovered earlier by Estoup (1916) and rediscovered by Condon (1928). It was not surprising that Cook and Skinner employed the Zipf function as a model for their data, particularly since there seemed to be a close fit. I became interested in the Zipf function because I supposed that it might help not only to describe word-frequency distributions but also to predict the type-token function (the relation between the number of word-types, n, and the number of tokens, N), and hence to predict the total number of types that would be obtained if tokens were sampled indefinitely. I supposed also that the parameters of the Zipf function could be used to index the "diversity" of a sample, i.e., the relative degree to which a sample is composed of different words (bearing in mind that the usual type-token ratio is a function of sample size). In a paper which I published about that time (Carroll, 1938), I explored this possibility but found that the Zipf function would be unsatisfactory. If the n different words (i= 1, 2,...n) of a sample of N tokens are arranged in order of decreasing frequency, the Zipf function asserts that the occurrence frequency, ν , of the ith word is N/ki, where k is an empirical constant whose value is ordinarily found to be about 10 in large samples. In this case, the probabilities of the n different words constitute a series of the form

$$P_i = [\frac{1}{k}, \frac{1}{2k}, \ldots, \frac{1}{ik}, \ldots, \frac{1}{nk}],$$

and if the function is to hold throughout the sample, then

$$\sum_{i=1}^{n} P_i = \frac{1}{k} \sum_{i=1}^{n} \frac{1}{i} = 1$$

and

$$\sum_{i=1}^{n} \frac{1}{i} = k.$$

Since it is shown in advanced calculus (e. g. Widder, 1947 p. 307) that

$$\lim_{n \to \infty} \left(\sum_{i=1}^{n} \frac{1}{i} - \log_e n \right) = \gamma = .57721566\ldots \text{(Euler's}$$

constant), for large values of n we may take

$$\sum_{i=1}^{n} \frac{1}{i} = \gamma + \log_e n.$$

Setting this equal to k = 10, we find that n = 12367; that is, that there would have to be 12,367 different words if the function is to hold throughout a sample. For the least frequent word, $\nu_n \geq 1$, that is $N_{p_n} = N/nk \geq 1$, and thus $N \geq 123,670$ for a sample in which the Zipf function holds uniformly throughout with k = 10. It can readily be seen that in general $N \geq nk$ if the Zipf function is to hold uniformly throughout a sample. If the Zipf function is dependent on sample size it would seem unsatisfactory for describing word-frequency distributions with any generality. Nor is it satisfactory for predicting the type-token function or the total size of the vocabulary underlying a sample. It should also be noted that the original Zipf function is a single-parameter one (unless one also introduces an exponent other than unity for the variable i). Although various improvements and modifications of the Zipf function have been offered (Mandelbrot, 1953; Simon, 1955), I am not aware that these provide any assistance in solving the problems stated above, namely,

predicting the type-token function and predicting the
asymptotic size of vocabulary. Nevertheless, in 1938 I
was still willing to believe that the Zipf function could
hold in an approximate way for small samples, and I derived
from it an equation for the type-token function which
seemed to fit small samples of data quite well. This
equation may be written as

$$n = \frac{N}{k} [1 - \gamma + k - \log_e (N/k)]; \quad\quad\quad [1]$$

it assumes, incidentally, that the frequency of the least
frequent word is 1, as is ordinarily the case. At the
same time I sought, without success, to find a better
rationale for the word-frequency distribution, and I tried
various empirical equations for the type-token function.
As I recall, one function that I rejected was the logarithmic type-token function--the function that would
assert that the ratio of the logarithm of the number of
types to the logarithm of the number of tokens is a
constant. It is clear that this function cannot be
correct; although it may fit data for medium-sized samples
(with N ranging, say, from 2000 to 10,000), it cannot fit
data for small samples, and it implies that vocabulary
increases indefinitely as N increases. I mention this
simply because the logarithmic type-token ratio has been
seriously advanced by some writers (Chotlos, 1944; Herdan,
1957; 1960, p. 26). Devooght (1957) derived a form of
logarithmic type-token function from Mandelbrot's modification of the Zipf law, but had to make the assumption of
an infinite vocabulary size.

In the meantime, another mathematical model for
describing word-frequency distributions has been offered,
namely, the lognormal distribution. Some writers have
supposed that the lognormal distribution was first proposed by Williams (1940, 1946), but he was concerned only
with a certain form of logarithmic series for sentence
lengths and for the distribution of species of insects.
Apparently, the lognormal distribution, as applied to
certain data of Zipf, was first proposed by two British
econometricians, Aitchison and Brown (1957, pp. 101-102).
Even before 1957, however, it was discovered independently by an American psychologist, Davis Howes (personal
communication). While working as a U. S. Air Force
psychologist and having been asked to apply the lognormal
distribution to some data of an entirely different
character, he inadvertently applied it to a word-frequency
distribution that he happened to have at hand, and was

startled to notice the excellent fit that he obtained.
Since then he has applied this distribution to numerous
sets of data on word-frequencies, both from standard word-
counts and from counts of words in aphasic speech (Howes,
1964). In Europe, the suggestion of Aitchison and Brown
has been followed up in the work of Somers (1959) and
Herdan (1960), who have found the lognormal model to yield
good fit to word-frequency distributions. This model was
one of those considered by Rapoport (1964) as applied to
samples of texts from normal and aphasic speakers.

Nevertheless, the work of Howes, Herdan, Somers, and
others has not led to a solution of the problems mentioned
above, namely, the specification of a type-token function
and the determination of an asymptotic value for the total
vocabulary in a sample of infinite size. In attempting to
apply the lognormal distribution to data assembled at
Brown University for a "standard corpus" of American
English printed in the year 1961 (Kučera and Francis, 1967
it came to my attention that previous research had failed
to honor the fundamental distinction between sample and
population, applying the lognormal distribution to finite
samples as if they were infinite populations. In a chapte
that I wrote for the Kučera and Francis publication
(Carroll, 1967), I showed that the fit of the lognormal
model to sample data was much improved if account was
taken of the distribution expected for a given sample size
I was also able to predict with considerable accuracy n
(the number of types) that would be found for a sample of
given size (N) drawn from a theoretical distribution with
parameters estimated from the sample.

Since, at the time of writing the paper for the
Kučera-Francis volume, I had not completely worked out
the mathematical details involved, this paper will present
those details. Further, it will apply the lognormal distribution to the word-frequency data of the Lorge Magazine
Count (Thorndike & Lorge, 1944).

I am not yet prepared to make the claim that the lognormal model is superior to other models, such as the Zipf
Mandelbrot formulation or the related Yule-Simon formulation. The latter models have the advantage that they are
based on information-theoretic, stochastic, or psychological process postulates. Nevertheless, I suggest that the
lognormal model cannot be properly compared with the other
models unless it is correctly applied. Moreover, it is
possible that an adequate logical or psychological

216

rationale for the lognormal model can be developed. Also, the lognormal distribution is a two-parameter model and thus may have more flexibility and utility than the original Zipf function in fitting actual data.

Mathematics of the Lognormal Model as
Applied to Distributions of Probabilities

The mathematical properties of the lognormal distribution, and some of its statistical properties, have been presented by Aitchison and Brown (1957). It will be seen, however, that it has some special properties when applied to distributions of probabilities. This is because probabilities computed from a sample are systematically biased estimates of the probabilities in the theoretical population underlying the sample.

In the present section, logarithms to the base e will be denoted by the symbol ln, while common logarithms will be denoted log.

According to Aitchison and Brown (1957, pp. 7 ff.), if X is an essentially positive variate $(0 < x < \infty)$ such that $Y = \ln X$, Y is normally distributed with mean $\mu*$ and variance σ'^2. (For the present, we attach an asterisk to μ and a prime to σ in order to distinguish them from common logarithm values defined below.) Then X is lognormally distributed, or X is $\Lambda(\mu*,\sigma'^2)$, and Y is $N(\mu*,\sigma'^2)$. The distribution functions of X and Y are then, respectively,

$$\Lambda(x) = \Lambda(x|\mu*,\sigma'^2) = P\{X \le x\} \qquad [2]$$

and

$$N(y) = N(y|\mu*,\sigma'^2) = P\{Y \le y\} \qquad [3]$$

Clearly,

$$\Lambda(x) = N(\ln x) = N(y), \qquad (x > o)$$

and

$$d\Lambda(x) = \frac{1}{x\,\sigma'\sqrt{2\pi}}\,\exp\left\{-\frac{1}{2\,\sigma'^2}(\ln x - \mu*)^2\right\}dx \qquad [4]$$

describes the frequency curve with a single mode at

$$x = e^{\mu* - \sigma'^2}.$$

The distribution possesses moments of any order. By Aitchison and Brown's formula, the first moment around the origin is

$$\lambda_1' = \exp\left(\mu* + \frac{1}{2}\,\sigma'^2\right).$$ [5]

This is equal to the total area of the first-moment <u>distribution</u>, for as they point out, the lognormal distribution possesses moment distributions, a property not found in the usual normal theory. They show (p. 12) that the jth moment distribution of a Λ-distribution with parameters $\mu*$ and σ'^2 is also a Λ-distribution with parameters $(\mu* + j\sigma'^2)$ and σ'^2 respectively.

Further, if X is $\Lambda(\mu*, \sigma'^2)$, then 1/X is $\Lambda(-\mu*, \sigma'^2)$, and $\ln(1/X)$ is $N(-\mu*, \sigma'^2)$.

Let $\phi' \equiv \ln(1/X)$; then ϕ' is $N(-\mu*, \sigma'^2)$. If we define $\mu' \equiv -\mu*$, then ϕ' is $N(\mu', \sigma'^2)$. The area of the first-moment distribution is, therefore, $\exp\left(\frac{1}{2}\sigma'^2 - \mu'\right)$.

Alternatively, working in common logarithms, define $\phi = \log(1/X) = \log \pi$, where π is the word-probability in the population. Then, ϕ is $N(\mu, \sigma^2)$, μ and σ being in common logarithms corresponding to μ' and σ'. The area of the first-moment distribution then becomes antilog $[\frac{1}{2}(\ln 10)\,\sigma^2 - \mu]$.

The formulations presented thus far may be depicted graphically. In Fig. 1, the upper frequency curve is for $\phi = N(\mu, \sigma^2)$; to correspond with materials to be presented later, the parameters have been set as $\mu = -3.0092$ and $\sigma = 1.4606$, all in common logarithms for convenience. A scale for the normal deviate $\xi = (\phi - \mu)/\sigma$ has also been provided. The lower frequency curve is the first-moment distribution, with parameters $(\mu' - \sigma'^2)$ and σ'^2, respectively (in natural logarithms), or $[\mu - (\ln 10)\sigma^2] = \mu_t = [\mu - 2.3026\sigma^2]$, and σ^2, in common logarithms. For the present data, these parameters are -7.9214 and 1.4606, respectively, and a normal deviate scale ξ_t based on these parameters has been provided. (The mean of the first-moment distribution, incidentally, is $[\mu' - \sigma'^2]$ rather than $[\mu' + \sigma'^2]$ because of the definition $\mu' = -\mu*$ and the consequent reflection of the scale about the origin.)

The interpretation of the basic-frequency curve for a theoretical lognormal distribution of word-frequencies is

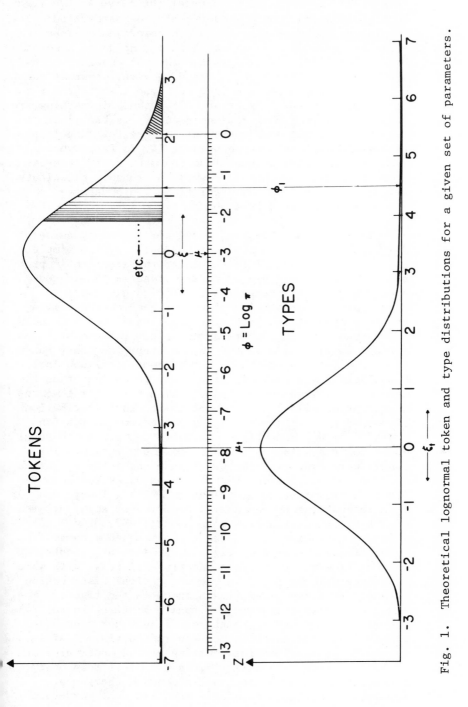

Fig. 1. Theoretical lognormal token and type distributions for a given set of parameters.

relatively simple. The area under the curve to the right
of a given point, say ϕ_a, represents the proportion of the
population composed of words whose logarithmic probabilities are greater than or equal to ϕ_a, or whose theoretical probabilities π are greater than or equal to π_a =
antilog (ϕ_a). It will be noticed, however, that as the
curve is drawn, a certain (shaded) area lies to the right
of $\phi = 0$, or $\pi = 1$. Mathematically, there is nothing wrong
with this as long as x remains positive (albeit less than
1), in $\pi = \frac{1}{x}$, but a word-probability greater than 1 is
impossible because π is bounded at 1. In fact, word-
probabilities of 1 or near 1 do not make sense, because
words possessing such values would presumably constitute
all or nearly all of the population. This apparent paradox will be resolved in a moment.

The interpretation of the lower frequency curve of
Fig 1, the "first moment distribution," is also simple.
It is the frequency distribution of the logarithmic probabilities of word-<u>types</u>, when each type is considered
separately. The area to the right of a given point ϕ_a
represents the proportion of word-types that have loga-
rthmic probabilities greater than or equal to ϕ_a of being
found when word-tokens are drawn randomly from the theoretical population depicted in the upper frequency curve.
Half of all the word-types in the theoretical population
have logarithmic probabilities equal to or less than the
mean of the first-moment distribution. The first-moment
distribution will henceforth be called the distribution
of word-types. Its area, N_t, given by the expression
$\exp(\frac{1}{2} \sigma'^2 - \mu')$ or $\text{antilog}_{10}(1.1513\sigma^2 - \mu)$, is the total
number of types in the theoretical distribution. The
single word-type with the greatest probability π_1 in the
theoretical population, therefore, occupies an area of
$1/N_t$ in the word-type distribution, with a lower bound of
ϕ_1 corresponding to the normal deviate for an upper area
of $1/N_t$ in a distribution with mean $(\mu - 2.3026\sigma^2)$ and
standard deviation σ. In the token-frequency curve (the
upper frequency curve of Fig. 1), this value ϕ_1 cuts off
an area A_1 which represents the probability π_1 with which
this type will be found in the theoretical distribution of
tokens. (For the parameters assumed in the figure, ϕ_1 =
-1.3526, corresponding to a normal deviate ξ_t in the type
distribution of 4.4973, cutting off an upper area of
1/291953, or corresponding to a normal deviate ξ of 1.1342
in the token distribution, cutting off an upper area of
.128315.) This probability π_1 is much less than unity;
the apparent paradox mentioned above is, therefore,
resolved. That is, the single most frequent word-type

has a logarithmic probability which lies between ϕ_1 and 0 (or a probability which lies between antilog ϕ_1 and 1), and, except in the case of abnormal values of the parameters μ and σ, there can be no words with probabilities greater than 1.

Successive areas of $1/N_t$ can be cut from the word-type distribution to yield the lower and upper bounds of ϕ for word-types numbered 2, 3, ... , N_t (i.e. with decreasing values of ϕ) in the word-type distribution, and the corresponding probabilities in the token distribution can be determined. (In Fig. 1, vertical lines have been drawn to indicate the area in the token distribution occupied by each of the first few word-types.) Although in theory this process can be continued until the N_t-th word-type is reached, it is computationally unfeasible when N_t is very large. After the probabilities of about the first 100 most frequent word-types have been determined, one may define successive equally-spaced small intervals $\Delta\phi$ on the scale of ϕ, such that $\Delta\phi = \phi_h - \phi_g$, ($\phi_h > \phi_g$), having a corresponding area A_t in the type-frequency distribution, and a corresponding area A_Δ in the token distribution. Then the number of types, m_Δ, lying within $\Delta\phi$ in the type distribution is $A_t N_t$. The average probability of the types in the interval $\Delta\phi$ is

$$\pi_\Delta = A_\Delta \, / \, m_\Delta, \qquad\qquad [6]$$

and $\phi_\Delta = \log\pi_\Delta$. For the extreme lower tail of the token distribution, ξ_g is set at $-\infty$ and ξ_h at some arbitrary value such as -6.00.

The above procedure specifies a complete theoretical population of tokens and the first-moment distribution of types. It will still be the case, however, that at $\xi = -\mu \, / \, \sigma$, $\phi = 0$ and the token distribution will include a certain area, A_o where $\phi \geq 0$, $\pi \geq 1$. If it is desired to eliminate this area to produce a truncated lognormal distribution, this area can be subtracted from the probability of the most frequent word-type, and the remaining probabilities (including that remaining for the most frequent word-type) multiplied by the constant factor $1/(1-A_o)$ in order to make them sum to unity. (With the parameters usually found, ϕ_1 is always less than $\phi = -\mu/\sigma$ and thus, $A_1 > A_o$.)

An alternative procedure which has not yet been fully investigated but which promises to give better fit for the

words of highest frequency is to delete an area at the
upper extreme of the type distribution corresponding to
one-half word-type (with a corresponding deletion in the
token distribution) and then to cut successive areas $1/N_t$
from the word-type distribution in the same manner as
described above, adjusting probabilities for the deleted
area.

Finding the Expected Word-Frequency Distribution for a Sample of Size N

Suppose we draw a sample of N tokens. A certain
number of word-types, f_1, will occur once ($\nu = 1$); a
certain number, f_2, will occur twice ($\nu = 2$), and in
general we have a series of values f_ν, each giving the
frequency (f) with which a given occurrence-frequency
(ν) is found. Then it will be the case that

and
$$\sum_\nu^\nu f_\nu = n \text{ (the number of word-types in the sample)}$$

$$\sum_\nu^\nu f_\nu \nu = N \text{ (the number of tokens).}$$

Our object is to predict the values of f_ν, and hence n,
when we draw a sample of size N from a theoretical lognormal distribution with given parameters μ and σ (either
from a complete or a truncated distribution).

It may be noted that in a sample, the empirical
probability, p*, of a word-type is ν/N, and its logarithm
is ϕ*. However, p* is a biased estimator of π and hence
ϕ* is a biased estimator of ϕ. That this is so is seen
most easily from the fact that when $\nu = 1$ (i. e., the
occurrence-frequency of the least frequent word in the
sample is 1), the value of p* is $1/N$, a value which is on
the average greater than the average value of π for the
word-types with $\nu = 1$. (In the limiting case where N = 1,
p* is 1.) When previous researchers have attempted to
apply the lognormal distribution directly to sample data,
they have in effect applied it to p* or ϕ* = log(p*). The
degree of bias in estimating π from p* varies inversely
with N and with p*.

In general, the occurrence-frequency, ν, with which a
type with a given value of ϕ will appear in a sample of
size N is expected to be $N\pi$ or N(antilog ϕ). If, however,

222

within a given interval $\Delta\phi$ there exists in the theoretical
distribution a certain number of types, m_Δ, with approximately equal values of ϕ_Δ (= log π_Δ), we may expect the
frequencies, ν, to occur according to the Poisson distribution. That is, the expected frequencies, f_ν, of types
occurring $\nu = 0, 1, 2, \ldots \nu*$ times in a sample of size
N is given by the series

$$\frac{m_\Delta}{\exp(N\pi_\Delta)}\left[1, \frac{(N\pi_\Delta)}{1!}, \frac{(N\pi_\Delta)^2}{2!}, \ldots, \frac{(N\pi_\Delta)^{\nu*}}{\nu*!}\right]. \qquad [7]$$

$(N\pi_\Delta)$ is the expected mean number of occurrences, and also
the expected variance. Terms in the series beyond that
which is approximately equal to $(N\pi_\Delta)$ will tend to decrease
to zero; successive terms are to be computed until they
are sensibly close to zero, say, less than .01, such that
the sum of terms is approximately equal to m_Δ. If $(N\pi_\Delta)$
is greater than about 20, a normal curve approximation to
the Poisson distribution can be used with mean and variance
equal to $(N\pi_\Delta)$. Thus, three procedures may be used, computationally, to predict the frequencies of occurrence of
types in a sample of size $\underline{N}$:

(1) For the most frequent types, say, the first 100,
or wherever single types are identified with $N\pi > 1$, the
expected occurrence frequency, ν, is $N\pi$.

(2) For groups of types ($m \geq 2$) with roughly equal ϕ
and such that $N\pi \geq 20$, the frequency of occurrence, ν, for
each type may be estimated by the normal curve approximation to the Poisson distribution. (For greater accuracy,
$(N\pi)$ may be set higher than 20.)

(3) For groups of types ($m \geq 2$) with roughly equal ϕ,
such that $N\pi < 20$, or for single types, such that $N\pi < 1$,
the number, f_ν, of such types occurring ν times is determined according to the Poisson distribution, [7].

The frequencies in the total sample are then obtained
by pooling the results over the above procedures, applied
to all types or class-intervals of types in the theoret-
ical-type distribution. Procedures (1) and (2) above
yield the ν to which $f_\nu = 1$ is assigned for each word-
type considered, while procedure (3) yields the fre-
quencies, f_ν, with which the m_Δ types in the interval $\Delta\phi$
will occur $\nu = 0, 1, 2, \ldots \nu*$ times. Pooling the

results involves summing f_ν for each value of ν over all types or all intervals $\Delta\phi$. In the end, one has a frequency distribution giving f_ν for each value of ν. The sum of the f_ν gives n, the expected number of different words, and as a check, $\Sigma f_\nu \nu$ should be approximately equal to N.

For finite N, the resulting distribution of ν (or $p* = \nu/N$) will deviate systematically from a lognormal distribution; or correspondingly, the distribution of $\phi* = \log p*$ will deviate systematically from a normal distribution. (To depict the distribution, it is convenient to plot the cumulative areas for given $\phi*$ on normal probability coordinates against $\phi* = \log p*$.) Notably, the lower portion of the cumulative distribution curve will bend downward from the curve (straight line) for the underlying theoretical population, due to the attenuation of the frequencies of the less frequent word-types.

To characterize the expected sample distribution, it might thought most justifiable to fit at least a third-degree polynomial because of the double curvature. It has been found convenient, however, simply to fit by least squares a linear equation to the points on normal probability coordinates. My first attempts in this regard used the points without weighting them by their frequencies, but this procedure made it difficult to fit expected sample distributions to actual sample distributions without producing wide discrepancies in the expected and observed numbers of types. Therefore, I hit upon the procedure of weighting the points by the frequencies f_ν, thus giving greater weight to the points for the less-frequent words and producing closer fits between expected and observed data for the lower portion of the lognormal plot. Specifically, let Y_ν be the normal deviate corresponding to the cumulative area in the expected or observed sample distribution at a point

$$\phi*_\nu = \log \left[\frac{\nu + (\nu + 1)}{2N}\right].$$

Then the best-fitting line is the linear regression of Y_ν on $\phi*_\nu$, the points being weighted by f_ν. That is,

$$\hat{Y}_\nu = a + b\phi*_\nu, \tag{8}$$

where

$$b = \frac{\sum f_\nu \, \phi^*_\nu \, Y_\nu - \left(\sum f_\nu \, \phi^*_\nu\right)\left(\sum f_\nu \, Y_\nu\right) / \sum f_\nu}{\sum f_\nu \, \phi^{*2}_\nu - \left(\sum f_\nu \, \phi^*_\nu\right)^2 / \sum f_\nu} \qquad [8a]$$

and

$$a = \sum f_\nu \, Y_\nu - b \sum f_\nu \, \phi^*_\nu \qquad [8b]$$

In these computations, the last point, i. e. for the largest frequency, is omitted because the value of Y_ν is $+\infty$, so that $\Sigma f_\nu = n - 1$. Then a sample standard deviation may be defined as

$$s = \frac{1}{b}, \qquad [9b]$$

and a sample "median" is

$$Mdn = -\frac{a}{b}. \qquad [9a]$$

Both are in the metric of ϕ^*. It should be carefully noted that thus defined they are not necessarily equal to the actual median or standard deviation of the sample token distribution. They are simply convenient parameters for characterizing the distribution.

The above procedures are for the expected sample token distribution. It is also possible to depict the sample type distribution, i.e., by plotting the cumulative proportions of the types against ϕ^* on normal probability coordinates and to compare this with the line for the theoretical type distribution. For finite N, it will be found that the expected sample type distribution deviates systematically (and quite markedly even for N in the neighborhood of 10^6, say) from the theoretical line.

The type-token function. It will have been noticed that the previously-described procedures afford a prediction of the number of types to be expected in a sample distribution of size N drawn from a theoretical distribution with given μ and σ. By starting from a given theoretical distribution and making predictions for samples of different sizes, it is thus possible to delineate the type-token function.

It is also possible to develop an analytical expression for the type-token function, by noticing that the

Poisson distribution gives, for any interval $\Delta\phi$ containing m_Δ types in the type distribution, the number of types expected to occur 0 times in a sample of size N. We can sum these values over all intervals and subtract the result from the known value of the total number of types in the theoretical type distribution, N_t. If the intervals are infinitesimal, the number of types in a sample of size N can be expressed (for parameters in natural logarithm) as

$$n_{(t, N)} = \exp\ (\tfrac{1}{2}\sigma'^2 - \mu') - \frac{1}{\sigma'\sqrt{2\pi}}\int_{-\infty}^{0} \exp$$

$$[-\tfrac{1}{2}(\tfrac{\phi' - \mu'}{\sigma'})^2 - \phi' - Ne^{\phi'}]\ d\phi' \qquad [10]$$

This is derived as follows: Using the first term of the Poisson distribution, we have for a given interval of ϕ' the number of types not occurring in a sample of size N,

$$n_{0,\Delta\phi} = m_\Delta\ \exp(-N\pi_\Delta).$$

But

$$m = z_\xi(\Delta\phi)/\sigma'\pi_\Delta = z_\xi(\Delta\phi')\sigma^{-1}\ e^{-\phi'}$$

Therefore,

$$n_{0'\Delta\phi} = z(\Delta\phi)\sigma'^{-1}\ e^{-\bar\phi'_\Delta}\ e^{-Ne^{-\bar\phi'_\Delta}} = \frac{1}{\sigma'\sqrt{2\pi}}\ \exp$$

$$[-\tfrac{1}{2}\left(\frac{\bar\phi'_\Delta - \mu'}{\sigma'}\right)^2 - \bar\phi'_\Delta - Ne^{-\bar\phi'_\Delta}]\ \Delta\phi'$$

Allowing the increments to become infinitesimal and taking the integral, we have the total number of types that are not expected to occur in a sample of size N as equal to

$$\frac{1}{\sigma'\sqrt{2\pi}}\int_{-\infty}^{0} \exp\ [-\tfrac{1}{2}(\tfrac{\phi' - \mu'}{\sigma'})^2 - \phi' - Ne^{\phi'}]\ d\phi'.$$

Unfortunately, it appears that this definite integral cannot be evaluated except by numerical analysis.

<u>Estimating the parameters of the theoretical distribution underlying observed sample data</u>. Thus far, the only practicable procedure discovered for estimating the parameters of the theoretical distribution underlying sample data is an iterative one. First, values of Mdn_ϕ and s_ϕ for the observed sample distribution of size N are computed using formulas [8] and [9]. The object is then to arrive at values of μ and σ for a theoretical token population such that the values of Mdn_ϕ and s_ϕ for an expected sample distribution for size N will be as close as desired to the values found for the observed sample distribution. Suppose trial values $_i\mu$ and $_i\sigma$ are postulated for the theoretical population, that the observed values for the sample are $_oMdn_\phi$ and $_os_\phi$, and that the postulated parameters yield expected values $_iMdn_\phi$ and $_is_\phi$ for a sample of size N. It has been found that the iterations will converge quite rapidly if the next trial values are taken as

$$_{(i + 1)}\mu = \frac{_oMdn_\phi}{_iMdn_\phi} (_i\mu) \tag{11}$$

$$_{(i + 1)}\sigma = \frac{_os_\phi}{_is_\phi} (_i\sigma) \tag{12}$$

Applications

<u>The Lorge Magazine Count</u>. Through the courtesy of Davis Howes, I have been supplied with corrected and edited data from the Lorge Magazine Count of 4,591,122 words from <u>The Saturday Evening Post</u>, <u>Woman's Home Companion</u>, <u>Ladies' Home Journal</u>, <u>True Story</u>, and <u>Reader's Digest</u> (Thorndike and Lorge, 1944, pp. 252-253). As in the case of the Brown University Corpus (Kučera and Francis, 1967) this count was made "by counting separately every combination of letters found." Thus, "<u>arm</u>, <u>arms</u>, <u>arm's</u>, <u>arms'</u>, <u>arming</u>, and <u>armed</u> were counted separately."

From formulas [9a] and [9b], for the Lorge Magazine Count Mdn = -3.2327, s = 1.2953. There were 74,677 types in this sample of 4,591,122 words, and there were 1198 points in the frequency distribution, of which 1197 were used in the calculations for Mdn_ϕ and s_ϕ, weighted by their respective frequencies f_ν.

The initial parameters postulated for the theoretical token population were taken from results obtained for the Brown University corpus, for which $\mu = -3.2273$ and $\sigma = 1.4151$ had been determined, using a "complete" (i.e., non-truncated) lognormal distribution. Table 1 gives the results obtained at various stages of the iterations to the point where the agreement between expected and observed values of Mdn and s was satisfactorily close. As may be noted in the table, the final values of μ and σ were -3.0092 and 1.4606, respectively. These are, in fact, the values employed in drawing Fig. 1, already discussed. Fig. 2 shows, on lognormal coordinates, the line for the theoretical population of tokens, the expected distribution of tokens for a sample of size $N = 4,591,122$, and the observed distribution of tokens. For the most part, the fit between expected and observed distributions is good. Marked deviation occurs only for the four or five tokens with largest frequencies. In addition, the agreement between the predicted and observed numbers of types (75,071 and 74,677, respectively) is very close. The theoretical parameters predict that in the total population there would be 291,953 types in all; it should be noted that despite the large size of the sample, it included only about 25.6 percent of the theoretical number of types.

Fig. 3 gives the line for the theoretical population of types, and the predicted and observed distributions of types in the Lorge Magazine Count sample. The agreement between the predicted and observed distributions is close enough to suggest that the lognormal distribution is a valid model for these data.

Because of the rather large discrepancies between predicted and observed frequencies for the few most frequent types, calculations were also performed on the assumption of a theoretical token population truncated at $\phi = 0$. Table 2 shows the theoretical parameters assumed at various stages of the iterations, as well as the results to the point where the predicted and observed statistics agreed satisfactorily. However, the use of a truncated theoretical population produced little improvement in the agreement between the predicted and observed frequencies of the most frequent types. Table 3 presents comparative data for the first ten types under the two assumptions.

Table 1

Results for the Lorge Magazine Count on the
Assumption of a "Complete" Lognormal Distribution

Iteration	μ	σ	μ_t	N_t	Mdn	s	n_t
1	-3.2273	1.4151	-7.8382	341019	-3.4210	1.2600	91667
2	-3.0498	1.4547	-7.9224	306324	-3.2691	1.2906	78458
3	-3.0158	1.4600	-7.9240	295061	-3.2393	1.2946	75688
4	-3.0097	1.4608	-7.9233	292725	-3.2332	1.2955	75170
5	-3.0092	1.4606	-7.9214	291953	-3.2327	1.2954	75071
observed sample:					-3.2327	1.2953	74677

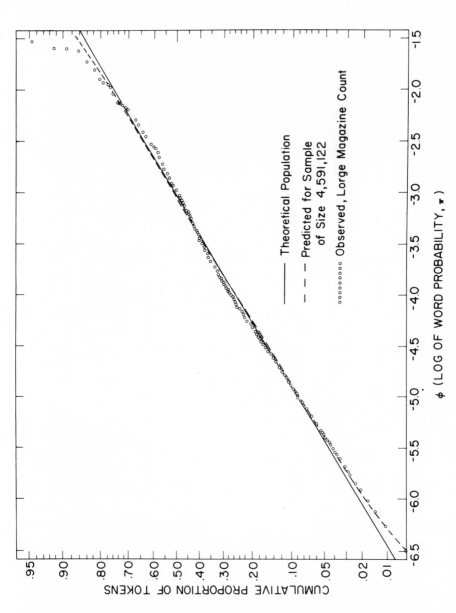

Fig. 2. Lognormal plot for the token distribution of the Lorge Magazine Count data, with the line for the theoretical population and the curve for the predicted token distribution

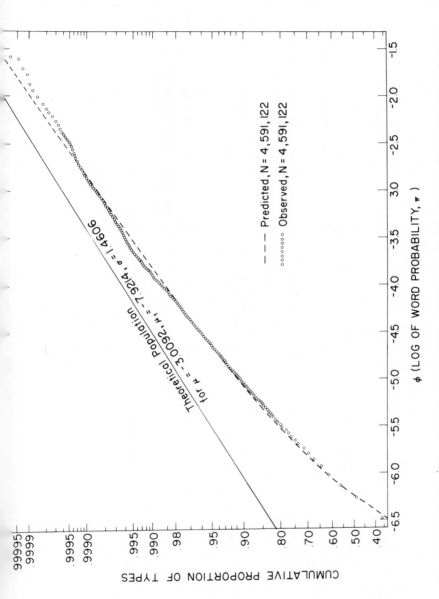

Fig. 3. Lognormal plot for the type distribution of the Lorge Magazine Count data, with the line for the theoretical population and the curve for the predicted type distribution.

231

Table 2

Results for the Lorge Magazine Count on the
Assumption of a "Truncated" Lognormal Distribution

Iteration	μ	σ	μ_t	N_t	Mdn	s	n_t
1	-3.0092	1.4606	-7.9214	291953	-3.2464	1.2905	75588
2	-2.9965	1.4660	-7.9454	295771	-3.2342	1.2950	75357
3	-2.9951	1.4663	-7.9460	295500	-3.2332	1.2952	75265
4	-2.9946	1.4664	-7.9460	295322	-3.2329	1.2952	75226
observed sample:					-3.2327	1.2953	74677

232

Table 3

Frequencies of the Ten Most Frequent Types, Lorge Magazine Count

	Observed	Predicted	
		"Complete" distribution with $\mu = -3.0092$, $\sigma = 1.4606$	"Truncated" distribution with $\mu = -2.9946$, $\sigma = 1.4664$
1	236472	589110	515873
2	138672	155971	160940
3	117222	105538	108818
4	115358	81568	84280
5	112601	67574	69006
6	89489	57527	59294
7	75253	50583	51987
8	58732	45014	46742
9	55667	41074	41785
10	52107	37524	38486
Total	1,051,573	1,231,483	1,177,211

References

Aitchison, J., and Brown, J. A. C. The lognormal distribution. Cambridge: Cambridge University Press, 1957.

Carroll, J. B. Diversity of vocabulary and the harmonic
series law of word-frequency distribution. Psychological Record, 1938, 2, 379-386.

Carroll, J.B. On sampling from a lognormal model of word-
frequencey distribution. Pp. 406-424 in Kucera, Henry
and Francis, W.N. Computational analysis of present-
day American English. Providence: Brown University
Press, 1967

Chotlos, J. W. Studies in language behavior: IV. A
statistical and comparative analysis of individual
written language samples. Psychological Monographs,
1944, 56, 75-111.

Condon, E. U. Statistics of vocabulary. Science, 1928,
67, 300.

Cook, Stuart W., and Skinner, B. F. Some factors influencing the distribution of associated words.
Psychological Record, 1939, 3, 178-184.

Devooght, J. Sur la loi de Zipf-Mandelbrot. Académie
royale de Belgique, Bulletin de la Classe des Sciences,
Ve Series, 1957, 43(4), 244-251.

Estoup, J. B. Gammes stenographique. Paris, 1916.

Herdan, G. The numerical expression of selective variation
in the vowel-consonant sequence in English and Russian.
In Studies presented to Joshua Whatmough on his
Sixtieth Birthday. The Hague, 1957.

Howes, Davis. Application of the word-frequency concept
to aphasia. Pp. 47-75 in A. V. S. de Reuck and Maeve
O'Connor (Eds.), Ciba Foundation Symposium on Disorders
of Language. London: Churchill, Ltd., 1964.

Kučera, H. and Francis, W.N., Computational analysis
of present-day American English. Providence, R.I.:
Brown University Press, 1967.

Mandelbrot, Benoit. <u>Contribution à la théorie mathématique des jeux de communication.</u> Paris: Institute of Statistics, University of Paris, 1953.

Rapoport, Amnon. <u>Comparison of four models for word-frequency distributions from normal and aphasic speakers.</u> Ph.D. dissertation, University of North Carolina, 1964.

Simon, Herbert A. On a class of skew distribution functions. <u>Biometrika</u>, 1955, 42, 425–440.

Somers, H. H., S. J. <u>Analyse mathématique de langage: Lois générales et mesures statistiques, I.</u> Louvain, Belgium: Editions Nauwelaerts, 1959.

Thorndike, E. L., and Lorge, I. <u>The teacher's word book of 30,000 words.</u> New York: Bureau of Publications, Teachers College, Columbia University, 1944.

Widder, David V. <u>Advanced calculus.</u> New York: Prentice-Hall, Inc., 1947.

Williams, C. B. A note on the statistical analysis of sentence length as a criterion of literary style. <u>Biometrika</u>, 1940, 31, 356–361.

Williams, C. B. Yule's 'characteristic' and the 'index of diversity.' <u>Nature</u>, 1946, 157, 482.

Zipf, G. K. <u>The psycho-biology of language.</u> Boston: Houghton Mifflin, 1935.

Footnotes

[1] This paper, which deals with the same general topic as the one read at the Conference on Language and Language Behavior, has been revised in order to offer historical material, mathematical formulations and empirical data that were not available for the oral presentation.

[2] The author, formerly a member of the faculty of the Graduate School of Education, Harvard University, is now a Senior Research Psychologist at the Educational Testing Service, Princeton, N. J.

SOME SIMPLE RULES FOR SELF-ADAPTIVE

MECHANICAL RECOGNITION OF VOWELS[1]

John F. Hemdal[2]

The purpose of the historical approach to the recognition of speech by computer has been to determine and
measure the invariant properties of speech which reside in
the acoustical signal. Unofrtunately, about the only
invariability in speech is its variability. The listener
is apparently not disturbed by this variation, but a
digital computer must operate with discrete and precise
information. In order to determine this precise information it seems possible that an examination of the sources
of parameter variability will reveal mechanical procedures
for accounting for the variability, i.e., it should provide
clues to various normalization procedures. The object of
a mechanical speech-recognizer is to present a written
equivalent of a speech input. Furthermore, the computer
is to approximate as closely as possible the transcribing
behavior of at least one listener. The recognizer should
attain this close approximation in the face of the same
variability that confronts the listener.

A classic representation of the first and second
formant variability for the vowels of English is given by
76 speakers in the Peterson-Barney (1952) study. Figure
1 presents formant frequency location as a function of
vowel label for ten vowels pronounced by 76 speakers in
a /h - d/ environment. The first observation to be made
concerning these data is the considerable vowel overlap.
That is, there are vowels which have the same or nearly
the same first and second formants, but which have
different labels. These vowels are recognized by a
listener as distinct (at least under certain conditions),
which indicates that the vowels are not completely
characterized by absolute physical properties.

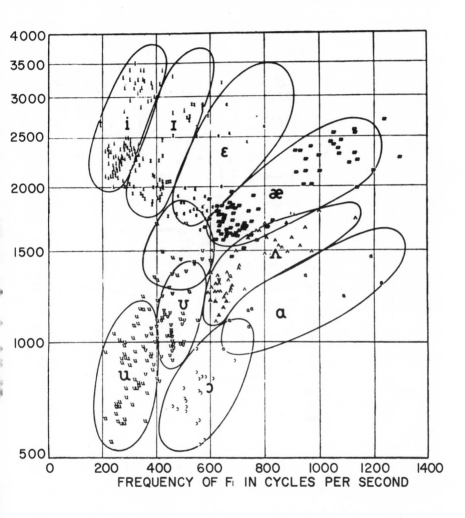

Fig. 1. Distribution of vowel production values on F1–F2 plane for 76 speakers (from Peterson & Barney study).

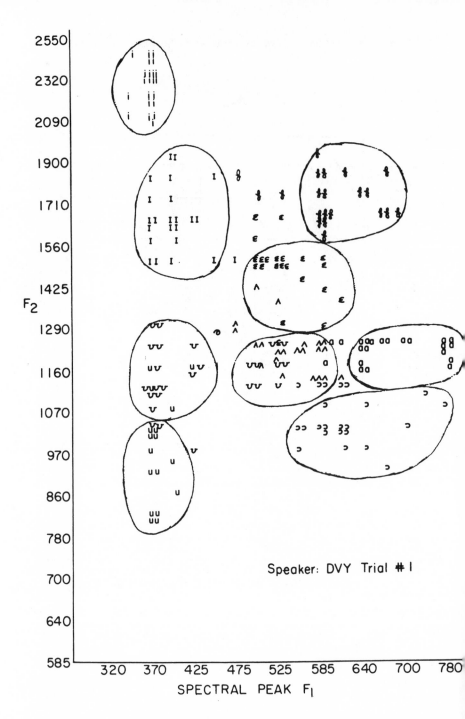

Fig. 2. Distribution of vowel production values on F1-F2
plane for speaker DVY, Trial No. 1.

A second observation shows that, although the overlap would produce some errors, a reasonable recognition accuracy can be attained by using complicated boundaries, such as the oval contours shown in Fig. 1. This cannot be an acceptable solution to the problem of mechanical recognition, however, since each vowel was produced in the same consonantal environment. Any change in this context tends to increase the variability and decrease the accuracy. Even more important is the failure of this boundary set as a simulation of human vowel perception. It is easy to see that the accuracy of recognition based on boundaries such as these would vary greatly from speaker to speaker to a degree not present among human listeners.

One of the first steps in an investigation of mechanical recognition is the determination of the sources of variability and their relative importance in scattering the data. Two sources of parameter scatter have been mentioned, inter-speaker differences and phonetic environment. The relative effect of the sources of variability may be measured by the degree of parameter overlap, i.e., the ratio of different phonetic items with similar physical properties to the separable items (see Fig. 2).

In order to illustrate how this ratio is used to compare inter-speaker variability with contextual effects, we can examine the scatter of vowel data of 76 speakers for the /h - d/ context and compare it with the scatter of data of one speaker in all possible CV and VC contexts. The contours enclosing vowel production areas of a single speaker are generally smaller, and the formant overlap is less. This fact suggests that differences between speakers are greater than differences in phonetic contexts.

Any extension of the speech data samples, say, to longer words or continuous speech, would increase the variability, as is shown by Fig. 3, taken from a study by Shearme and Holmes. The overlap portrayed here is extreme. Note particularly the vowels /i/ and /I/. A computer cannot separate these two vowels on the basis of F1 and F2 alone. This fact would be discouraging for a program in mechanical recognition, except that the cause of the overlap and parameter shift is not shown. In other words, the control

239

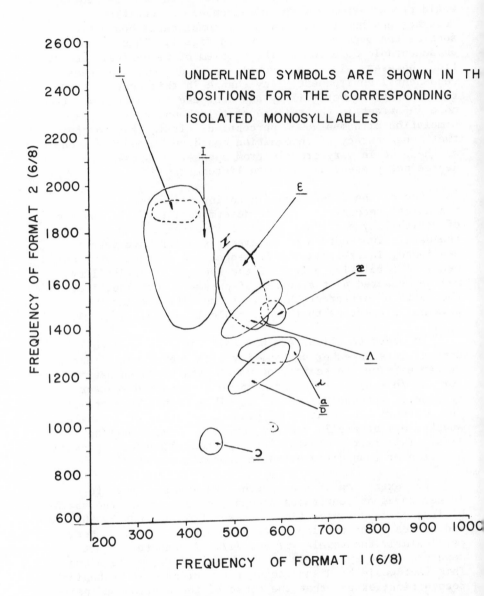

Fig. 3. Distribution of vowel production values on F1–F2 plane for continuous speech of one speaker (from Shearme & Holmes study).

expressed in this experiment was not sufficient to
determine the conditions of the vowel space. Not only
is the direction and degree of parameter shift important,
but also the stability and reproducibility of the shift
and the factors responsible for the shift. This program
in mechanical recognition is an attempt to design experiments in which only one possible cause of variation at a
time can operate. The source of variation then becomes
the independent variable, and the distribution and shift
of the vowel parameters are the dependent variables. It
is hoped that the resulting parameter shift from each
cause is a stable shift and that each source of variability
is independent. Thus, if a given consonantal environment
tends to lower the second formant of speaker A in a CVC
monosyllable, then the same environment should tend to
lower F2 for the continuous speech of speaker B. The
feasibility and economy of a mechanical speech recognizer
depend on the consistency of this effect.

This program, then, is a series of experiments in
speech production in which only one source of parameter
variation, the independent variable, is allowed to change,
if at all possible. Note that not all of the sources of
production variability are known. The factors that do
contribute to a variation of parameters that are known
include: the speaker: the speaker's sex, physical
condition, age, articulatory configuration; the time of
day; the instructions given the speaker; the list of
material (whether it is to be read, repeated or memorized
and so forth, or whether it is continuous speech or
isolated words); the acoustic conditions at recording; the
equipment used; the method of measuring acoustic parameters;
and many others.

The first step is to see if these sources of variability can be held constant. Every one of the above
factors was held constant, except that the speaker
attempted to duplicate his production on three different
days. The first two were a week apart, and the last, two
days apart. Thus, the same speaker on three different
occasions was given the same instructions to repeat the
same CVC word list in the same room, on the same recorder,
and so on. The data were processed for all three readings
at the same time and the measurement of parameters was
carried out by digital computation. This is perhaps the
maximum control that can be exercised on speech production
short of achieving reinforcement control, and it is not

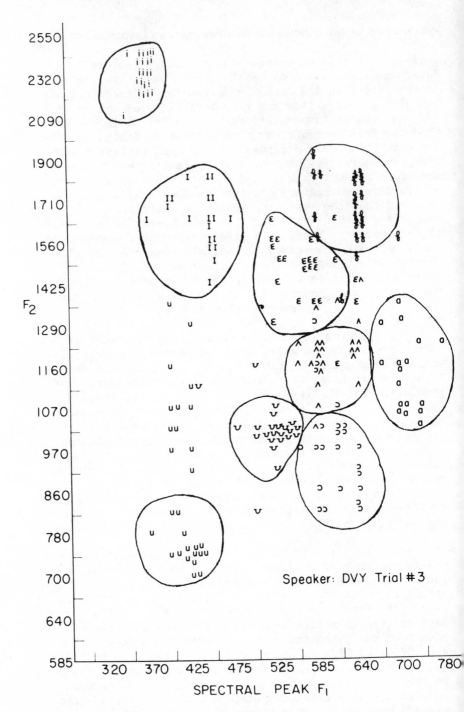

Fig. 4.   Distribution of vowel values on F1-F2 plane for
speaker DVY, Trial No. 3.

242

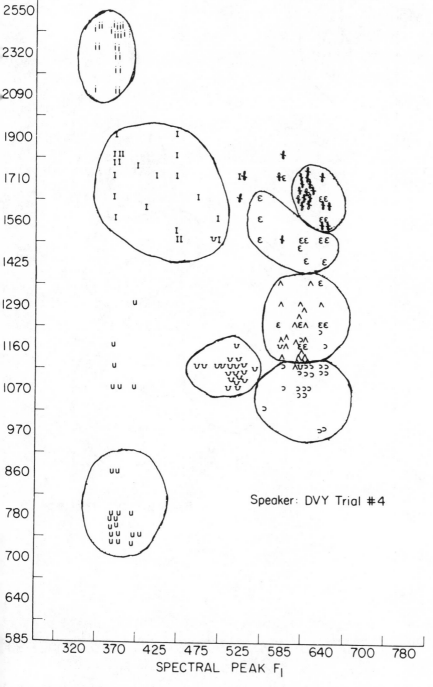

Fig. 5. Distribution of vowel production values on F1-F2
plane for speaker DVY, Trial No. 4.

243

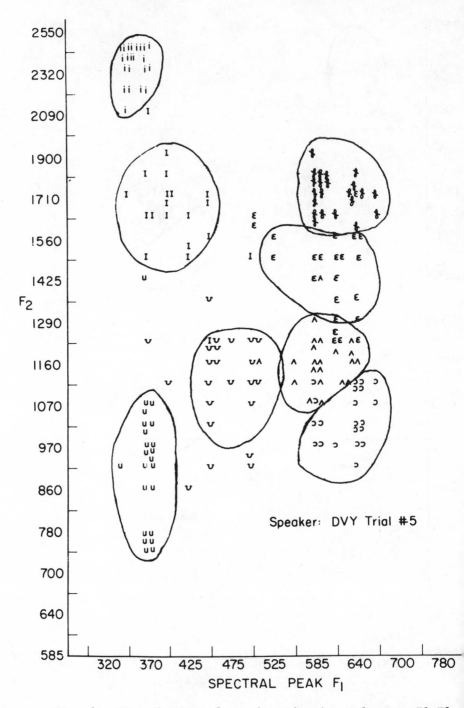

Fig. 6. Distribution of vowel production values on F1–F2
plane for speaker DVY, Trial No. 5.

yet apparent that that much control is desirable in a
speech recognition program.

Figure 4 shows the third trial of speaker DVY. Note
the position of the contour enclosing most of the vowel
/U/. It is adjacent to and nestled between /ʌ/ and /ɔ/.

Figure 5 shows the same speaker's vowel production
the following week. /U/ and /ɔ/ are more widely separated.
In addition, the contour enclosing the vowel /I/ is larger.

Figure 6 shows the same speaker two days later. If
Fig. 5 and Fig. 6 were superimposed, the differences would
be much clearer. For the most part, the vowel areas are
the same. There are some problems, however. When both
sets of data are taken together, there is a large degree
of variation and overlap between the vowels /ʌ/ and /ɛ/.
These vowels did not overlap on individual days. Optimal
recognition of this speaker's vowels depends, then, upon
shifting the boundaries slightly from day to day. In
addition, the day-to-day change in the distribution of
the production parameters may be greater for more complex
stimuli. So far, these data indicate that given a single
set of conditions of vowel production, including the
requirement that the production of the speech does not
spread out over a long time, the overlap and variability
are small enough that the computer optimally recognizes
the vowels. Every separate production of the vowels may,
however, require a new set of decision boundaries. In the
recognition of continuous speech it may not be possible to
find stable boundaries, even in the same speech production.

Any change in the factors of speech (mentioned
earlier), which in turn implies a different production,
requires a change in the decision boundaries. The problem
of mechanical speech recognition is to find a means of
determining proper boundaries automatically, that is, on
the basis of the properties of each separate speech
production. Complex boundaries (complex in terms of the
physical variables) can be programmed into the computer,
but the need to shift the boundaries for each separate
production almost demands that the decision boundaries be
very simple. Some perceptual studies also indicate that
very complex decisions by listeners are not made. The
future possibilities of mechanical recognition depend
upon finding simple boundaries which can be easily shifted
and yet which yield adequate results.

245

Speech communication takes place between at least two persons, implying that <u>perception</u>, as well as production, is important to the process. Thus, recognition boundaries must be related to the perceptual referents of at least one listener. This point is fully appreciated and no attempt is made to slight its importance. However, to paraphrase Jakobson, a person speaks in order to be heard, in order to be understood. Therefore, some initial decisions can be formed on the basis of the distributions of the parameters of production. Nevertheless, the only criterion of success of a mechanical recognizer is that it approximates the recognition behavior of at least one listener, and any mechanical scheme must be evaluated in these terms.

With this description of the problem we may now look at some more formant positions of CVC monosyllables. Figure 7 is a plot of F1 and F2 for 84 words produced by speaker JRP at one sitting. These 84 words are so generated that all possible CV and VC combinations are present. The various ovals surrounding production values of F1 and F2 are drawn to include nearly all voicings of the same vowel and yet remain non-overlapping. These ovals are complex, but ideal or optimum as far as accuracy is concerned. They provide for the lowest error-rate, but they are probably not realistically related to perception and they are not simple enough to avoid very complicated programming changes when production conditions change.

Jakobson, Fant and Halle (1952), suggest what to look for when examining the distribution of speech parameters. For example, in the discussion of the distinctive feature compact/diffuse, they say: "In the case of vowels this feature manifests itself primarily by the position of the first formant: when the latter is higher (i.e., closer to the third and higher formants), the phoneme is more compact." Now, since this is a binary feature, the statement seems to imply that, were F1 alone plotted, there would be a bimodal distribution in production and if F1 alone were varied, there should be a binary characteristic in the perceptual behavior. In fact, many critics of the distinctive feature theory insist that such a bimodal distribution is a necessity of the theory. However, Jakobson and Halle go on to say: "The opposition compact vs. diffuse in the vowel pattern is the sole feature capable of presenting a middle term in addition to the two polar terms. On the perceptual level,

246

experiments that obtained such middle terms through the mixture of a compact with the corresponding diffuse vowel seem to confirm the peculiar structure of this vocalic feature. . ."

In later discussions Halle prefers two binary decisions to a single tertiary feature, and talks of vowels which are noncompact and nondiffuse. This distinction between tertiary and binary is merely academic unless it makes a testable difference at some level. Furthermore, Jakobson and Halle refer only to the vowels in [bat], [bet], [bot], [but], and [bit], not including the vowels [bought] and [beet]. Later, Halle (1957) and Jakobson and Halle (1961) included the feature tense vs. lax and these two vowels.

At this point their system has eight vowels divided into four tense vowels: four lax, four acute, four grave, four diffuse, and four compact. In addition, Halle also considers the vowels /e/ and /o/, for which he develops the distinction noncompact-nondiffuse, although upsetting the symmetry and efficiency of the feature system just a bit.

Most of the data included in this study came from speakers with a midwest dialect; it was noted from the data that the vowels /e/ and /o/ are physically more like simple diphthongs. It is interesting to contemplate the effect of describing these two sounds in the system as diphthongs characterized by a transformation from a compact to a diffuse vowel. In anticipation of the value of this viewpoint, the vowel F1-F2 plane has been plotted without including /e/ or /o/. This change in concept eliminates the need for a noncompact-nondiffuse distinction and reduces the number of features to three, the least number required for eight vowels.

It is not certain that the distribution of the production parameters in a binary fashion is necessary for the validity of the feature theory. However, it is a fact that the monosyllable data do suggest a two-valued distribution along the first formant. If it is possible to describe /e/ and /o/ by their transition of the first formant, then we should achieve a bimodal distribution along F1 for the remaining eight vowels.

247

Figure 7 shows that it <u>is</u> possible to perform a
Halle-type bisection, dividing the diffuse vowels from
the compact vowels on the right according to the value
of the first formant. The vertical dotted line represents
a line of constant F1. If this is chosen as a boundary
for the compact/diffuse decision, there will occur three
compact errors for an accuracy of about 96 percent. If we
move this boundary to the right 25 cps, we will have three
diffuse errors and the same accuracy. This boundary
satisfies the requirements of simplicity and ease of
change by computer. It is also accurate enough for computer recognition, and this accuracy may improve, pending
the results of the listening tests.

Figure 8 shows the F1-F2 vowel distribution for
speaker GDA. Again a line of constant F1 provides an
accurate division of compact vs. diffuse vowels. There
are four errors, and the accuracy of the decision is
greater than 95 per cent. The frequency of the boundary
is approximately 435 cps, down from the value of 475 cps
for speaker JRP in Fig. 7.

Speaker GWH. One diffuse error at a boundary of 510
cps or one compact error at a boundary of 540 cps are
found (see Fig. 9).

Speaker CS. Two compact errors at a boundary of 510
cps are observed (see Fig. 10).

Speaker JLK. Two compact and three diffuse errors
at a boundary of 485 cps, for an accuracy of about 94
per cent, are obtained (see Fig. 11).

Speaker DVY Trial No. 2. No errors for a boundary
from 500 to 550 cps are found (see Fig. 12).

The accuracies obtained by a decision boundary set at
a constant first formant are excellent. An earlier study
(Hughes & Hemdal, 1965) also has shown that perhaps as
many as 50 per cent of the computer errors were also
production errors. That is, listener tests indicated
that nearly half of the vowels in error were identified
differently than the speaker intended. Of course, much
of the parameter measurement was performed automatically
by a computer, and this may be another source of error.

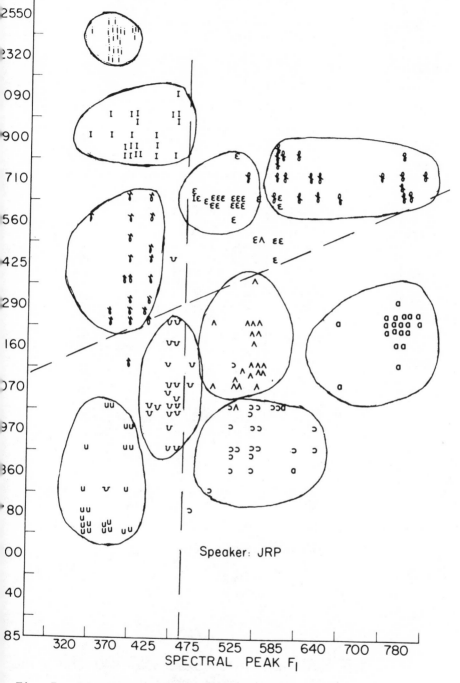

Fig. 7.   Distribution of vowel production values on F1–F2 plane for speaker JRP.

249

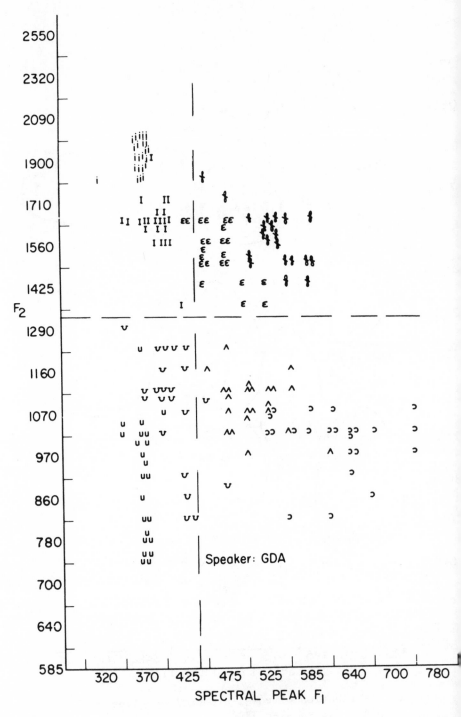

Fig. 8.   Distribution of vowel production values on F1-F2 plane for speaker GDA.

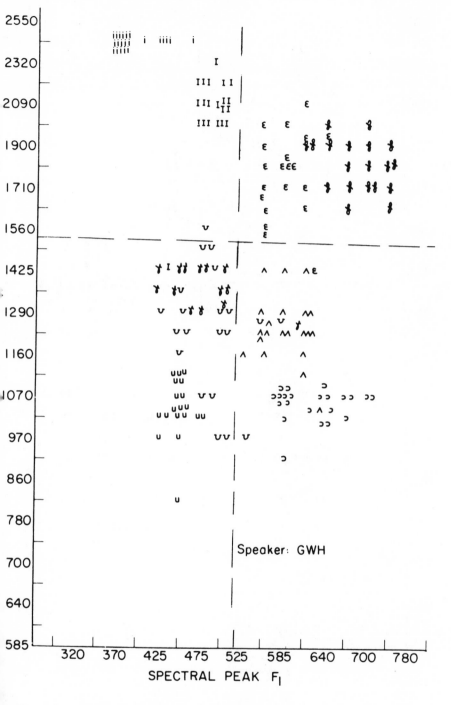

Fig. 9. Distribution of vowel production values on F1–F2
plane for speaker GWH.

251

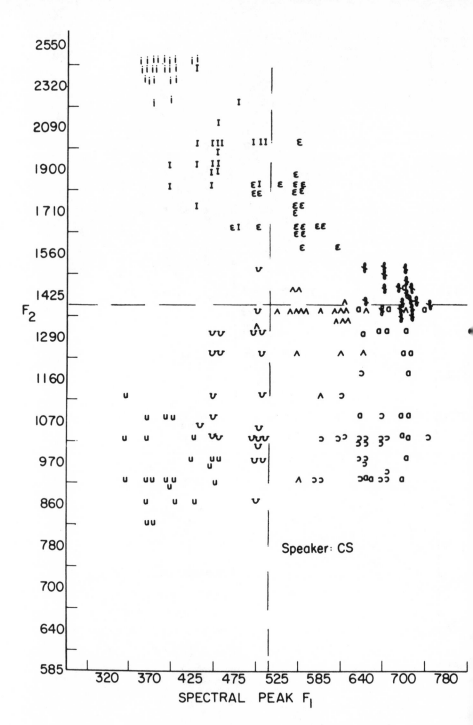

Fig. 10. Distribution of vowel production values on F1–F2
plane for speaker CS.

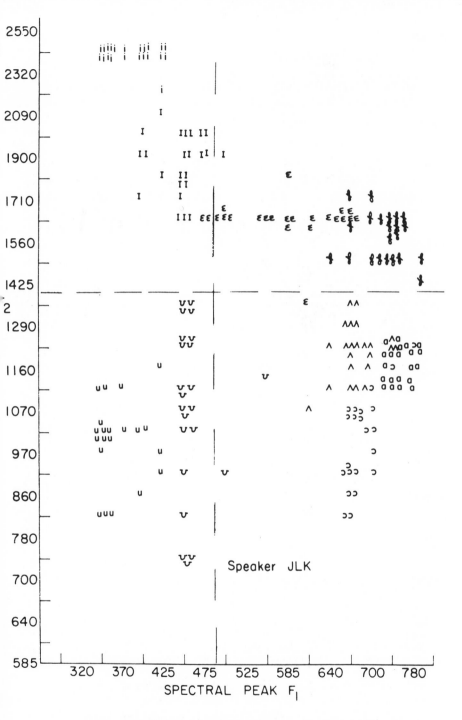

Fig. 11. Distribution of vowel production values on
          F1-F2 plane for speaker JLK.

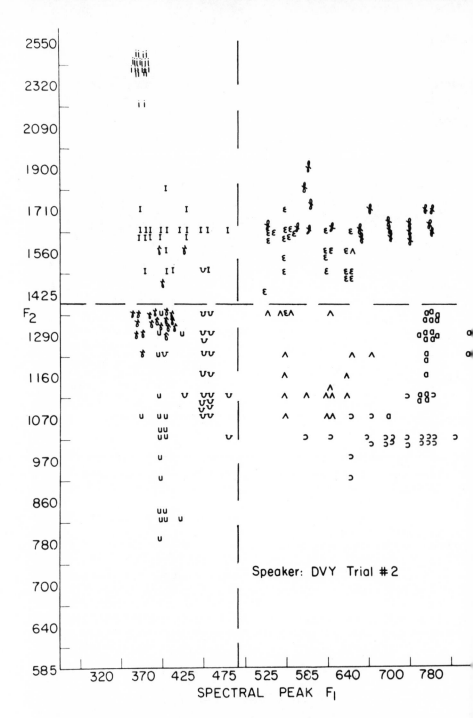

Fig. 12.   Distribution of vowel production values on
F1-F2 plane for speaker DVY, Trial No. 2.

Fant (1960), in a study of the F-patterns of compound tube resonators and horns, calculated the hypothetical formant frequencies of an open tube of length 17.6 cm., approximately equal to the average length of the male vocal tract. This tube, with an average speaker's cross-sectional area, produces a first formant of 500 cps which Fant refers to as the neutral reference. It may be interesting to speculate on a possible connection between this reference and the clustering of the compact/diffuse boundary around 500 cps.

The only change in the conditions of production were the speaker and the time of production. A good case is made for using a line of constant F1 for the compact/diffuse boundary in a computer recognition program, at least for monosyllables. But the frequency value of this line changes from speaker to speaker. Is it constant for a given speaker, i.e., is this boundary one of the invariants of speech production? To answer the question, an examination was made of the productions of speaker JFH in 1964 and in 1966, and the production of speaker DVY in 1966, a week apart and two days apart. In this latter set of three repetitions, all possible control on the conditions of production was maintained, except the separate occurrences.

Figure 13 presents the 1966 data of speaker JFH. There are six compact errors resulting from a boundary placement at 465 cps, or eight diffuse errors at 450 cps.

Figure 14 presents the 1964 data of the same speaker. There are five diffuse and three compact errors at a boundary of 510 cps, a difference of around 50 cps in the distribution of the separation of vowels along F1. This is a significant change in the frequency of the boundary, since error rates increase rapidly for small changes in this value. These data were taken two years apart, so it is necessary to determine if this is a long term shift in values and whether such changes occur on a day to day basis. For this answer we go to the three repetitions of speaker DVY, Trials No. 3, No. 4, and No. 5 in Figs. 4, 5, and 6.

Figure 4 shows the greatest error rate. The minimum error is about 15 per cent, primarily because of proximity of /U/ to /ɔ/. The best boundary does appear to be around 520 cps.

255

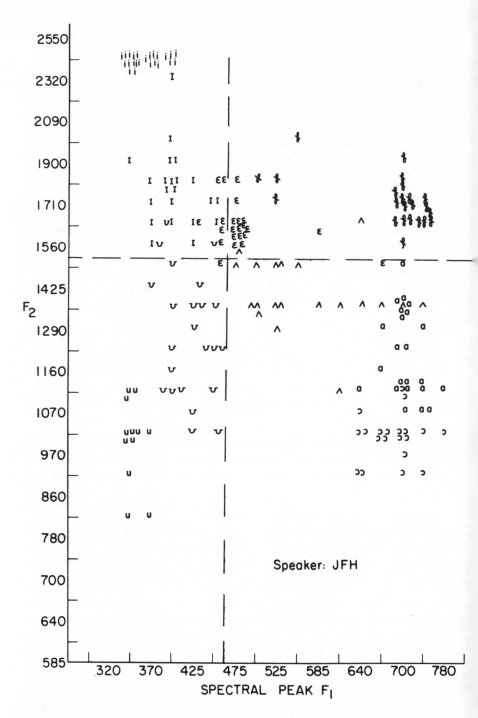

Fig. 13.   Distribution of vowel production values on
F1–F2 plane for speaker JFH, 1966.

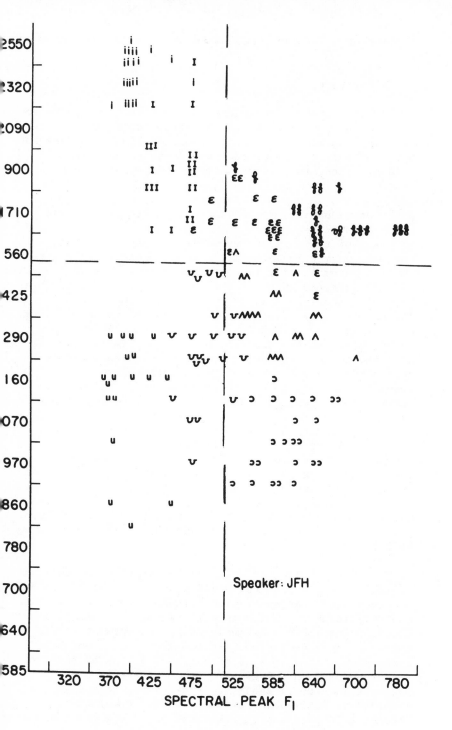

Fig. 14.   Distribution of vowel production values on
F1-F2 plane for speaker JFH, 1964.

257

Figure 5 yields five errors at 540 cps for an accuracy of 94 per cent.

Figure 6 shows three errors when the boundary is set again at 520 cps. Although the error rates vary considerably, the location of the compact/diffuse boundary does not. If a frequency of 520 cps is chosen and all three trials lumped, the overall accuracy is greater than 90 per cent.

For mechanical recognition the most useful boundaries between vowel groups are those that are simply expressed in terms of the physical variable of measurement primarily because, as mentioned earlier, these boundaries have to be shifted automatically for each new speaker. Both the shift and the information about the speaker which is needed for the shift should be easily obtainable. Thus, a compact/diffuse boundary of a line of constant F1 is particularly attractive and the accuracy is very good. This tempts one to speculate on the significance of the bimodal cluster of data and to inquire into a possible relation to vowel perception. Future studies with synthetic vowels will be conducted in an effort to determine if a relation exists between this production boundary and perceptual boundaries.

This result also prompts one to ask whether there are other similar production distributions that will allow simple boundaries for other features. Consider the feature acute vs. grave. Jakobson and Halle consider F2 to be the primary determiner of acute vs. grave, and they suggest as a measure for this feature the ratio of the difference between F1 and F2 to the difference of F2 and F3. The ratio corresponds to a boundary sloping up from left to right.

A straight line of gentle slope in this region will divide the acute from the grave vowels in Fig. 7 with an accuracy of 98 per cent. The left-most vowel above this boundary is an /ɔ/ which is differentiated from all other vowels in having a relatively low third formant. This vowel need not be included in the grave/acute boundary discussion. Therefore, a boundary of a line of constant F2 may be used as the grave/acute boundary with no increase in error. Again it is necessary to see if the boundary is applicable across a speaker population. Returning to previous figures, the following grave/acute boundaries and accuracies are obtained:

In Fig. 8 (Speaker GDA) Constant F2=1325 cps, yields no errors.

In Fig. 9 (Speaker GWH) F2=1530 cps, three errors, 96 per cent accurate.

In Fig. 10 (Speaker CS) F2=1400 cps, ten errors, 88 per cent accurate.

In Fig. 11 (Speaker JLK) F2=1400 cps, one error, 99 per cent accurate.

In Fig. 12 (Speaker DVY No. 2) F2=1390 cps, three errors, 96 per cent accurate.

In Fig. 13 (Speaker JFH 1966) F2=1525 cps, seven errors, 91 per cent accurate.

In Fig. 14 (Speaker JFH 1964) F2=1525, four errors, 95 per cent accurate.

The conclusion again may be stated that it is possible to satisfy the requirements of simplicity and maintain sufficiently high accuracy. It is also interesting to note that the grave/acute boundary is very close to 1500 cps, the second formant calculated by Fant for the neutral reference vowel based on average vocal tract dimensions. Perhaps the measurement of an individual's neutral vowel is related to the location of this boundary junction.

In this study it has been shown that parameter variability in vowel production can be controlled. It has also suggested several methods of describing the characteristics of production. We do not know yet whether these simple boundaries have any relationship to vowel perception. Experiments conducted with synthetic vowels should give us this information. If we consider that the first and second formants are perceptual continua, then the two simple boundaries imply that the listener attends to these continua independently and need only make a binary decision on them.

It should be emphasized that these boundaries constitute only a model of recognition of vowels in carefully pronounced nonsense syllables. They are parameters of production under these conditions and not of perception. In addition, they may not be extendable

to the production of actual words or continuous speech;
however, it will be a part of our methodology to attempt
to relate each separate source of parameter variability
to these simple boundaries.

References

Fant, Gunnar. Acoustic theory of speech production. The
    Hague: Mouton, 1960. Pp. 72-73.

Halle, M. In defense of the number two. Studies presented
    to Joshua Whatmough on his sixtieth birthday. The
    Hague: Mouton, 1957. Pp. 65-72.

Hughes, G. W., & Hemdal, J. F. Speech analysis. Purdue
    Res. Found. Tech. Rep. TR-EE65-9, 1965.

Jakobson, R., Fant, G., & Halle, M. Preliminaries to
    speech analysis: The distinctive features and their
    correlates. M. I. T. Acoustics Lab. Tech. Rep.,
    1961, No. 13.

Jakobson, R., & Halle, M. Tenseness and laxness. In D.
    Abercrombie, D. E. Fry, P. A. D. McCarthy, N. C.
    Scott, & J. L. M. Trim (Eds.) In honour of Daniel
    Jones: Papers contributed on the occasion of his
    eightieth birthday. Longman's Green & Co., 1962.
    Pp. 550-555.

Peterson, G. E., & Barney, H. L. Control methods used in
    a study of the vowels. J. acoust. Soc. Amer., 1952,
    24, 175-184.

Footnotes

[1]This report is an edited form of the address
presented at the Conference on Language and Language
Behavior, CRLLB, University of Michigan, Ann Arbor,
October, 1966.

[2]The author is a member of the research staff at the
CRLLB.

AN EXPLORATION OF SOME PERSONALITY VARIABLES
IN AUTHENTIC PRONUNCIATION OF A SECOND LANGUAGE[1]

Alexander Z. Guiora, Harlan L. Lane, and Lewis A. Bosworth[2]

Speakers of a second language may differ greatly in
the authenticity of their pronunciation, even when they
have similar backgrounds, training, and proficiency.
Unsystematic attempts to account for this difference sometimes include intelligence, language aptitude, discrimina-
tive capacity, or anatomical capabilities. The experiment
to be reported here initially explores a rather different
possibility: namely, that personality differences may
play a major role in the observed differences in authenticity of pronunciation. The study may also illustrate,
more generally, the desirability of collaborative research
between the discipline of clinical psychology and the
language sciences, an interaction that, heretofore, has
been virtually nonexistent.

Undoubtedly, many variables make up the composite
picture of pronunciation authenticity. It is unlikely
that any single identifiable personality variable is a
necessary and sufficient condition for pronunciation
authenticity. Nevertheless, the comments of language
teachers, and the observation of authentic and non-
authentic speakers of a second language suggest the
importance of some personality variables more than others,
and make it possible to single out a few such personality
characteristics, however tentatively, for systematic
study. In particular, we hypothesized that the personality characteristic of empathy plays a significant role
in the acquisition of native-like authenticity of pronunciation; specifically, people who can be described as
high empathizers may achieve a greater degree of authenticity than those who are low empathizers.

In order to pursue this possibility, a measure of
empathy and a measure of authenticity were required. Both
attributes are difficult to define and to measure reliably
and validly, but there is a body of thought concerning
them that provides the basis for a beginning.

261

The element of sharing, i.e., of gaining understanding through some kind of intimate relationship, seems to be an essential part of the empathic act. This sharing implies more than a mere recognition of another's feelings or a relationship based on identification, per se. Thus, Katz (1963) distinguishes between empathy and sympathy, an important distinction often overlooked: "In empathy we focus our attention on the feelings and the situation of the other person...when we sympathize we are pre-occupied with the assumed duality or parallel between our own feelings and the feelings of others" (p. 8). The need to differentiate empathy from identification is also suggested by Greenson (1960), who views empathy as a kind of emotional knowing. The emphasis is on an emotional level of reaction to the object, a reaction that is based on processes in psychological development that are prior to the operation of the mechanism of identification. This view is clearly advanced by Sullivan (1947) in his discussion of empathy; he relates this process to the direct and immediate apprehension by the infant of its mother's mood.

Since empathic capacity is based upon the earliest form of object-relation, a relation which precedes the development of structured boundaries between the self and non-self, it may be clearly differentiated from the capacity of inference. In contrast to the process of inference, where the affective element is significant mainly in the negative sense of a potentiality for distortion of the cognitive function, the empathic capacity is based upon, and operates as a mode of, comprehending, in which the affective experience is primary. There is in the empathic act a temporary suspension of ego functions in favor of an immediate, precognitive experience of another's emotional state as one's own. This fusion of self and non-self is, in a sense, a regressive process, yet the link to cognitive control is not fully severed. The empathic experience emerges from a primitive mode of object relation but does not remain solely as a diffuse global feeling. It progresses, so to say, through a cognitive filter which transforms affective experience into comprehension of the meaning of the experience: in the object, in the self, and in the self-object inter-action. The active use of the passive-receptive aspect of empathy is implicit also in Flescher's (1963) description of empathy as "sharing another person's feelings with the purpose of understanding him."

In the light of the foregoing discussion, the following definition of empathy is offered in the terms of its
discussion in clinical psychology: Empathy is a process
of comprehending in which a temporary fusion of self-
object boundaries, as in the earliest pattern of object-
relation, permits an immediate emotional apprehension of
the affective experience of another, this sensing being
used by the cognitive functions to gain understanding of
the other (Guiora, 1965).

For the present purpose it was desirable to define
authenticity of pronunciation so as to exclude various
related components of spoken fluency in a second language.
Clearly, grammatical accuracy (including phonological
accuracy) is to be treated separately. Richness of vocabulary, appropriateness of style, and control of idioms,
often cited as components of oral fluency, were also to
be distinguished from authenticity of pronunciation;
sample utterances from two speakers which are identical in
all these respects may, nevertheless, be considered by
native-speaker judges to approximate native-like pronunciation in different degrees. Precisely what the cues are
that such judges employ and, hence, what the physical
dimensions of authenticity are, remains to be discovered,
but we may say with some confidence that judgments of
authenticity are relative to some internalized norm for a
dialect, and that sub-phonemic cues (both segmental and
suprasegmental) are critically involved.

In order to explore the relation between authenticity
of second-language pronunciation and certain personality
variables including, significantly, empathic capacity, we
recruited an experimental population of 14 high school
teachers of French who were reasonably homogeneous in
their proficiency in the French language; these 14 were
selected, after administration of the Modern Language
Proficiency Test (French) and a personal information
questionnaire, from 40 high school teachers of French who
were participating in an NDEA Summer Institute. An
extensive battery of tests was administered to the Ss,
including measures of personality, interest patterns,
general aptitude and intelligence, and perceptual functioning. In the first category of tests we administered the
Pensacola Z Scale, which seeks to measure hostility,
anxiety, dependency, and rigidity; the Minnesota Multi-
phasic Personality Inventory; and the Rorschach Test. For
measures of interest patterns we used the Allport-Vernon

263

Scale and the Strong Vocational Interest Test. Our
measures of intelligence and language aptitude included
the Miller Analogies Test, the Wechsler Adult Intelligence
Scale, and the Modern Language Aptitude Test. Measures of
perceptual functioning included the Closure Flexibility
Test, the Kramer Affect Test, and a measure of the
intelligibility of English when spoken with a foreign
accent.

In order to obtain our dependent variable, a measure
of pronunciation authenticity, we recorded two samples of
each of our Ss' French--one when the S was asked to
describe a series of pictures, and another when he read a
selected passage. These samples were excerpted so that
utterances comparable in content could be recorded and
presented to a panel of native French judges for rating.
A rating scale was constructed which allowed ratings of
each sample on a scale of eight, ranging from one (very
poor) to eight (native speaker). Initial experiments with
the scale demonstrated reasonably high inter- and intra-
judge reliability.

The 14 Ss in the experimental group were then ranked
on the combined measure of pronunciation authenticity, and
this rank-order was correlated with each of the independent
measures described above. In particular, we were interested in the relation between scores on pronunciation
authenticity and those on an instrument we constructed for
the purpose of measuring empathic capacity. This instrument derived from a recent report by Haggard and Isaacs
(1966) which stated that, when strips of film of psycho-
therapeutic sessions were shown at reduced speed (from 24
frames per sec. to 4 frames per sec.), facial expressions
denoting affective states become discernible. These
transitory facial expressions are called MME's (micromomentary expressions). We hypothesized that the ability
to perceive minimal cues in interpersonal interaction was
an important component of empathic capacity, and that
individual differences in the threshold level for the
perception of MME's would reflect corresponding differences in empathic capacity. We selected a strip of film
in which Haggard and Isaac's judges detected only a few
MME's at normal speed but many at slower speeds, and we
presented the film to our Ss in a descending order of
speeds. The Ss were instructed to make a tick mark (on
sheets provided) each time they saw an MME, and the number
of marks made by each S during the showing of the film at
each speed were later tallied. The score assigned to each

S for this test was his average deviation from the mean
number of MME's seen by our sample population at each
speed; thus, some Ss were identified as exceptionally high
MME perceivers, and some as exceptionally low ones.

At the time of this report our analysis of the interrelationships among the various measures of personality
and their relation to the measures of authenticity has not
yet been completed. We can report, however, some negative
and positive preliminary findings. At this point, it
appears that scores on most of the psychological tests
listed above do not correlate significantly with scores
on the measures of authenticity. One noteworthy exception
to this generalization is the significant relation found
(a rank order correlation of 0.6) between measures of
empathic capacity, described above, and those of pronunciation authenticity. Pending the final accounting in the
present study, these initial findings encourage us to
further develop measures of empathic capacity and of
authenticity, in order to assess the magnitude and
replicability of this relationship.

References

Flescher, V. On empathy, intuition and countertransference.
    Unpublished manuscript, 1963.

Greenson, R. Empathy and its vicissitudes. *Int. J.*
    Psychoanal., 1960, *41*, 425-429.

Guiora, A. Z. On clinical diagnosis and prediction.
    Psychol. *Reps*., 1965, *17*, 779-784.

Haggard, L. A., & Isaacs, K. S. Micromomentary facial
    expressions as indicators of ego mechanisms in
    psychotherapy. In L. A. Gottschalk & A. H. Auerbach
    (Eds.), *Methods of research in psychotherapy*. New
    York: Appleton-Century-Crofts, 1966.

Katz, R. *Empathy*: *Its nature and uses*. New York: Free
    Press of Glencoe, 1963.

Sullivan, H. S. *Modern conceptions of psychiatry*. New
    York: William Alanson White Foundation, 1947.

Footnotes

[1]This report is an edited version of the paper presented at the Conference on Language and Language Behavior. It is based on research supported by a contract with the Office of Education, U. S. Department of Health, Education, & Welfare, under provisions of P. L. 83-531, Cooperative Research, and Title VI, P. L. 85-864, as amended.

[2]The authors are members of the research staff at the CRLLB.

TOWARDS A DESCRIPTION OF STRESS-TIMING IN SPOKEN ENGLISH[1]

George D. Allen[2]

Rhythm is characteristic of human behavior. From heart beats and rapid eye-movements to longer daily and monthly cycles, our activities show temporal regularity. Speech also has its rhythm, but different languages have different rhythmic organizations. Linguists, for example, classify languages as either "stress-timed" or "syllable-timed," just by listening to them: English and German are said to be stress-timed, while Spanish and Japanese are syllable-timed. Most descriptions of speech rhythm have been based on intuition, however, and no matter how well educated the intuition may be, it remains intuition. Even the terms "stress" and "syllable," basic as they are in the language of speech scientists, have defied consensual definition. The nature of speech rhythm is still unclear, and so the present paper discusses experiments designed to show that we can distinguish between stress-timing and syllable-timing, and to describe the stress-timing of English.

A definition of stress-timing or syllable-timing usually takes the following form: a language is stress- (syllable-) timed if its stresses (syllables) tend to be regularly spaced in time. In the light of what is known about human motor and perceptual behavior, however, this definition is rather uninformative. That is, we know enough about human behavior and English speech to predict that the stresses of English will tend to be regularly spaced. First, the major stresses of English are produced, or at least accompanied, by "pulses" of respiratory muscle activity (Cooker, 1963; Ladefoged et. al., 1958; Stetson, 1951). Since many motor activities are naturally rhythmic (Miyake, 1902), we might expect these pulse movements also to be rhythmic. Second, studies on the perception of time and rhythm (Fraisse, 1963; Woodrow, 1951) show that people impose temporal organization on sequences of stimuli, sometimes perceiving rhythms and accent patterns that are not present in the physical signal. Therefore,

listeners probably are predisposed to hear rhythm in
speech. Since we already know that the stresses of
English are produced by muscles that probably move
rhythmically and are perceived by listeners who are all
too ready to hear rhythms, an acceptable description of
English speech rhythm must now tell us more than that "the
stresses of English tend to be regularly spaced in time."

Speech rhythm probably originates in muscle movements,
for both stresses and syllables are associated with
extensive and regular motor activity, and no other
linguistic unit without large associated movements
functions as a rhythmic center. In the report of "tone-
timing" in Ịjọ the only published report of a rhythm
other than stress- or syllable-timed, the author mentions
that stress in Ịjọ is predictable and highly correlated
with high and changing tones (Williamson, 1965). Therefore, even this one reported tone-timed language probably
has increased muscle activity associated with the rhythmic
beats. If linguists can distinguish consistently between
stress-timed and syllable-timed languages, however, these
associated movements must have different rhythmic organizations.

An experiment is being designed to see if different
rhythmic organizations can be found in the prosodies
alone and if these differences lead to the same classification of languages as that based on stress- and
syllable-timing. Recordings of conversations in various
languages will be passed through an electronic circuit
that destroys segmental information but leaves fundamental
frequency and instantaneous speech power unchanged. The
conversations will sound as though they were recorded
through a wall or over a very noisy telephone (cf.
O'Malley and Peterson, 1966. Both linguists and untrained
listeners will listen to these conversations and will be
asked to classify them rhythmically. The linguists will
be asked to use the stress- versus syllable-timed
distinction in their classifications, but untrained
listeners will have to use some intuitive criterion.
Agreement between the results of this experiment and the
traditional classification of the various languages as
stress- and syllable-timed will indicate not only that
the rhythmic distinctions are reliable, but also that the
important correlates of rhythm lie in the prosodies.
Disagreement among subjects in classification will prove
that speech rhythm involves linguistic units other than

stresses and syllables. The unlikely finding of agreement among subjects on a classification different from the traditional one would force us to take a long look at the intuitive validity of stress- and syllable-timing.

Another behavioral measure that will distinguish between stress-timing and syllable-timing is suggested by an earlier study (Allen, 1966). The hypothesis underlying this study was that peripheral muscle movements are appropriate kinesthetic responses to a rhythmic stimulus and that such movements can be used to locate the down beats of speech rhythms. Subjects tapped their fingers in time to the rhythms of several utterances and the times of their taps, relative to the utterances, were recorded. Subjects heard each utterance a number of times and tapped many times to every syllable, whether down beat or not. Although the stated purpose of the experiment was to locate the beats precisely in the speech wave, the result- ing data also showed that subjects tap more easily to the beat syllables, and that, in English, these beats are the stressed syllables.

Before any experiments were run, the experimenter categorized all the syllables of all the utterances accord- ing to his intuition of their roles in the rhythms of the utterances. Syllables with full stress were called type A; those with reduced stress or no stress but still play- ing the part of a beat or a counterpoint in the rhythm were type B; the rest were type C. After the tapping experiment the subjects wrote down the utterance rhythms as they perceived them, and there was good agreement between the experimenter's and the subjects' perceptions of the rhythmic beats. This typology defined the degree to which a syllable is a rhythmic beat. Reliability in tapping to a syllable was measured by the variance of the subjects' tapping responses to that syllable, that is, the degree to which his taps were spread around his average tap location in the syllable. The more tightly clustered his taps were, the smaller their variance--and, therefore, the more reliable they were. This variance in tapping was averaged within the different classes of syllables for all subjects and was seen to be lower for the stronger rhythmic beats. Finally, a "stress score" was obtained for each syllable of the utterances by having five trained linguists transcribe the prosodies of the utterances and then counting the total number of stress marks assigned to that syllable. Since each linguist

transcribed each utterance twice, stress scores ranged
from zero to ten. The stress scores were averaged within
the different syllable classes for all the linguists and
were found to be greater for the syllables which were
rhythmic beats. A comparison between the rhythmic typolog
of the syllables and the results of the tapping and stres
scoring experiments is summarized in Table 1 (type B1
syllables carry a primary rhythmic beat; type B2 syllables
are counterpoint beats).

These results show the degree to which stress, rhythm
and ease of tapping correlate for the English utterances
studied. This correlation suggests that the range of
variance in tapping to syllable beats may be used as a
valid measure of the rhythmic type of a language. That
is, if the same study were carried out cross-linguisticall
different correlations should result for different languages. The range of variance in tapping presumably is
great for English; the data show the variance for
unstressed syllables to be double that for stressed syllables. This range might be slightly different for English
speech samples drawn from a formal address, in which
syllables and stresses are more clearly enunciated, or
from a more animated conversation, with choppy and run-on
sentences. In a syllable-timed language, however, each
syllable is more nearly the rhythmic equal of every other
syllable; therefore, the range of variance in tapping
should be much less than it is for English. In other
words, if the tapping and stress-scoring experiments were
performed on a syllable-timed language, stress scores for
different syllables might remain widely divergent, but
variability in ease of tapping should be less from one
syllable to the next.

In the definition of stress-timing as "a tendency
toward equal spacing of stresses," the "tendency toward
equal spacing" remains unexplained. A tendency is a
cause-effect process, yet we know neither the nature of
the cause not the size of the effect. We shall now
suggest three interpretations for this tendency, along
with possible underlying causal mechanisms. Then we
shall describe a set of experiments to determine which of
these interpretations is most likely to be true for
English.

Table 1

Average Tapping Variance Versus Average Stress

Score for Types A, B1, B2, and C Syllables

Syllable Type	Average Variance in Tapping Experiment	Average Stress Score
A	1048 msec^2	8.6 (out of possible 10)
B1	1328	3.4
B2	1683	.94
C	2161	.028

We have been assuming a simplified model of speech rhythm in which only syllables and stresses "compete" as rhythmic beats, with both having some tendency toward equal spacing. To the extent that one or the other of these units wins this competition for the central position in the rhythm, the language will be stress- or syllable-timed. With this model in mind, the statement by Halliday that "the ratio of the average durations of one-, two-, and three-syllable feet [in English read aloud] was ... about 5:6:7" (1963, p. 6) is evidence that stresses, which mark off the feet, dominate syllables as rhythmic centers, and that English is therefore stress-timed. But there are other influences on the durations of syllables and inter-stress intervals, and our experiments must take account of all of them.

The three most important influences on the durations of syllables and interstress intervals are tempo (average speech rate), phonetic composition, and prosodic contour. When we talk faster, all syllables and interstress intervals shorten. If the rhythm meanwhile remains unchanged, the temporal relationship between the interstress intervals also presumably remains the same, each interval shortening in proportion to this increase in tempo. But within each interval, different syllables are affected differently, unstressed syllables shortening more than stressed ones. At extremely high speech rates, unstressed syllables may disappear entirely.

Likewise, different syllables and interstress intervals are composed of different articulatory-phonetic sequences. The different kinds and combinations of speech sounds vary in their intrinsic durations, and so different sequences of sounds take different amounts of time. For example, the two-syllable word "basket" often has greater duration than the three-syllable word "battering," because of the long /sk/ combination in "basket." Like syllables, different phonetic types are also affected differently by changes in tempo.

Durations of speech segments are also influenced, though probably less, by the prosodic contour, that is, the placement and degree of stress, the inclusion of various kinds of juncture, and the intonation.

272

Since a "tendency toward equal spacing" is a tendency away from something else, our discussion of the temporal characteristics of the spacing of stresses must first establish a baseline for comparisons. It was pointed out above that, in the absence of any tendency toward equal spacing of stresses, the interstress intervals will be different in duration. In order to detect such a tendency we must hold tempo, phonetic material and prosodic contour constant, or else control for whatever changes they bring about in the interstress interval lengths. In the following description of three possible tendencies toward equal spacing, tempo is assumed to remain roughly the same from one utterance to the next, and different utterings of the same phonetic material are assumed to have the same prosodic contour.

The first kind of tendency toward equal spacing we shall call the "null tendency," because the only determiners of the length of time between two stresses will be tempo, the internal phonetic composition of the interval and its prosodic contour. If we hold these three determiners constant, this kind of tendency will cause the length of an interstress interval to remain the same in different environments. For example, consider the pair sentences "Carol has returned from Europe" and "Barnaby has returned from Europe." The time lapse between the stresses on the syllables "turned" and "Eur" is a function of the articulatory processes required to produce the extra syllable "from" and all of the associated phonetic material. The time lapse may or may not be a function of the material in the rest of the sentence. If it is not, the null tendency is true for stress-timing in English.

There are two interesting ways in which the interstress interval might depend upon its environment, and these two ways would result in the other two kinds of tendency with which we shall concern ourselves. Looking at the example of Carol and Barnaby, we can see that (probably) the time lapse between "Bar" and "turned" is greater than that between "Car" and "turned," because "Barnaby" is one syllable longer than "Carol". Here "tendency toward equal spacing" can be interpreted to mean that "-turned from Eur-" will be longer when it follows "Barnaby has re-" than when it follows "Carol has re-". This tendency might result from temporal memory in the proprioceptive system, i.e., an ability of the muscles involved in stress production to remember when their last

two actions occurred, even if they had acted at a rate
different from the average.

But such a temporal memory might equally produce the
opposite tendency: the time lapse between "turned" and
"Eur" might be <u>less</u> after "Barnaby has re-" than after
"Carol has re-." This tendency would be better called a
"tendency toward constant tempo" than a "tendency toward
equal spacing," however, for it will compensate for an
overlong interstress interval by shortening the following
interval.[3]

The three interpretations of the "tendency toward
equal spacing of stresses" can be summarized, then, as
follows:

H1) The Null Hypothesis--The location of a stress
in an utterance is unaffected by the location of any other
stress in that utterance.

H2) The Hypothesis of Correlated Interval Size--If
the time interval between two stresses in an utterance
increases, the duration of the succeeding interstress
interval will also increase.

H3) The Hypothesis of Constant Tempo--If the time
interval between two stresses increases, the duration of
the succeeding interstress interval will decrease.

Three experiments are presently being designed that
will establish which of these hypothetical tendencies is
true for English. All three experiments make use of what
we shall call "minimal pairs of utterances," that is,
pairs of utterances, U_1 and U_2, of the following form:

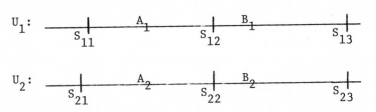

where S_{ij} is the jth stress of utterance U_i; A_i and B_i
are the first and second interstress intervals of U_i,
respectively; B_1 is phonetically identical to B_2; and A_1

is <u>not</u> phonetically identical to A_2. Our three hypotheses can then be rewritten as:

H1) B_1 equals B_2 in length, regardless of the relative lengths of A_1 and A_2.

H2)   If A_1 is longer than A_2, then B_1 is longer than B_2.

H3)   If A_1 is longer than A_2, then B_1 is shorter than B_2.

It is important that tempo be held constant from one utterance of a minimal pair to the other, for the effects of changes in tempo are very much like effects of the second kind of tendency, the tendency toward correlated interval sizes. As tempo increases, all interstress intervals decrease, so that a change in B_i caused by a change in tempo will correlate with a similarly caused change in A_i. But we are interested in effects of one interval duration upon <u>succeeding</u> ones, and so we want to show that the B_i's are different in length just because the A_i's are different in length.

There are two approaches that might be taken to control for changes in tempo. The first is to calibrate the normally observed variation in tempo from one utterance to another in speech situations like the ones contemplated for the experiments. This observed variation in tempo would serve as a baseline with which to compare variations in B_i. We know that variations in the durations of B_i will be correlated with variations in the durations of the A_i because both variations are correlated with normal variations in tempo. Any significant additional variations can be attributed to a stress-timing effect of the A_i.

A second means of controlling for tempo changes is the inclusion, at the beginning of each test utterance, of another stress interval, phonetically identical for the two utterances of each minimal pair, whose duration would serve as an indication of the tempo of that utterance. Since no interstress interval precedes this interval, variations in it would be assumed to be due solely to changes in tempo. All interstress interval durations could then be compared with this initial duration. This second method of control gives more information than the first in that the first method can be derived from the second simply by ignoring the first interstress interval.

Once a set of minimal pairs of utterances has been composed, they will be read under three different experimental conditions. In the first experiment subjects will read all of the utterances from a list in which the two utterances of each pair are separated by one utterance from some different pair. The interposition of one unrelated utterance between the two utterances of a minimal pair will eliminate any short-term memory of the durations of the interstress intervals of the first member of the pair before the second member is read. Tempo will not change much, moreover, in so short a time. In the second experiment the two members of a minimal pair will be conjoined by the word "and" to form single sentences, and the resulting sentences will be read in a list. Tempo will remain constant, but there should be considerable memory of B_1 when B_2 is read. For the third experiment the various minimal pairs will be imbedded in paragraphs. Fairly large changes in tempo will occur in the readings of these paragraphs, but the speech will be much more "normal" or "conversational." Because the tendencies we are investigating are equated with differences in the durations of B_1's and B_2's, short-term memory of the length of B_1 during the reading of B_2 might reduce the measured effect of such tendencies. We therefore expect the experimental effects to be greatest in the third experiment and least in the second, with the effects in the first experiment somewhere in between.

The data from these experiments will be the durations of the interstress intervals of the various minimal pairs. By including in the set of all pairs many different kinds of syllable and phoneme strings we can determine the effects of these other phonological units in interval duration. In this way we can examine closely the nature of the dominance of stress in the rhythm of English.

In order to measure the time lapses between successive stresses, however, we must first be able to locate the "beats" of the stressed syllables as points in time. We shall now show that this can be done precisely enough for our purposes. Previous investigations of English rhythm used two different behavioral measures of syllable beat

location. Miyake (1902), Classe (1937), and Hollister
(1939) had subjects tap their finger in time to the rhythm
of syllables. The resulting behaviors were fairly consistent from one investigation to the next. Newcomb (1961)
had subjects move an audible click around in syllables
until they felt the click coincided with the syllable beat.
The derived click locations showed some relation to the
places where subjects had tapped. Together, these studies
pointed to a syllable-beat location related to a maximum
of physiological and acoustic energy in the production of
the syllable. The investigators felt that the onset of
the nuclear vowel of the syllable is a peak toward which
the articulation of the initial consonant builds and after
which the syllable energy tapers off. Thus, the onset of
the nuclear vowel (or the release of the last consonant
before the nuclear vowel) was seen as the location of the
syllable-beat.

Although there was agreement in principle from one
study to the next, the published data did not always
support the alleged relationships. Incomplete experimental
design precluded generalized conclusions, and uncalibrated
errors in the apparatus threw doubt on some of the parti-
culars. In order to clarify this problem of syllable-beat
location, we therefore designed experiments in finger-
tapping and click-locating in such a manner as to clarify
differences between subjects, differences between dialects,
and differences between phonetic syllable types. The
tapping experiment was mentioned earlier when we wrote of
distinguishing stress-timed from syllable-timed languages.

The need for reliable estimates of the location and
variability of response, be it a tap or a click-placement,
required that subjects give many responses to the same
(i.e., phonetically identical) utterance. Since many
responses were required, and since it is impossible to
obtain two or more phonetically identical utterances in a
normal conversation, utterances were selected from recorded conversation and played many times for the subjects.[4]

Preliminary investigations showed intersubject
differences in tapping to be quite large, and so only
three subjects were used. The use of such a small number
of subjects had the double advantage of allowing every
subject to respond to every syllable. This complete
design was statistically desirable. The subjects used in
the click-placing experiment were two of the three subjects employed in the tapping experiment.

From an hour-long recorded conversation with the three subjects nine utterances were chosen, three from each subject's speech, satisfying the following constraints:

(1) Each utterance was bounded at both ends by a major rhythmic juncture so that the utterances were rhythmically "complete".

(2) There was some variation in rhythmic structure over the several utterances.

(3) There was a broad sampling of phonetic types of syllable-onset in the rhythmically accented syllables so that the relation between beat-location and phonetic material would be clarified.

(4) Each utterance was fairly even in loudness, so that audibility was not affected in shifting attention from one part of the utterance to another.

(5) Utterances were long enough to have interesting rhythmic patterns but not be inefficient to play over and over.

These utterances were recorded at 7-1/2 inches per second on 30-inch loops of high-quality magnetic tape.

In the first experiment subjects tapped their finger to a specified syllable on each playing of the loop; fifty taps were recorded for each syllable. In the second experiment subjects moved a click around in the syllable until they felt that the click coincided with the place where they had tapped their fingers in the first experiment; fifteen placements were given for each syllable by each subject. Experimental apparatus and schedules of stimulus presentation for the tapping and click-placing experiments are given in a study by Allen (1966).

The fifty taps and fifteen click placements to each syllable formed distributions whose means were compared as locators of the syllable-beat. As we noted earlier, comparison of the variances of the distributions gave information about the rhythm or stress associated with the syllable.

The means of the tapping distributions were found to
differ depending on which subject was tapping and which
syllable he was tapping to. The displacement in time
(bias) of the mean of the subject's taps from the moment
of onset of the nuclear vowel of a syllable was different
for different subjects and for different initial consonant
sequence durations. Bias was calibrated for a given
subject by having him tap to a regular sequence of clicks;
the average displacement of his taps from these clicks was
found to compare fairly closely with the average displacement of his taps from the onset of the nuclear vowels of
syllables. Comparison of the average displacement of a
subject's taps from the onset of the nuclear vowel of a
syllable with the duration of the initial consonant sequence of that syllable yielded Pearson correlations of
.66, .33, and .20 for the three subjects. Since displace-
ments were almost always forward in time (i.e., taps
preceded the vowel-onset), we may state the results of
the tapping experiment as they relate to syllable-beat
location as follows: The onset of the nuclear vowel can
be taken as the beat to which the subject is tapping. The
amount by which his taps will precede the vowel-onset is a
function primarily of the subject and of the duration of
the consonant sequence preceding the vowel in the syllable.

The distributions of click-placements also exhibited
biases, but these biases were harder to calibrate. The
mean click placements for the two subjects were not
statistically different, but, although click placements
were close to the tapping locations, these two were
statistically different, and there was no clear relationship between click placements and either tapping locations
or nuclear vowel-onset.

The magnitude of variations in bias and of differences
between tapping locations and click placements within and
between subjects is about one to four centiseconds.
Because differences in interstress interval durations
due to stress-timing effects should be at least this great,
we can use the onset of the nuclear vowel as the location
of the syllable beat with not too great a loss of accuracy.

Let us now summarize what we have written above.
After showing that the usual definition of stress- and
syllable-timing is inadequate, we discussed two experiments
that will show how reliably people can classify languages

279

as stress-timed and syllable-timed, and whether our rhythmic behavior differs from language to language, according to this classification. These experiments will tell us how valid the stress- versus syllable-timed distinction is in linguistics and how various languages should be classified.

Since English is supposedly a stress-timed language, stresses in connected English speech should show a tendency toward equal spacing. After indicating some of the important influences on the duration of speech segments, we described three experiments that will tell just what kind of "tendency toward equal spacing" the stresses of English show. The hypothesis under consideration is that successive interstress interval durations may be (1) uncorrelated, (2) positively correlated, or (3) negatively correlated. Each of these three possibilities leads to a different interpretation of the underlying rhythmic process. The experiments we described will use pairs of utterances chosen to control best for extraneous changes in the durations of the interstress intervals studied.

Finally, we showed that the time of onset of the nuclear vowel of a stressed syllable may be taken as the location of the down beat of the rhythmic foot to which that syllable belongs. The interstress intervals studied in the experiments mentioned above will then be the intervals between two successive stress beats.

References

Allen, G. <u>Two behavioral experiments on the location of the syllable beat in spoken American English</u>. (Doctoral dissertation, University of Michigan) Ann Arbor, Mich.: University Microfilms, 1966. No. 6708203.

Classe, A. <u>The rhythm of English prose</u>. Oxford: Blackwell, 1939.

Cooker, H. S. <u>Time relationships of chest wall movements and intraoral pressures during speech</u>. (Doctoral dissertation, State University of Iowa) Ann Arbor, Mich.: University Microfilms, 1963. No. 64-3357.

Fraisse, P. <u>The psychology of time</u>. New York: Harper & Row, 1963.

Halliday, M. A. K. The tones of English. Archivum
     Linguisticum, 1963, 15 (1), 1-28.

Hollister, R. D. T. Relation between hand and voice
     impulse movements. Speech Monogr., 1937, 4 (1),
     75-100.

Kozhevnikov, V. A. & Chistovich, L. A. Speech: articula-
     tion and perception. Moscow, Leningrad, 1965 (JPRS:
     30, 543, April 1967).

Ladefoged, P., Draper, M. H., & Whitterridge, D. Syllables
     and stress. Misc. Phonet., 1958, 3, 1-14.

Miyake, I. Researches on rhythmic action. Stud. from the
     Yale Psychol. Lab., 1902, 10, 1-48.

Newcomb, W. B. The perceptual basis of syllable boundary.
     Unpublished manuscript, General Dynamics Corporation,
     Rochester, New York, 1961.

O'Malley, M. H. & Peterson, G. E. An experimental method
     for prosodic analysis. Phonetica, 1966, 15 (1),
     1-13.

Peterson, G. E. & Lehiste, I. Duration of syllable nuclei
     in English. J. acoust. Soc. Amer., 1960, 32 (6),
     693-703.

Stetson, R. H. Motor phonetics. Amsterdam: North-
     Holland, 1951.

Williamson, K. A grammar of the Kolokuma dialect of Ijo.
     New York: Cambridge University Press, 1965.

Woodrow, H. Time perception. In S. S. Stevens (Ed.),
     Handbook of experimental psychology. New York:
     Wiley & Sons, 1951. Pp. 1224-1236.

Footnotes

[1]This report is based on research supported by a
contract with the Office of Education, U. S. Department
of Health, Education & Welfare, P. L. 83-531, Cooperative
Research, and Title VI, P. L. 85-564, as amended.

[2]The author is a member of the research staff at the
Center for Research on Language and Language Behavior.

281

[3]Since this writing two unrelated studies have been found whose data support the validity of this kind of "temporal memory" for English and Russian. Kozhevnikov and Chistovich (1965) found that the random variations in the durations of repeated Russian sentences were less than the sum of the variations of the component syllables (cf. Chapter 3, §3, pp. 91 ff. and especially Fig. 3.13, p. 99). Therefore the variations of the successive syllables are negatively correlated. Peterson and Lehiste (1960), although they write that sentence durations vary widely among speakers, show that within one speaker's utterances the standard error of the durations of his test-frame sentences was about 4% of the total length of the sentence (6.9 : 174). This figure agrees closely with the Kozhevnikov and Chistovich data and is about half the value that would be predicted from other studies on variations in repeated time intervals (cf. Woodrow, p. 1225). There does seem to be an internal clock operating at a level higher than motor articulation.

[4]Subjects tapped while listening to these recordings, and so it must be understood that the syllable-beat investigated in these experiments is a perceived syllable-beat. Nevertheless, although a speaker might not tap in the same place while speaking as he would if he listened to a recording of the same utterance, there still should be some close kinesthetic relation between the two kinds of taps.

WHAT IS HAPPENING IN PHONETIC RESEARCH[1]

Peter Ladefoged[2]

It would be in the spirit of the Center for Research on Language and Language Behavior if we had a small experiment to begin with, an experiment to find out what you would like me to talk about. On the other hand, within the traditions of all psychological experimentation, it will be a forced-choice experiment, and I will give you two choices only, which you will mark A or B. If you mark "Don't know," then you leave. There are two things which, in all seriousness, I had prepared to talk about. I can't fit them both in, so I would like to know because I just don't know this audience enough to know what would be most profitable. The first thing I had in mind is: what are the interesting questions in phonetic research, i.e., what should the phonetician be doing now? (And the brief answer, which I would elaborate, is that he should be working on what is the nature of a distinctive-feature theory, and what is the relation between competence and performance). The other choice would be to try to answer the question that people often ask me: "How much does it cost to set up an experimental phonetics laboratory?" A short answer to this question is about $9,000 per year for the first three years, and rising exponentially.

As for the first--and more important question--I am afraid that much of what I will say will not be news to many of you who are doing precisely these things. One of them is related to the paper we have just heard [George Allen, Toward a Description of Stress-Timing in Spoken English], which is in some sense, as I'm sure you know and will point out, the relation between competence and performance. So, before dealing with that one, which is in a way more interesting, let me say a few words about the distinctive-feature theory.

Most people will agree with what is becoming a common view that all descriptions of the phonologies of a language involve, in some sense, some form of the distinctive-features theory. Now, I don't mean that they involve a Jacobsonian one, or anything like that. Rather, I simply

283

mean--and this is a remark that Chomsky has made--that if you describe a language, at some stage you refer to things as being "voiced" as opposed to "voiceless", "alveolar," or "acute" as opposed to "grave", "strident" as opposed to "non-strident", "fricative" as opposed to "non-fricative". It doesn't matter what labels you use or whether you put them in binary terms. Any phonetic description ultimately involves talking in terms of categories.

The real question concerning this is: Is it profitable to talk as if there were a limited number of categories? Whatever the categories are, is it true, as I think Martin Joos said, that languages differ in innumerable ways? J. R. Firth also said that you couldn't compare languages in that way. And, in the traditional position, I think Charles Hockett, in his manual of phonology, makes the point that you can't set up a taxonomy of phonetic features which will be sufficient to cover all languages of the world. I would maintain that you have to behave as if it were possible, or else you cannot do anything about comparing one language with another. In fact, you can't ever relate your description to some kind of reality.

I don't think it turns out to be difficult, as people sometimes make out, provided you observe the distinction (which Morris Halle was probably the first to make absolutely explicit) that, in order to talk about oppositions within one language, you need distinctions like "voiced" as opposed to "voiceless", as compared with the distinctions you need in order to talk about differences between languages. That is, many languages do have a contrast between "voiced" and "voiceless", whatever you prefer, but English may have less voicing in it than French, as a kind of stock example. So that you could have a limited number of categories for talking about phonemic types or positions and, later on in your description, you could say there were 60 degrees of voicing in French as compared with about 10 degrees, or whatever you like, in English. This, I think, relates to what is currently called, in generative phonology, the two levels of systematic phonemics and systematic phonetics. The talking about oppositions on the level of "voiced"-- "voiceless" is on the systematic-phonemic level and is all that one needs when describing the lexicon of a given language. The other one, saying it is 60 degrees as compared with 10 degrees in some other language, would be the oppositions you need at the systematic-phonetic level.

I would, of course, in my concepts of generative phonology, like to go one step further and actually relate them. I think it is essential that one does relate them to physical phonetics, so that we have a kind of three-step effort: from systematic phonemics and systematic phonetics through to physical phonetics (physical phonetics being actual sounds). And generative phonology should be one that generates (in a literal sense that is usually a speech synthesizer or something like that) actual sounds.

Then, of course, as soon as you have progressed that far, you are not talking about the differences between languages. Now you have to give them particular values, and they correspond to differences between individual speakers. But, unless you do go so far as to make the phonological description realizeable, i.e., in terms of actual sounds, you cannot say that you have a complete phonological description. It is completely untestable and becomes quite unreal because you have no way of knowing whether another description, which had all the same labels but in reversed positions (or in distinctive-feature terms wrote <u>plus</u> for every <u>minus</u>, or something like that), would be equally valid, unless you actually can at some stage give physical content to these measures.

From the phonetician's point of view we are concerned with the last two stages. We are concerned with the level of systematic phonetics and the physical phonetics. Now, I don't want to talk about the way of going across them, from the one to the other, at the moment. If you don't know it, I suggest that you might like to hear that there is some significant work, not in terms of distinctive features in the traditional sense, i.e., the Jakobsonian sense, by some people in the Joint Speech Research Unit of the British Post Office in England. The Post Office, is responsible for the telephone company and, so, to a lesser extent, this Unit corresponds to the British Bell Laboratories, or something like that. One of the projects by these people has been to show that you can, from a phonetic transcription, type into a computer and the computer has what corresponds to a "look-up" program. It looks up the values corresponding to each of these segments. For example, you type in <u>cat</u>. It looks up the value for /k/, the value for /ae/ and the value of /t/. It computes the transition between them and then generates signals which will operate a speech synthesizer. In fact, the program now includes generating prosodic information. You type in full stops, question marks regarding them, etc., of course, as phonetic elements, and the computer will interpret them and give the resulting sentences the correct intonation and, to a limited sense, the correct rhythm.

Now, the speech that they produce is a long way from being perfect, but this strikes me as one of the interesting things that phoneticians ought to be doing, namely, in a literal sense, what Haskins Lab talked about years ago--the synthesizing of speech by rules. The Haskins rules were not computable, i.e., you couldn't put them into a computer. They were never explicit. The first published set of these rules (and the paper includes a total set of rules and values for the computer) is, I believe, the work by Holmes, Mattingley and Sherm.

Now, let me get on to the other question: "What is the relation between what is called linguistic competence and linguistic performance?" A speaker's competence has been said to be his knowledge of the language. I don't like the term "knowledge" in that sense because it is, of course, not explicit knowledge, and it is using the word "knowledge" in a very unusual way. Rather, it concerns the rules that govern his usage of the language, as opposed to the rules that govern his behavior as a speaker. As for rules that govern his usage, we can take again a Chomsky-type example. There are a whole set of words, like demonstration, contemplation, etc., where you get demon - stration with a reduced vowel, and contem - plation, as contrasted with a whole set of words like relaxation and condensation. I think it's true with most Americans that one vowel is not a reduced vowel in any kind of sense, whereas the other one is. Now, this is part of a speaker's competence in the sense that he obeys a set of rules. And you can formulate what the rule is that distinguishes between these two sets of words. In case you haven't guessed what the difference is--I must admit that I didn't realize by a long way what the difference was--the sure difference is that one set is derived from words like demonstrate and demonstration, whereas the other is derived from words like relax and relaxation. Because the derived structure contains relax (it contains the full vowel), it remains when you add the ending; whereas, when the ending is added in the other set, the vowel is probably already reduced or, at least, partially reduced before that time. So that's my competence. I know this, though not explicitly. I couldn't have verbalized it until it had been pointed out to me. But I know it in the sense that, in words like

286

penetration and eradication (I have a whole list of such
words), one behaves as if they all followed into the set.
I behave that way but, on the other hand, I can't possibly
believe that when I say one of these words I generate my
utterance by going through those rules. There is a great
gap between my performance as a speaker, and my knowledge.
This seems to be one of the interesting things that one
should investigate: what is the relationship between
linguistic units of the kind that one needs to express the
facts of the language like that, and the performance units
that one needs to express how the speaker is performing.

Since you may not know about a speaker's performance,
let me tell you very quickly about one or two experiments
that are going on. I think the first thing that I want
to separate out is the difference between what a speaker
can do, from what a speaker does do. What I'm interested
in is what a speaker normally does in his usual speech.
Incidentally, if I had time, I would have liked to talk
about performance, not as a speaker only but as a listener
also. Now, I won't separate out what a listener can do
from what he normally does do. The examples there are
easier to distinguish. I mean, it's quite easy to show
that listeners can, in experimental conditions, differentiate between very small elements of time in sequences
that are going on if you play them things over and over
again. I don't think that they normally do do that and,
if you put them in other circumstances where they are
forced to listen to the words more as words and get some
kind of content from them, they can't distinguish between
small orders of time.

But really I think it's more profitable to discuss
the experiments about how a speaker controls his ordinary
speech. Let me again draw your attention, in case you
don't know it, a recent Russian work by Kozhevnikov and
Chistovich, which is causing quite a lot of interest among
phonetic circles. (We now require it as a textbook for
our courses in experimental phonetics.) I made a note
because I thought it worth knowing that it has been
translated into English, a publication of the Joint
Publications Research Service of the Department of
Commerce. (Its number if you want to get it is 30, 543,
and it's worth having a look at.) Now, one of the things
which I have said it before, but which they have expressed
rather neatly (and I picked the idea up more explicitly
from them) is that, from the performance point of view,

you might say the same sentence at a slow rate, as compared
with a fast rate. If I say, for example, "The cat sat on
the mat" (slowly), as compared with, "The cat sat on the
mat" (faster), or something like that, we say that these
two sentences are the same. I think they probably are.
I think if we want to describe them, it would be an
impossible linguistic task if we said that each time the
rate was the thing that made things come out with a
difference. Actually, the sentences differed in ways
other than just the rate, for they had different units
involved. Now, suppose they have the same units involved.
It would mean that the units were coming along differently: in one case slowly, and in the other case spinning
out more rapidly. This is the hypothesis that they have
suggested. And if this is true, an interesting kind of
experiment is possible. That is, make a number of recordings of a number of speakers uttering sentences like that
and then measure the duration, first of all, say, of the
ratio of each phoneme to the sentence as a whole. Now,
that ratio should be constant, if the phoneme were what
you said things in terms of. When you send out more
phonemes more rapidly, that should simply mean that the
ratio of the phonemes to the sentence as a whole should
remain constant.

Well, of course, it doesn't. I mean, anyone can see
that you just say the sentence very slowly and you don't
lengthen all phonemes equally. Well, what do you lengthen
equally? What words or what segments of words or
syllables are there that remain constant so that you can
say that the timing is in terms of these? I think that
you can say that, in view of the last paper that we've
just had, our preliminary results show that probably the
smallest unit that remains constant is something that, in
terms of British phonology, would be called a <u>foot</u>, that
is, a unit with a single-stressed syllable, and with an
associated unstressed syllable. It isn't even a syllable
that remains constant, because it's the stressed syllable,
and the unstressed syllable is associated with it. I
don't want to be pressed on whether that's really true or
not, because this experiment is currently in progress and
there may turn out to be some hitches in it.

There is another experiment going on at UCLA on a
speaker's electromyographic activity. That is a recording
of what the muscles actually do in an effort to find out
about the invariance of the command to the muscles. Again,

I can cite a simple example. Take words like "bee" and "bah" and "boo," or "bid" or "did," or words of this kind, and ask, "Is it true that there is a single command sent to the lips for the consonant b̲ and another command sent out for a rounded vowel, if there is a rounded vowel?" It turns out that you can't predict the results that we get in terms of a single command for each phoneme. It turns out that the command for "boo" differs as a whole from the command for "bee" and "do," because speakers produce things in terms of larger chunks. If that is so, what is this relationship? What is this thing called linguistic competence? Quite plainly, in another sense, as Morris Halle remarked again, a phoneme is a non-fictional unit in the sense that all the laws of sound changes are expressed in terms of phonemes or traditional variance of phonemes, if nothing else. Can we say anything about the relationship between how a man performs and what his linguistic competence is? I'm afraid I can't give an answer because I said that all I was going to try to do was suggest that there are a number of problems.

Footnotes

[1]This report is based on a transcription of the tapes. Because of the factors of time and distance, the Editor assumed the responsibility of editing the tapes and preparing this report. Where there were difficulties in understanding the technical content of the message from the tapes, the Editor had the assistance of both George Allen and John Hemdal, who appeared on the program with Dr. Ladefoged. Furthermore, the Editor rephrased sections, in which the speaker was referring to material he had written on the blackboard, in order to make them more understandable to readers of this volume.

[2]The author is a professor of phonetics at the University of California, Los Angeles.

INTELLIGENCE TESTS AND EDUCATIONALLY-RELEVANT MEASUREMENTS[1]

Loren S. Barritt[2]

The concept of general intelligence and the instruments which provide its operational definition have been with us for a long time (McNemar, 1964; Burt). Recently, however, a concern about the use of intelligence tests with minority group children has caused at least one large school system (New York City) to remove these tests from use (Loretan, 1966). I do not propose to deal with the specific issues raised by "civil rights" groups about these tests but prefer, rather, to deal with the broader questions which ought to be asked about the utility of intelligence tests in school settings.

Quinn McNemar addressed himself to these broader issues recently in his presidential address to the APA (McNemar, 1964). He began by asking the rhetorical question, "Lost our intelligence? Why?" The double entendre was, I am sure, intentional. McNemar defended intelligence tests against the onslaught of civil rights groups, "legislators," "school people" and statistically naive researchers. Any attempt on my part to interpret his remarks must of necessity lose something in translation. His argument seems to boil down to this:

(1) General intelligence tests are able to predict school achievement as well as, or better than, anything else available, including differential aptitude batteries, and measures of creativity. They are, therefore, useful "tools."

(2) Because they predict so well, we ought not to abandon intelligence now that it is being attacked. If we do, we might wind up with something which is not as "socially useful".

The above statements are generally accepted by psychologists and educators who deal with these instruments. I find myself in disagreement with this point of view.

It is my conviction that intelligence tests are not useful tools in an educational setting and, further, that there is little danger in abandoning the tests because we can do much better. It is the purpose of this paper to explicate the reasons why intelligence is not a useful educational concept, and to suggest better alternatives.

Professor McNemar's paper is a useful point of departure for an examination of the issues because it is the work of a highly respected scholar in the field who has set forth the generally-accepted reasons for the tests. His paper is a useful foil for this discussion.

Intelligence Tests Are Good Predictors

Certainly it must be acknowledged that intelligence tests are capable of predicting success in school, as well as, or better than, other psychological tests. The ability to predict does not by itself, however, guarantee the value of an instrument. This issue is a critical one because it is generally accepted that the demonstration of correlation with some relevant criterion is sufficient evidence for the value of a test. I would dispute such a claim.

My disagreement is based on the conviction that the scientist, who works on educational problems and who claims social utility for his procedures, cannot divorce himself from normative questions. Education is a value-loaded enterprise, and all those who investigate it participate in making value decisions. The point is well-illustrated in the present case. It is necessary to consider the goal of any test before deciding what evidence is required to demonstrate its value or utility. It seems clear that the goals of education are not adequately served by a test which does no more than predict future success.

It is the purpose of education to change behavior by providing the most succinct, effective treatments possible. To do this it is necessary to have information about intra- and inter-individual differences, and their interaction with various learning programs. A test which only predicts the likelihood of future success does not provide this information.

Let me illustrate this point with an analogy to the medical profession.

The medical model is the right one in the present case because the goals, diagnosis and treatment, are consonant with those in education. Suppose a doctor were to give you a test of general health. If he said, "You have a low score; your chances for life are not very good." Such a prediction might be extremely accurate but most of us would find the information useless because it doesn't identify the areas of difficulty and hence suggests no program of treatment for remediation of the problem. Fortunately, doctors don't operate with a single test but, rather, use several tests which examine specific areas of functioning. A diagnosis is made based upon this infor- mation. A program of remediation can then be built upon this differential diagnosis. This is the procedure which we should seek to emulate in an educational setting.

Prediction by itself is not helpful. As Cronbach (1958) has said: "Predicting outcome has no social value unless the psychologist or the subject himself can use the information to make better choices of treatment. The prediction must help to determine a treatment for every individual."

I. O. Interpretation

The I. O. which an intelligence test yields not only provides no information about diagnosis and treatment but there is evidence (Rosenthal and Jacobson, 1966) that it can effect the behavior of teachers toward children with- out their being aware of it. One might say that this is the fault of the teacher who doesn't know how to use the score, which is, in one sense, true. Teachers are not technically sophisticated with respect to test interpre- tation. But what could the technically sophisticated say about the I. O. that would be different from the teacher's reaction? What is the appropriate interpretation of an I. Q. score?

The answer to these questions must rest upon the definition or meaning of intelligence. The construct of intelligence has proven rather difficult to define and it has even become acceptable to deny the need for definition (McNemar, 1964; Hayes, 1962, p. 299). Most, perhaps all, of the difficulties discussed in this paper can be traced to this lack of definition.

Measurement is the process of assigning numerals to represent properties (Campbell, 1920). It is a shorthand which permits the manipulation of properties that would otherwise be inaccessible. Though psychologists have been unable to clarify what is meant by intelligence, it has nevertheless been measured. How do we know it is intelligence that has been measured? Because our measurements correlate with other intellectual attainments. The circularity is well known.

What does not seem to be recognized, however, is that, as a result of this lack of clarity in definition teachers, when asked to translate the shorthand back into behavior, provide their own definition for intelligence. This is done implicitly, but done, nonetheless. These definitions all carry to one degree or another the idea of inherited ability which, at least in some measure, is a part of most psychological definitions of intelligence.

The fixity of intelligence is built into the I. Q. and contributes to misinterpretation. What can a teacher do to change nature or the I. Q.?

It is popular today to denigrate the view that intelligence is primarily an inherited characteristic. This viewpoint is not reflected in the I. Q. scores themselves, which are still stable over time (by design) and, consequently, resistant to change with learning. It is difficult for anyone technically sophisticated, or not, to interpret an I. Q. as anything but a score, fixed, in part, by inheritence, which identifies bright, average and dull children. In an educational setting, where our aim is to expand the intellect, it would seem beneficial to discontinue the use of tests which are misleading in this way.

Even if one believes in the primacy of nature over nurture and the fixity of intellectual development, there is cause to question whether this conception is a useful one for an _educational_ program. Education ought to be guided by a search for effective treatments. Until there is clear evidence that we _cannot_ teach certain children to amplify their intellectual skills (and when we get this much information we will probably have the ability to alleviate any such handicaps), we ought to continue to try. It might be said that education seeks to overcome nature with nurture. This may be an impossible task, but if one strives toward this end there is no need to fear that we haven't aimed high enough.

293

Educationally Relevant Measurements

The utility of intelligence tests has been challenged here on two grounds. First, that the prediction of future success is not useful in an educational setting unless there is some prescription for treatment provided and, second, that scores are inherently misinterpretable and lead teachers et al to unfortunate conclusions about children.

It is not untrue to say that intelligence tests provide teachers, with answers to questions which were never asked. Our technical skills seem to lead us astray. Obviously in such cases the tail is wagging the dog.

Education asks about the relationship between treatments and outcomes. What is seeks is information which will help to maximize treatments to enhance outcomes. These are questions about causes and effects. Correlational studies do not provide evidence to resolve such questions. What is required are experimental studies of the relationships between student characteristics, educational treatments and outcomes. These studies might well use information from correlational research to build hypotheses about these relationships. Intelligence tests might provide a reservoir of skills to be measured in conjunction with treatments to determine the nature of the interactions.

The development of treatment-relevant tests should be accompanied by a change in the procedure for reporting test scores to teachers. At present, scores are reported with reference to some group of people who are supposed to be relatively similar to the students we are testing. Further, this assumption is usually a tenuous one. This reference point has little value in the development of treatment programs. The reason for this in the case of the I. Q. is clear. The property we have tried to measure is not represented by the system we have chosen for the translation of raw scores. We have related scores to people. What we have is a kind of sociological yardstick. What we need is a system for reporting scores that is related to the treatments which will be prescribed. We need norms which relate scores to skills, rather than to some nebulous mean of a large group.

The principle involved in the translation of raw scores by reference to averages for groups is directed at specifying what should be expected of children at some point in their life. It tries to represent the individual performance but ends up describing a group. The value of studying groups to describe individuals seems limited at best. The specifying of the group mean as a point of reference does not accomplish the goal of representing individual performance norms.

To relate scores to skills would certainly require a more rigorous delineation of that which needs to be mastered and taught. It would further require precise definitions of skills so that meaningful numbers could be derived.

Let me summarize. What I am suggesting is a change in the procedures for validating educational test scores. Since we want to know about the relationship between treatments and outcomes, we must use procedures that speak to such questions, i.e., experimental procedures. Further scores should be reported with reference to the skills, rather than the people, tested. The development of skill-norms is possible with the changes in procedure suggested above.

Language and Language Behavior

Language facility is the coin of the realm in schools. You either have it or you fail. Most intelligence tests place heavy emphasis upon language skills. It seems reasonable to expect that a good beginning toward the goal of educationally-relevant assessment will be attained by measurement of language variables.

It should be clear that if and when we begin to measure those aspects of language performance that are related to educational treatments we will at the same time be improving our understanding of human cognition. It should also be clear that by using experimental tryout procedures in the classroom we can begin to take insights directly from the laboratory and test their value in classrooms.

This is precisely the kind of interaction between laboratory research and educational treatments that the Center for Research on Language and Language Behavior can make, and has already made, possible. I think it

295

significant that this very room [TV Classroom] is used daily for both our subjects in carefully-controlled psychological experiments and also to teach children to read.

Education attempts to teach skills which can amplify the human mind (Bruner, 1965). Psychology has developed procedures for the study of human behavior. There is virtue in the combination of these enterprises. Education, with its goals can direct psychology with its procedures to more relevant and useful research. A closer cooperation is to the benefit of both groups. Psychology has allowed itself to lose sight of the fascinating problems of human learning and performance. Education has often chosen the most expedient non-solution for its considerable problems. A wedding of the two areas should make it easier to justify research into relevant problems with appropriate techniques. A center for research on language and language behavior is a natural place for the ceremony to take place.

References

Anastasi, Anne, "Psychology, Psychologists and Psychological Testing", American Psychologist, 1967, 22, 297-306.

Bruner, Jerome S., "The Growth of Mind", American Psychologist, 1965, 20, 1007-1017.

Burt, Cyril, "The Evidence for the Concept of Intelligence". British Journal of Educational Psychology, 1955, 25, 158-177.

Campbell, N. R., Physics, The Elements, Cambridge University Press, London, 1920, 565 pp.

Carroll, John B., "Factors of-Verbal-Achievement", Proceedings of the 1961 Invitational Conference on Testing Problems, Educational Testing Service, 1962, 11-18.

Carroll, John B., "The Nature of the Data, or How to Choose a Correlation Coefficient", Psychometrika, 1961, 26, 4, 347-372.

Combs, Arthur W., "Intelligence from a Perceptual Point of View", <u>Journal of Abnormal and Social Psychology</u>, 1952, <u>47</u>, 662-673.

Cronbach, Lee J., "The Two Disciples of Scientific Psychology," <u>American Psychologist</u>, 1957, <u>12</u>, 671-684.

Ferguson, George A., "On Learning and Human Ability". <u>Canadian Journal of Psychology</u>, 1954, <u>8</u>, 95-112.

Ferguson, George A., "On Transfer and the Abilities of Man", <u>Canadian Journal of Psychology</u>, 1956, <u>10</u>, 121-131.

Guilford, J. P., "Three Faces of Intellect". <u>American Psychologist</u> 1959, <u>14</u>, 469-479, in <u>Readings in the Psychology of Cognition</u>, Anderson and Ausubel (ed.), 1965, 194-214.

Hayes, Keith J., "Genes, Drives, and Intellect", <u>Psychological Reports</u>, 1962, <u>10</u>, 299-342.

Loretan, J. O., Alternatives to intelligence testing. <u>Proceedings of the 1965 Invitational Conference on Testing Problems, Educational Testing Service</u>, 1966; 19-30.

McNemar, Quinn, "Lost: Our Intelligence? Why?", <u>American Psychologist</u>, 1964, 19, <u>12</u>, pp. 871-882.

Rosenthal, R., & Jacobson, Lenore. Teachers' Expectancies: Determinants of Pupils' IQ Gains. <u>Psychological Reports</u>, 1966, <u>19</u>, 115-118.

Sigel, Irving E., "How Intelligence Tests Limit Understanding of Intelligence", <u>Merrill-Palmer Quarterly</u>, 1963, <u>9</u>, 39-56.

Vernon, Phillip E., "Ability Factors and Environmental Influences". <u>American Psychologist</u>, 1965, <u>20</u>, 723-733.

Whiteman, Martin, "Intelligence and Learning", <u>Merrill-Palmer Quarterly</u>, 1964, <u>10</u>, 297-309.

Footnotes

[1] This report is based on research supported by a contract with the Office of Education, U. S. Department of Health, Education & Welfare, P. L. 83-531, Cooperative Research, and Title VI, P. L. 85-564, as amended.

[2] The author is a member of the research staff at the Center for Research on Language and Language Behavior, and an assistant professor in the Department of Education, University of Michigan.

IMPROVING LANGUAGE PERFORMANCE OF YOUNG CHILDREN:

A PROGRESS REPORT

Evan R. Keislar and Carolyn Stern[1]

There are two strongly-held positions with regard to
how the young child should obtain his first basic learnings,
and how he should acquire language to which he needs to
respond and with which he can control his environment.
One school of thought holds that it is the function and
obligation of the parent to make sure that the child is
exposed to these learning experiences in his own home. A
young child provided with a normal environment will develop
the requisite behaviors "naturally". From this point of
view, there is no need for any type of formal education
for the pre-kindergarten child.

The second approach holds that a great many young
children are disadvantaged upon entering formal schooling
just because their homes do not provide the requisite opportunities to nurture this unfolding of innate abilities.
For such children, the enriching experiences routinely
provided by middle-class parents must be supplied by a
professional agency in the form of a compensatory or
intervention nursery program.

Once the latter position is accepted, there is still
a great deal of room for discussion as to what type of
program is most appropriate or effective in remediating
the deficiencies. A wide variety of formal programs for
the culturally-disadvantaged child are now being carried
on around the country. These may be viewed as lying along
a continuum defined in terms of the degree of structure
provided. At one extreme is the position exemplified by
many nursery schools where the curriculum is regarded
primarily as a substitute for the normal middle-class home
environment. The child is placed within a social setting
where he must learn to relate to his peers as well as to
adults. By virtue of this experience, it is argued, the
child will be prepared to meet future school demands,
including those of facility with language.

At the other extreme is the view that language deficiencies can best be compensated in a systematically-structured program, such as that of Bereiter and Engelmann (1966). Their procedures include a total curriculum which occupies the major portion of the child's nursery school day. The emphasis is on a type of patterned repetition through which the child's mastery of the basic academic skills of reading, writing, and arithmetic are formally developed.

Along various points of this continuum, between the two extremes just described, are to be found the programs of Gray and Klaus, George Peabody College; Weikart, Perry Preschool Project, Ypsilanti, Michigan; Hodges and Spiker, University of Indiana; and Sprigle, Jacksonville, Florida, among many others.

The Preschool Research Program at the University of California, Los Angeles, has adopted a structured approach to improving language performance of the young culturally-disadvantaged child which differs from other similar programs in three important ways. First, the total amount of time in which the child is involved in the programmed activities is only 15 minutes a day. Secondly, the materials are designed to be administered by a "non-professional" adult, such as a teacher's aid, who can supervise a small group of children, while the teacher is conducting the usual preschool curriculum with the remainder of the class. Finally, the program is focussed specifically on improving the child's use of language. Instruction is organized to reflect three fundamental uses of language: expressive (how the individual communicates his thoughts, emotions, and wants to others); receptive (how the individual responds to the instructions, commands, and verbalizations of others); and mediational (how the individual uses his own language in solving a wide variety of problems).

A series of studies is being carried out in a systematic effort to achieve two related goals: the generation of viable programs to promote instruction in the three areas described above, and the testing of a number of hypotheses directly relevant to the preparation of such programs.

New instruments for language assessment

Of critical importance is the ability to define the desired outcomes in a clear and objective fashion. To this end it has been necessary to construct a number of new instruments to assess the child's language performance, before as well as after instruction.

The first of these measures is an auditory discrimination task which avoids a critical weakness in existing instruments of this type. In many tests, the child's ability to discriminate sounds is measured in terms of how well he can classify pairs of auditory stimuli as either the "same" or "different." Culturally-disadvantaged preschool children find this task very difficult. A test which involves the comparator function will have low validity insofar as scores reflect the child's inability to understand the instructions, rather than how well he can discriminate the stimuli.

The Children's Auditory Discrimination Inventory (CADI) uses 38 pairs of pictures. One of each pair represents a familiar object, called by its appropriate label; the other a nonsense picture to which a nonsense di-syllable has been arbitrarily assigned. (See Fig. 1.) The child is told "This is a table and this is a pable. Put your finger on the table." An equal number of real and nonsense words are called for, but in random order.

The words selected were based on a hierarchy of difficulty of phonemic consrasts, ranging from exceedingly gross discriminations (e.g., girl - hujuj) to minimal pairs (e.g., fish - fith). The real words and pictures were pretested with a comparable population and found to be well within the children's response repertoire. The nonsense stimuli were selected from those rated low in association value in a study with a similar population. In the preliminary work with this instrument, internal reliability of .74 was obtained with a population of 85 kindergarten children.

A second instrument, the Visual Discrimination Inventory (VDI), is concerned with the assessment of the child's ability to discriminate visual stimuli. Most

Fig. 1. Sample Item from Children's Auditory Discrimination Inventory.

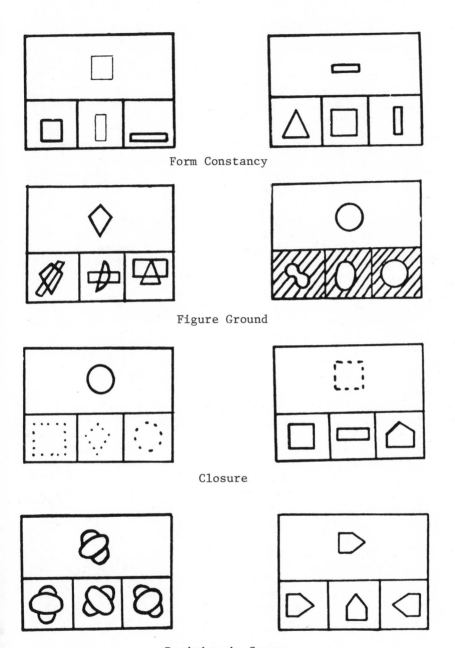

Form Constancy

Figure Ground

Closure

Position in Space

Fig. 2. Sample Item from Visual Discrimination Inventory

303

available tests of this skill require the child to produce
a written response which usually demands a high order of
motor control. Again the measurement of discrimination
is confounded by irrelevant characteristics of the response.
To provide a more valid test, the VDI requires the child
to indicate his ability to discriminate forms by a simple
selection response. The four areas under which the
discrimination tasks are subsumed are: form constancy,
figure-ground, closure, and position-in-space. Samples
of each of these types of items are shown in Fig. 2.
There are 52 items in the test, which takes approximately
10 minutes to administer.

In a short preliminary sequence, training in the
selection task is provided. The children are taught to
match one of three pictures with a model, using familiar
objects such as a cat, ball, etc. Only after ten correct
selections in a row have been made is the child given the
Visual Discrimination Inventory. The reliability of this
instrument, based on 209 children (47 three-year-olds,
87 four-year-olds and 75 five-year-olds) was .91 when
corrected for attenuation.

To provide a measure of expressive language, a
sequence of four tests, ordered in complexity, has been
devised. At the lowest level is a task which requires
only simple imitation. The Echoic Response Inventory for
Children (ERIC) presents the child with a series of
utterances, each of which has been analyzed for difficulty
by transformational analysis. The rationale for the
echoic responding test is that a chain of verbal responses
present in the child's repertoire is a much simpler matter
to produce than one which is an unfamiliar stimulus
pattern. Many studies have confirmed the facilitating
effect of familiarity on the retention and reproduction
of verbal stimuli. (Cf. Underwood and Schulz, 1963.)
This instrument should provide a measure of the levels of
sentence complexity which the child is capable of producing. Two equivalent forms have been prepared. (See
Table 1 for sample sentences used in each form.) The
internal reliability of the test in a pilot study with
80 children was .78.

Table 1.

Sample Items from Echoic Response Inventory for Children.

Form A	Form B
1. Dogs bark	1. Birds fly.
5. He pushed the door too hard.	5. He bounced the ball too high.
10. Ouite a good show is playing.	10. Ouite a large dog is barking.
15. If it's late, I have to hurry.	15. If it's late, he has to run.
20. If the ground is wet the children won't be able to play in the park.	20. If the weather is cold the children won't be able to swim at the beach.

The second level of difficulty in the use of expressive language is represented by the labeling task of the Expressive Vocabulary Inventory (EVI). The 40 items used in this test were selected from a list of 125 words which most children are expected to know when they enter kindergarten. It differs from the Peabody Picture Vocabulary Test in two ways. First, by providing a more adequate sampling of words for the young child it should be a more reliable instrument for this age group. Secondly, the child is required to produce the word which is appropriate for the picture, rather than to point to one of four pictures which goes with the word spoken by the examiner. In addition, the EVI has been designed to include progressive forms of verbs, prepositions, adjectives, and adverbs, as well as nouns. This test has recently been revised to provide even more representative sampling over these different parts of speech. Samples of picture descriptions, accompanying stimulus questions, and responses expected are presented in Table 2.

The quantity and quality of the child's verbal output is said to differentiate socioeconomic groups. Bernstein (1960, 1961, 1964) and John (1964, 1965) emphasize the flexible and elaborate language styles of advantaged children. In contrast, disadvantaged children are said to have "restricted" languages, i.e., to use fewer adjectives, adverbs, and progressive verb forms, especially action verbs, and to be deficient in nouns describing phenomena with which they do not have personal experience.

Several investigators have attempted to obtain empirical data to verify these assumptions. At the Institute of Developmental Studies, research studies (cf. Deutsch, et al, 1964) have used operant conditioning techniques in an unstructured situation to stimulate verbalization. In contrast, Feldmann and Weiner (1962) devised a highly-structured procedure in which children are asked to retell a story told to them about a sequence of pictures. In the first instrument, the stimuli are too uncontrolled and in the second they are too restricting.

Table 2.

Sample Items from Expressive Vocabulary Inventory

Item No.	Description of Picture	Question	Scoring Key Word
1.	fish	"What is this?"	"fish"
5.	boy swimming	"What's the boy doing?"	"swimming"
9.	cat in a box	"Where's the cat?"	"in"
33.	large and small ball	"This ball is smaller, what is this ball?"	"larger"
38.	circle and square	"This is round. What is this?"	"square"

As an alternative approach, the Preschool Language Project is trying out a semi-structured type of Verbal Output Inventory. In this instrument, children are shown five black-and-white pictures, one at a time. (See Fig. 3.) There are two country scenes, a middle-class urban scene, an urban slum street scene, and a picture of a typical zoo. For each picture, the children are instructed: "Just look at the picture" for a five-second interval before speaking; then they are to name as many things as they can. When they have stopped labeling they are asked to tell what they think is happening in the picture. Finally, they are encouraged to imagine what they think is going to happen next.

A study was carried out with this instrument in a 2 x 2 design, using ethnic and social-class variables. All the words produced by the children were recorded on magnetic tape and, except for hesitations and conjunctions, analyzed both in terms of total output and variety. The relationship between these two measures was so close ($r = .97$) that only the total output scores were used for the analyses. No significant differences for race or socioeconomic status were found. Bean (1966) also found no reliable difference in verbal output as a function of socioeconomic variables.

Approximately 60% of the speech of all the children in the sample consisted of nouns, with all the other parts of speech accounting for the other 40%. No significant differences attributable to either socioeconomic status or ethnicity were found in the part of speech-usage patterns, nor in the relationship of verbal output to the semantic content of the pictures.

The fourth test of expressive language performance being developed at UCLA is a Structured Story-Telling Test which provides the child with the opportunity of producing his own story, on the basis of pictorial stimuli. Two sets of related pictures (one two-picture and one three-picture sequence) are presented, and the child is asked to tell a story for each of the sequences. The scoring system being used at present assigns one point to each complete sentence, one point for each complete thought, and one point for recognition of continuity within the two- or three-picture sequence.

Fig. 3.   Sample Stimuli: Verbal Output Inventory for
          Children.

In the four instruments described above, the quantity and quality of the child's expressive language are assessed. In another series of tests, the child's receptive language performance is evaluated. Here attention is focussed upon whether or not the child responds correctly to the verbalizations of others. In the tests of auditory and visual discrimination, an introductory program is provided to teach the child to respond appropriately to the task instructions; only after there is evidence that the child has achieved an adequate level of performance on the receptive aspects of the task is there an attempt to assess the ability to discriminate in either of the sensory modalities. These instruments may thus be considered as tapping the very simplest level of receptive language usage.

At a higher level are a series of tests which comprise a Language Comprehension Inventory. In a subtest aimed at evaluating the child's ability to respond to prepositions, the child is asked to place a checker in the appropriate relationship to a small box (in, on, behind, etc.) or two boxes (between). Another subtest provides the child with a booklet, each page of which consists of a model, and two or three choice alternatives. The child is asked to look at the model and then mark the picture which is exactly like it. A third subtest assesses the child's familiarity with the concepts of home and family in two ways: one requires the child to manipulate two sets of cards so that he matches a number of different animals with their respective habitats; a second task requires the child to indicate whether or not a group of figures constitutes a family unit.

Verbal mediation may well be considered the highest level of language usage. The way children use their own language to help them solve problems, as well as their ability to cope with those simple logical operations controlled by sentential connectives, such as "both-and", "either-or", and "not", are tested in a series of subtests involving conjunction, disjunction, and negation. Another subtest in this series asks the child to draw inferences and solve problems on the basis of data given.

The battery of evaluation instruments is designed to assess the child's ability to use language in expressive, receptive, and mediational tasks. While in all of the tests there is an important element of experience-related

310

vocabulary acquisition, the terms used are considered so basic that they should be within the active repertoire of all children, regardless of the degree of deprivation involved.

EXPERIMENTAL STUDIES

In the designing of instructional programs, it is often necessary to make decisions with reference to which of two or more procedures to adopt. Often choices are made quite arbitrarily on the basis of hunches which have no more empirical validity than the toss of a coin. Many times choices involve trivial questions which do not merit extensive experimental study. Also, in many cases such choice decisions are found to be non-critical, and one procedure is as effective as another. It has been pointed out (Keislar, 1967) that research is often incompatible with product development. This is fortunately not the case in the Preschool Research Program carried out at the University of California, Los Angeles, where a number of experimental studies, paralleling the preparation of the instructional programs, have been carried out.

A question of special concern for the education of young children is whether or not two-dimensional materials, that is, the pictorial representation of objects and events, are as effective instructional media as three-dimensional stimuli. For a long time, teachers of this age group have maintained that it is essential for young children to be able to manipulate, smell, feel and touch the real objects so as to develop meaningful concepts about them. Such materials obviously have an important place in the total curriculum, but they pose serious housekeeping problems for the classroom teacher.

To compare the efficiency of learning with two- and three-dimensional materials, an experiment was carried out with 50 culturally-disadvantaged four-year-old children. All children were pretested and randomly assigned to either the picture or the object treatment. The instructional programs for both groups were identical in all other respects. A t-test comparison of the mean gains on the posttest showed no significant difference. Furthermore, the hypothesis that the true difference in the means is larger than .8 may be rejected at the .05 level of confidence. Since the gain made by both treatment groups

is so much larger (five points), it is safe to conclude
that the use of manipulanda would at best produce only a
negligible difference. When the practical problems
involved in the use of objects are weighed against the
ease of using and storing pictorial materials, these
results provide some basis for deciding to use a minimum
of manipulanda in the 15-minute structural language program.

One question frequently faced in preparing instructional programs is whether to teach one concept label
fully, with many instances, before proceeding to develop
a second concept label. There is evidence that mature
learners learn equally well, whether or not the material
is presented in a grouped fashion, but there are no studies
which confirm that this is also true of the very young
child.

Two related hypotheses, (1) that young children can
be taught concept labels through an auto-instructional
program and (2) that an ordered sequence will produce more
efficient learning, were tested with 36 disadvantaged
Negro children, ranging in age from 37 to 66 months.
Stratified random assignment to one of three groups was
made on the basis of pre-test scores. Two treatment groups
received five 10-minute daily lessons with the only
procedural difference between the two treatments being the
order of presentation of the frames. The third group had
the same pre- and posttests; in addition, the children in
this control group had a short daily conversation with the
experimenter, but no concept training. On the day following the last training session a posttest and transfer test
were administered; one month later, retention tests were
given over the same content.

No statistically significant difference between the
two treatments was found. Both methods of programming were
dependably superior (.01 level) to the control. The latter
group made a mean gain from pre- to posttest of 1.9 points,
whereas the groups receiving programmed instruction gained
13.9 and 12.9 points, respectively. The instructed groups
also made reliable gains on a transfer test to new
instances of the concepts, and maintained these gains after
a one-month retention interval.

Another question of concern in the construction of
programs aimed at the improvement of language usage is
whether a structured, pattern-practice procedure is more

effective than a presumably more interesting story context. This hypothesis was tested in an experiment comparing two methods of teaching correct sentence formation to 25 culturally-disadvantaged children. Both of the programs provided instruction over five days, and required two additional days for pre- and posttests. The daily lessons contained up to 90 individual items and lasted approximately 12 minutes. In the pattern-practice treatment, the sentences were carefully arranged in order of complexity, and presented in a sequence of problems to which a routine of responding was easily developed. A problem consisted of five frames. For the first three, the child echoed the sentence given by the examiner. The sentences followed a specific grammatical pattern of varying subject, verb, object or prepositional phrase. The fourth frame presented three pictures on the same card, and the task for the child was to select the one which was appropriate for the verbal utterance of the examiner. On the fifth frame the child was asked to produce the appropriate sentence without assistance.

In the story treatment, the same sentences were used when they were appropriate for the story context. However, to maintain continuity, the pattern of repetition had to be altered and a number of bridging sentences which required only a listening response had to be interpolated. The number of occasions for echoing the structured sentences was decreased so that the total time would be the same for both treatments.

Results showed that the structured repetition of the sentences in the pattern-practice treatment produced significantly more learning (.01 level) than the story form. This improvement transferred to new and different types of pictures. The story, contrary to expectations, did not seem to be more interesting to the children, at least for the short duration of this experiment, than the patterned repetition. The children could easily produce the beginning sentences and were gradually taught to produce the more complex forms, providing a program which proved to be sufficiently reinforcing to maintain active involvement.

Closely related to the study reported above was an investigation of the comparative effectiveness of two types of patterned procedures, involving a sequence of

sentences which formed two parallel stories. Two groups of
nine children were given the same four-day program consisting of 16 different pairs of pictures. In one treatment,
the experimenter spoke the appropriate sentence for one
picture of a pair and the child was expected to repeat it;
then E spoke the sentence for the second picture, and the
child repeated that sentence. For instance, a picture of
an apple was shown accompanied by the statement: "This is
an apple." The child repeated, "This is an apple." Then
the picture of a banana was shown and the statement:
"This is a banana." The child repeated this sentence.
The same procedure was followed for all the paired items
in the program.

In the second treatment, the procedure was the same
for the first picture of a pair, but the child would be
asked to produce the sentence for the second picture
without any help. While this treatment gave the child
only half as much practice at hearing the correct sentence,
he did get the experience of producing his own sentences.

The test required all the children to produce sentences to pictures without prompting. Some of these
pictures had been used in the training and some of them
were completely unfamiliar ones. Comparison of the means
of the two groups revealed that the children who were
exposed to the sentences for each of the pictures were
more successful in producing sentences without prompts in
the test situation. However, because of the smaller
number of children used in the study, the obtained
difference was not large enough to be statistically
significant.

At a more theoretical level, the mediational use of
the child's own language in problem solving was explored
in two studies. For the first experiment, 60 four-year-old
children were given two days of training in selecting the
correct one of three pictures which differed only in size
(see Fig. 4). The children were randomly assigned to one
of two treatments: Labeling or Non-Labeling. Children in
the Labeling Group were required to verbalize overtly
relevant labels (large, medium, and small) during the
selective learning task. Children in the Non-Labeling
Group performed the same task but were not required to
produce the label aloud. The Labeling Group performed

Fig. 4.   Sample stimulus: Size dimension, Selective
          Learning Task.

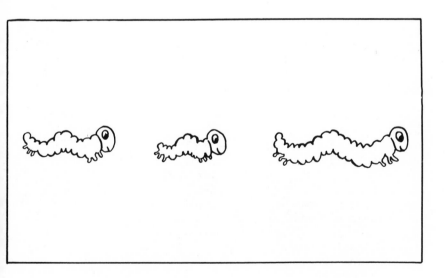

Fig. 5.   Sample Stimulus: Length dimension, Selective
          Learning Task.

significantly better than the Non-Labeling Group during training, as well as on a posttest which presented new problems with no instructions to verbalize.

This was not the case in an eight-day investigation with 72 five-year-old children, where the presentation of stimulus materials and verbal instructions was electronically controlled, and the task involved three values or levels of four different dimensions: size, thickness, length, and brightness. (See Fig. 5.) In all of these dimensions, the middle value was always labeled "medium", with the extreme values appropriate to the particular dimension, e.g., fat, medium, thin; long, medium, short. On the posttest, where no children were instructed to verbalize, no reliable differences in performance were found between the two groups. The performance of all children was consistently inferior when the intermediate-value in any of the four dimensions was the correct stimulus.

The studies demonstrated that young children could learn to use labels appropriately as cues to assist them in a problem-solving task. The effects of training carried over to a posttest where no instructions to verbalize were given. On the other hand, where the labels were diverse, and perhaps not thoroughly internalized, no facilitating effects were found. This might lead to the inference that labeling may produce interference effects; it is logical to assume that intensive language experience is essential to produce the maximum facilitating effect of appropriate verbalization during problem solving.

The major focus of the Preschool Language Project is a long-term experiment to measure the effectiveness of a semi-structured language plan with groups of culturally-disadvantaged children. It is important to note that each day's instruction occupies only 15 minutes of the child's total time in the school setting. Every child is given what amounts to individual attention; no school, no matter how expert and dedicated its staff, can provide a similar one-to-one pupil-teacher relationship, with the concomitant "high intensity" learning. The fact that the child's involvement in the program covers such a limited period of time ensures that the child will have plenty of opportunity for the many other very valuable learning opportunities which are part of the rich curriculum in the children's centers.

The structured language program applies pattern-practice procedures to help children develop the ability to produce sentences which conform to the school's conception of "good English." However, these standard forms are not represented as being the only correct and acceptable language. Children are not given the feeling that their own dialect is inferior or inadequate; rather, they are taught that, in school, certain language structures are more appropriate than others.

Criteria for Program Construction. Several principles have been accepted as guidelines in the preparation of the instructional sequences. These include commonly accepted principles of programming as well as conditions particularly relevant to the needs of this population.

1. Materials and devices used in the program should be tried out, revised, and improved until they prove effective.

2. A variety of tasks and modes of responding should be provided each day to maintain pupil activity at an optimum level.

3. The materials and equipment used in the instructional program should be relatively inexpensive, require a minimum of teacher preparation, and, therefore, be easily adapted to a variety of school settings.

4. The program must have sufficient control over the child's behavior so that he will produce the type of verbal response desired.

5. The child must be taught a sufficient variety of verbal responses under a diversity of conditions to enable him to generalize appropriately to novel situations.

6. In order to foster an ability to generalize to new situations, the prompting procedures used in the pattern training should be faded as rapidly as possible to force the child to perform independently.

7. The lessons, administered to groups of four or five children by a teacher-monitor, should take no more than 15 minutes per day.

Modes of Presentation. The instructional programs are presented through a number of different media or "interfaces."

1. An audio-visual group teaching-device is used in both research, and try-out of programmed materials. Ten children, each seated in a separate booth, see slides projected on a common screen, listen to taped commentary through earphones, respond by selecting appropriate pictures in multiple-choice fashion, and speak into activated microphones. Feedback to the child is provided by colored lights for the button-press response, and a signal to reinforce his overt speech. Data are automatically punched for each child for subsequent processing by a computer.

2. An inexpensive "learning center" provides five children at a time with individual tape recorders, operated through a master panel controlled by a teacher. These tape recorders have been modified so that the child can listen to a short story, record his own version of it, and then listen to his own voice re-tell the story.

3. A series of programmed picture work books allows the child to make selections in a sequence of frames and obtain immediate feedback by means of water-soluble colors in a special "magic" ink. These booklets are being used in conjunction with tape-recorded commentary as well as with a teacher working with a small group.

4. The Bell and Howell Language Master has been modified so that children listen to and classify auditory stimuli in a variety of ways. This "Judge" adaption permits the child to separate the items he knows from the ones he still needs to practice and, in a sense, permits him to construct a program individually tailored to his own needs.

5. To solve some of the problems inherent in the classroom management of manipulanda, and to make a viable puzzle program, an automatic device, capable of presenting five puzzles in a predetermined order, has been developed. It is thus possible to prepare an instructional program to teach children how to use their own language to help them assemble the puzzles.

6. Teacher-tutoring procedures for use in small groups are provided to instruct the child to manipulate three-dimensional objects, such as toy figures, furniture, etc.

7. Games, such as Lotto, Fish, Old Maid, and Dominoes, have been programmed to give children the opportunity to practice their new language learnings in a variety of highly-motivating situations.

Program Content. In the instructional sequences being prepared for the Children's Centers, the content has, for convenience, been divided into six basic areas and subsumed under familiar subject-matter labels.

1. Natural phenomena (science) include programs on weather, life and growth, shapes, forms, colors, animals, and habitats.

2. People and places (social studies) include family relationships, concepts of home and family, neighborhoods, and services.

3. Quantities (mathematics) present a very important type of language learning, including such basic express- ions as how much, how many, more than, less than, equal to, same, bigger, smaller, heavier, lighter, add, take away, etc. In addition, the concept of number and the numerals by which they are represented, are introduced. These concepts are applied in the teaching of money where naming, identifying, and recognizing the exchange value of various coins can be developed.

4. Problem-solving skills are fostered through the medium of simple three- or four-picture problem situa- tions. Children are taught to draw inferences and to use their own language in problem solving. Children also learn to use concepts of identity, affirmation, and negation. Here the ability to respond appropriately to "same" and "different" would carry over from the previous unit on quantities. Classification is another important element in problem-solving which crosses over content areas. Thus, there are classification activities in the learning of colors, sizes, shapes, and numbers, as well as in the learning of such concepts as transportation, clothing, toys, etc.

319

5.   Ordering or seriation is another type of problem-solving skill involving many subject fields, but it is such a basic and important one that it is given separate emphasis.   Seriation programs, such as counting, use number concepts; the orderly sequence from infancy to adulthood uses natural science concepts; the succession of day and night, and of the seasons, also provide materials for presenting the concept of order in nature.

In story plots there is also an inherent order. Children are required to order a set of picture cards so that they present a coherent story.   They begin with simple nursery rhymes which involve three or four pictures, and continue into complex story plots requiring as many as ten or twelve different cards.

As this chapter has indicated, the Preschool Language Project is exploring a number of basic research questions concerning the improvement of language instruction of culturally-disadvantaged children.   The individual experiments constitute part of a larger, three-year investigation in which the possibility of developing a structured language program for young children is being tested.

An essential aspect of the research involves the creation of a set of new instruments which can be used as objective pre- and posttest measures in assessing and evaluating the language performance of the preschool population.   A most important outcome is the preparation of a replicable two-year instructional program which will, hopefully, have demonstrable effectiveness and will be adaptable to a wide variety of preschool and primary grade settings.

References

Bean, Joan P.   The effects of socio-economic status on oral language skills.   Unpublished thesis, San Jose State College, San Jose, California, 1966.

Bereiter, Carl, & Engelmann, Siegfried.   Teaching disadvantaged children in the preschool Englewood Cliffs: Prentice-Hall, 1966.

Bernstein, B. Elaborated and restricted codes: Their social origins and some consequences. *American Anthropologist*, 1964, 66, 1-35.

Bernstein, B. Language and social class. *Brit. J. Sociol*, 1960, 11, 271-276.

Bernstein, B. Social class and linguistic development: a theory of social learning. In A. H. Halsey, J. Floud, and C. A. Anderson (Eds.), *Education, economy and society*. Glencoe: The Free Press, 1961.

Deutsch, M., Maliver, Alma, Brown, B., and Cherry, Estelle. Communication of information in the elementary school classroom. U. S. Office of Educ., Cooperative Research Proj. No. 908, 1964.

Feldmann, Shirley & Weiner, M. A report on the validation studies of the Reading Prognosis Test. Institute for Developmental Studies, Department of Psychiatry, New York Medical College, New York, 1962.

John, Vera P. Research related to language development in disadvantaged children. *Bulletin*, Information Retrieval Center on the Disadvantaged, New York, November 1965.

John, Vera P. & Goldstein, L. S. Social context of language acquisition. *Merrill-Palmer Quarterly*, 1964, 10, 265-275.

Keislar, E. R. Research possibilities in a produce development milieu. Paper read at American Educational Research Association Conference, New York, 1967.

Underwood, B. J., & Schulz, R. W. *Meaningfulness and verbal learning*. Chicago: Lippincott, 1960.

Footnote

[1]This paper was read by the senior (first-named) author. Both are members of the faculty of the Department of Education, University of California, Los Angeles.

CONTEMPORARY ISSUES IN APHASIA[1]

Ronald S. Tikofsky[2]

What I propose to do in this paper is to set forth some of the problems facing students with language distur- bance, following damage to the central nervous system, and to illustrate the interdisciplinary character of the field of "aphasiology". One of the current difficulties beset- ting the student of aphasia is the fact that he has to become quite thoroughly acquainted with the contributions made by a variety of disciplines in order to make sense out of the mass of data, accumulated history, and theory on the subject.

The study of aphasia actually began with the physician and anatomist and their concern for understanding mental processes and correlating them with brain function. This is a problem that faces us today in contemporary neuro- psychology. Recent work carried out by Weinstein and Teuber (1957 a, b), Penfield and Roberts (1959), and others in this hemisphere, and in Europe by Hécean (1962), Bay (1964), Conrad (1954), Russell, Espir (1961), and many more, plus the significant contributions of the Russian psychologist, A. R. Luria, particularly in his new work, The Higher Cortical Functions of Man (1966), attempts to inter-relate various forms of aphasia with local brain lesions. These efforts have produced important evidence concerning cerebral localization. New concepts, as to the relation between where damage in the brain occurs and type of behavioral and in particular linguistic change, have been put forward. This research has also resulted in new theories of what happens operationally in the nervous system to produce the various forms of aphasia. However intriguing this topic, it is not my primary concern in this paper. Rather, I would like to spend the time dealing with problems faced by three or four other disci- plines.

The first of these is the field of speech pathology. The speech pathologist's concern with aphasics relates to

his attempt to evaluate and change or shape their impaired
language behavior so that it will better approximate normal
language behavior. His next aim is to increase the
aphasic's efficiency of language performance, i.e., to
manipulate the impaired language so that (a) the aphasic
can better handle the language that he receives from his
environment, and/or that (b) he can use language which the
people in his environment can understand. Consider some
of the illustrations that are typical of the sorts of
things that the speech pathologist might deal with. The
telegraphic speech of the aphasic may be very effective
communication in the sense that the listener is very much
aware of what is intended by the speaker, that is, the
listener can make a correct or appropriate response to
the impaired verbal behavior of the aphasic because
enough of its structure and lexicon is present. On the
other hand, we see many fluent aphasics who, while they
articulate precisely and retrieve appropriate, i.e., real,
words from their vocabularies, to not put these words
together in a meaningful fashion and therefore make no
sense to the listener. The typical jargon aphasic, who
may articulate very well, produces appropriate sequences
of phonemes which are not real words. He is merely a good
producer of nonsense syllables. It should be noted,
however, that many of these phonetic sequences are
perfectly acceptable in the language. This poses an
entirely different problem for the speech pathologist than
that of the telegraphic speaker. The speech pathologist
must be concerned with understanding normal language
function and structure, as well as the nature of the
deficiency, in an effort to shape behavior so that there
is a better approximation to adequate communication.
This brings him into contact with problems in programmed
learning, verbal learning, conditioning of verbal behavior,
short-term memory, and the like.

Another area that has been deficient in the study of
aphasia is the discipline of linguistics. The linguist
should be concerned with the aphasic patient and his
disturbed language in an effort to structure models of
normal language systems. He can assist in determining
if the language deviation of the aphasic is ordered or
random behavior and, if orderly, describe the rules
governing such language behavior. As Dr. Goodglass (the
previous speaker) pointed out, the linguist may have to
distinguish between the structure and rules which govern

output, as compared to rules the aphasic may be using when he perceives language and attempts to decode it. These problems can be viewed either in terms of syntax and word retrieval, or according to their phonological aspects. It is necessary to examine the phonological "substitutions" that occur in the speech of many aphasics when they produce otherwise appropriate utterances. Jakobson argues that such substitutions can be explained by the aphasic's regression hypothesis. This hypothesis is currently being tested by speech pathologists and psycholinguists. At the moment, it appears as if the hypothesis with respect to perception will not fare very well, but as yet no acceptable alternative has been offered.

Psycholinguistics is another discipline which is becoming increasingly interested in the problem of aphasia. Psycholinguists attempt, in part, to combine the psychological study of language with the linguistic analysis of language structure in terms of models describing syntactic rules, competence, and performance in language. Thus, they are concerned with developing techniques for assessing, in a controlled fashion, the ways in which aphasics can manipulate language. They carry out such experiments as those described in the previous paper by Dr. Goodglass, and other experiments, such as those by Davis Howes (1964) on the distribution of word frequency and rate at which aphasics talk. Barrett (1960), in his doctoral dissertation, attempted to study the aphasic's ability to make grammatical transformations. Wepman and Jones (1966) and their colleagues are attempting to determine grammatical class usage by aphasics. I am now exploring the influence of grammatical complexity on aphasic short-term memory. In these experiments, sentence-length, in terms of number of lexical elements, is kept constant and the depth of the sentence, or direction of branching right or left, is systematically varied. Dan Carson, his wife and I (1966) are carrying out experiments dealing with the aphasic's ability to discover rules in concept-learning situations that are both verbal and nonverbal, and are testing his ability to generalize these rules to new sets of stimuli.

Each of the disciplines discussed above, as well as clinical and experimental psychology, add new and significant dimensions that can be applied to the study of aphasia from both a theoretical and practical standpoint. I am firmly convinced that the linguist and psycholinguist can, and will, make important contributions of relevance

to clinicians who must evaluate, diagnose, and treat the
aphasic.

The research carried out by the nonclinically-oriented
scholars tends to focus on important questions other than
how one classifies aphasics. We have a variety of
"diagnostic tests" to enable us to make adequate clinical
classifications of aphasic patients. However, we are not
yet in a position to be able to make adequate predictions
concerning the aphasic's response to "language therapy."
Further, there is virtually no research which allows for
the objective evaluation of the influence of treatment on
performance except "clinical intuition," and subjective
reports of the therapist and family. There are no tests
that enable us to determine, with any degree of confidence,
whether the patient has improved or whether we can make a
prediction as to how he will improve or in what areas
improvement can be expected. To achieve this end, that
is, the prediction of performance as opposed to classification, a new approach to diagnosis and evaluation is
necessary. The introduction of quasi-learning tasks,
which attempt to explore the capacity of the aphasic to
change his behavior, and the rate of this change, under
explicit sets of condition into our evaluative procedures,
may provide relevant information.

Treatment follows evaluation, and the speech pathologist must deal directly with the treatment process.
Attention must be directed at evolving techniques that
allow us to understand how we can shape and control the
aphasic's verbal behavior. The speech pathologist must
be prepared to depart from the standard drill procedures
commonly used in aphasia therapy. He must begin to do
serious research on the therapeutic process itself. Such
study requires research dealing with some of the following
questions: What are the appropriate types and schedules
of reinforcement to use with aphasics? How can learning
tasks be evaluated? What is the appropriate linguistic
level at which to initiate therapy? How can transfer from
the treatment session to ordinary conversation be achieved?
An important corollary is the very critical issue of
determining when the patient can no longer benefit from
continued treatment, that is, how do you know when the
patient has reached asymptote? Experimental evidence
obtained in our learning experiments will perhaps offer
some clues. Some aphasics will level off, i.e., reach an

325

asymptotic point which leads us to believe that, even with an additional hundred trials, the learning curve will be absolutely flat. Data from a series of pilot studies of the learning behavior of the aphasic have compelled us to take a second look at what aphasia represents beyond the language disturbance itself.

The approach that I and my colleagues are advocating does not represent a radical departure from the present view of aphasia. Rather it is approaching the problem from a different perspective. It is our contention that all forms of aphasia can be thought of from the point of view of information processing models, and that it represents a reduction of the efficiency with which a previously-acquired language system can be employed. Such a reduction can be evaluated in terms of the capacity and rate with which the aphasic handles language. Measures of rate and capacity can also be applied to the evaluation of the aphasic's ability to improve his language abilities. This approach can lead to some interesting theoretical questions as to differences between aphasics and non-aphasics. Much of the data generated by our aphasics on learning tasks looks very much like that from normals, if the numbers on the abscissa were eliminated and one just looked at the curves. Many of the learning curves we have obtained in the laboratory have the general shape and characteristics that one would expect from normal subjects, including college sophomores. In several instances some of our aphasics do as well as college sophomores (even those at the University of Michigan). This is rather disturbing.

The similarity in the shapes of the curves suggests that the aphasic is not operating in an unpredictable fashion. Rather, it suggests just the opposite, and permits us to hypothesize that the aphasic is endeavoring to compensate for his impairment by attempting to use his previously-acquired linguistic abilities. Closer examination of the data illustrates the generalized reduction in rate and capacity for both verbal and nonverbal symbolic tasks. Two things become apparent with such examination. First, for most tasks the curves generated by the aphasic populations we have studied never reach levels obtained by normals. Second, it takes aphasics much longer than normals to reach maximum-performance levels. That is, aphasics require more trials to reach asymptote than do normals. It is this difference in level of performance and time to reach maximum level between aphasics and normals that illustrates the utility of rate and capacity of information processing as techniques for the study of aphasia.

The results we have obtained thus far and the interpretation we have given to them lend credence to the view that the aphasic, in spite of his language disturbance, is, in his effort to communicate, employing mechanisms that are not different from those that the normal subject uses. Evidence from studies like those of Dr. Goodglass and Davis Howes, as well as others, allows for a similar interpretation. What the aphasic is suffering from, in part, is a restriction of the speed with which he can employ those mechanisms. He is also attempting to compensate for his lowered level of linguistic competence (not in a theoretical, but in a practical sense). It would appear, then, that the aphasic is not necessarily developing new strategies or compensatory mechanisms to lessen his impairment, but rather that he seems to be attempting to use the old familiar ways, which he is not able to do very efficiently. This slows him down, and, in part, it also accounts for the reduction in his capacity to deal with language. The aphasic patient is still trying to grapple with language in much the same way that he grappled with it before. Further, he is demonstrating to us that he is not behaving like a random system.

Two other important factors emerge from recent experimental investigations of aphasic behavior which tend to contradict some of our earlier notions about this population. Clinicians and test-makers have argued for years that the behavior of the aphasic could not be quantified. The reasons underlying such a view were that (a) the aphasic's behavior was too variable to produce reliable and stable data, and that (b) the differences between individual aphasics were so great that one could not talk about the aphasic population. The evidence reported in this session demonstrates that it is possible to obtain reliable data from aphasics, and to regard their behavioral patterns as characteristic of the population. We can now say with some degree of confidence that aphasic performance can be quantified, and, therefore, that we can describe the characteristics of this population in terms of its variability along specific behavioral parameters. We can also say with confidence that reliable and stable data can be obtained from aphasics in experimental tasks. This view argues that we should not ignore the variability of performance between aphasics, but, rather, that we should analyze it so that we can better understand the nature of the language disturbance. Thus, subsets of aphasics can be described in terms of common and quantifiable characteristics. However, we are still faced with the problem of determining the most appropriate parameters to employ for differentiating and describing the language disturbances in the aphasic population, as a whole and for subsets of the population.

Let me illustrate what I mean by a search for non-randomness and predictability in aphasic behavior. This example is from clinical observation, rather than from experimental data. Within the population of aphasics, there is a group that can be described as "talking aphasics". These patients usually have excellent articulation, but they produce meaningless speech, with both jargon and understandable words. Furthermore, they cannot stop talking once they start because they really do not know how to deal with language. Wepman has called them "pragmatic aphasics". Such a patient, if asked the "simple" question, "What did you have for breakfast?" might reply with: "Well, I had something, then tomorrow morning fishing inglub over there by the bus", and so on for as much as 10 to 15 minutes of uninterrupted, unintelligible output. The range and amount of speech they omit varies greatly, and, while it would seem, at first glance, to defy analysis, it certainly does not appear to be anything but a random string of words and jargon. Closer analysis shows this to be a false conclusion, for, while their phrases seem to make no semantic sense, the aphasics tend to put these inappropriately-chosen words into appropriate grammatical slots. One rarely finds an aphasic of this type interjecting an adjective into a verb slot, or a conjunction into a noun slot. These patients appear to maintain the syntactic order of the language system. They seem to be excellent producers of such Chomsky-type sentences as "Colorless green ideas sleep furiously."

Even the patients with telegraphic speech or the ones who cannot deal adequately with tense or number still maintain the basic sequential syntactic order of the sentence.

A similar phenomenona can be observed in the talking aphasic with word-finding difficulties, as he attempts to search for the appropriate word. He makes a statement, pauses as he searches for a word, and then will often do one of two things. He might use a word which is semantically inappropriate but syntactically of the correct grammatical form class, or else he may circumlocute. The circumlocuted phrases, when taken as a unit, often have the characteristic of the appropriate form class. For example, when the patient who says, "I want to go to the – the place where you buy things to eat," for "I want to go to the market," he is circumlocuting with a phrase which is the equivalent of the noun that would have been used. Such consistency in the aphasic's verbal behavior is impressive, and should receive much more attention from the student of language behavior than it has in the past.

I also want to mention briefly several factors that serve to complicate our analyses of aphasia. Problems in short-term versus long-term memory arise when considering word-finding difficulties and memory span in aphasia. On the one hand we are dealing with short-term memory when we ask the patient to make a specific response to a sequence of statements or repeat statements. On the other hand, when he is engaging in normal conversation, we are asking him to draw words from his long-term memory, that is, from his total lexicon, and to retrieve them and put them into some sort of sequence. We begin to see some of the problems in short-term memory when the aphasic gets lost in constructing a sentence, as he tries to find an appropriate word and forgets the first part of the utterance.

It would seem that some of the paridigms currently employed to study short-term memory in normal verbal behavior can with little difficulty be adopted to investigate the apparent retention and retrieval problems presented by the aphasic. This would also be true with respect to long-term memory studies.

The subject of aphasia offers, for the student of normal language and language behavior, a fertile field for investigation and study. It is indeed unfortunate that the psychologist, linguist and psycholinguist have not taken a more active role in the study of aphasia as a means of enhancing their understanding of normal language and cognitive function.

References

Barrett, Jr., R.P. Some grammatical characteristics of aphasic speech. Unpub. doctoral dissertation. The University of Mich., 1960.

Bay, E. Principles of classification and their influence on our concepts of aphasia. In: V. S. deReuck & M. O'Conner, eds., Disorders of language. Boston: Little, Brown and Co., 1964.

Carson, D. H., Carson, Florence E. & Tikofsky, R. S. An experimental approach to nonverbal learning by aphasics. Mental Health Research Institute, The University of Michigan, Ann Arbor, Mich. Preprint No. 193, July, 1966.

Conrad, K. New problems in aphasia. Brain, 1954, 77, 491-509.

Goodglass, H. A psycholinguistic study of aphasia. Paper read at First Language and Language Behavior Conference, Ann Arbor, Mich., October, 1966.

Hécaen, H. Clinical symptomatology in right and left hemisphere lesions. In: V. B. Mountcastle, Ed., Interhemispheric relations and cerebral dominance. Baltimore: The Johns Hopkins Press, 1962.

Howes, D. & Geschwind, N. The brain and disorders of communication. Quantitative studies of aphasic language. Res. Publ. Ass. New. Ment. Dis., 1964, 42, 229-244.

Luria, A. R. Higher cortical functions in man. (Translated by B. Hugh) New York: Basic Books, Inc., 1966.

Penfield, W. P. & Roberts, L. Speech and brain mechanisms. Princeton: Princeton University Press, 1959.

Russell, W. R. & Espir, M. L. E. Traumatic aphasia. London: Oxford University Press, 1961.

Weinstein, S. & Teuber, H. L.   Effects of penetrating
        brain injury on intelligence test scores.
        Science, 1957a, 125, 1036-37.

Weinstein, S. & Teuber, H. L.   The role of pre-injury
        education and intelligence level after brain
        injury.   J. Comp. physiol. Psychol., 1957b, 50,
        535-539.

Weyman, J. M. & Jones, L. V.   Grammatical indicants of
        speaking style in normal and aphasic speakers.
        Chapel Hill, North Carolina: The Psychometric
        Laboratory, University of North Carolina,
        Research Report No. 46, Dec. 1966.

Footnotes

[1]This paper is a slightly modified and edited version
of the one read at the Conference. This report was based,
in part, on research supported by a contract with the
Office of Education, U. S. Department of Health, Education, & Welfare, under provisions of P. L. 83-531,
Cooperative Research, and Title VI, P. L. 85=564, as
amended.

[2]The author is a member of the CRLLB and of its
Executive Committee, and is also chairman of the new
University of Michigan Doctoral Program in Psycholinguis-
tics.

A PSYCHOLINGUISTIC STUDY OF AGRAMMATISM[1, 2]

Harold Goodglass[3]

Aphasia gives us the opportunity to test whether the
components of language, which we infer from normal speech,
correspond to the lines drawn by pathological symptoms.
In this paper I will describe the results of some studies
which suggest that our preconceived categories do not
correspond to the results of pathology. Specifically,
that on close scrutiny of the apparent "grammatical"
difficulties of certain aphasics, their symptoms cut
across the confines of the term "grammar". By re-drawing
the definition of the symptoms, we hope to come closer to
grasping the mechanism which created them. At the same
time, in the course of these experiments, we learn something of the psychological prerequisites for normal
grammatical performance.

As you may know, many aphasic patients, while they
begin to recover a considerable speaking vocabulary,
continue to omit articles, relational words, and inflectional endings, all of which we refer to as "grammatical
function words". The variations in the form and severity
of grammatical difficulties have elicited a variety of
descriptive names, the most common being "agrammatism".
Milder degrees of difficulty take the form of "telegraphic
speech", so named because the omission of inessential
words and of inflectional endings suggest the terseness of
sentences in a telegram. Such a patient sounds like this
man who was interviewed during an admission to the hospital for gum surgery. Upon being asked by the interviewer
what brought him back to the hospital, he replied:

"Yes...ah...Monday...ah...Dad and Peter Hogan,
and Dad...ah...Hospital...and ah...Wednesday...
Wednes, nine o'clock and ah Thursday...ten o'clock
ah doctors...two...two...and doctors and...ah...
teeth...yah. And a doctor...an girl...and gums,
and I. (Upon question about his former employment
in a paper mill) Paper. Four hundred tons a day!
And ah...sulphur machines, and ah...wood...Two

332

weeks and eight hours. Eight hours...no! Twelve
hours, 15 hours...working...workin...workin! Yes,
and ah...sulphur. Sulphur and...Ah wood. Ah...
handlin! And ah sick, four years ago."

This sample is typical of severe motor aphasia with
agrammatism. In it we can detect the characteristics of
agrammatic speech as defined, from the linguist's point of
view some years ago, by Jakobson. Syntactic rules are lost;
there is no indication of grammatical coordination or
subordination; there are few inflectional endings; and
almost all grammatical function words are missing.

In contrast with the speech pattern of agrammatism,
where the output is impoverished, there are forms of aphasia
in which speech output remains fairly fluent, although
marked by errors of transposition of sounds and by difficulties in the selection of words. We call these patients
"fluent" aphasics. In classical terminology they belong to
the diagnostic groups of Wernicke's aphasia and amnesic
aphasia. In a speech sample from such a patient we may
observe that almost every utterance started includes a
subordinating construction, indicating a readiness to use
complex syntactic forms. Nevertheless, sentences may
remain incomplete because of the noun-finding difficulty
common in this form of aphasia.

If we were to list all the types of grammatical
difficulty attributed to aphasics, we would include the
following:

1. Omission of articles, prepositions, personal
   pronouns.

2. Inadvertent interchange of articles, prepositions,
   personal pronouns.

3. Substitution of verb stem or infinitive for
   inflected verb forms.

4. Loss of coordinating and subordinating syntactical
   constructions, with substitution of series of
   one-word or short-phrase "sentences", in which
   grammatical relationships are implied only by
   contiguity and sequence.

5. Loss of comprehension of the meaning of words which have primarily grammatical functions, and loss of comprehension of distinctions between inflectional forms.

6. Leaving sentences incomplete or mixing grammatically incompatible sequences.

Previous work on aggramatism

If we turn to the literature in this area we find a general assumption that grammatical disorders may be regarded as a unitary feature of aphasia, a point of view which is repeated in the recent writing of Roman Jakobson. He coined the term "contiguity disorder" to refer to the disruption of those speech processes which relate elements to each other.

Another issue which is dealt with is whether grammatical disorders in aphasia need apply concurrently to the expression and comprehension of grammatical distinctions. Salomon and Isserlin both contributed cases which illustrated the independence of the receptive and expressive aspects of grammatical performance. This independence raises some question about the construct "competence" which has recently been put forward by psycholinguists concerned with the child's acquisition of grammar. Competence refers to the intrinsic mastery of a rule which is supposed to underlie the child's ability to comprehend and produce any newly-learned grammatical distinction. However, if comprehension and expression may be independently impaired, the validity of this construct is seriously challenged, unless we accept competence for expression as distinct from receptive competence.

Finally, I would like to point out that current grammatical theories, particularly Chomsky's, but also Jakobson's, include predictions concerning the order of difficulty of various constructions, which are subject to experimental verification in aphasia. The material which we discuss has bearing both on the independence of expressive and receptive grammar, and on the order of difficulty of grammatical operations.

334

Aphasia and the rules of grammatical inflection

We embarked on an effort to define the precise
linguistic operations which are difficult for the motor
agrammatic patient. I would like to summarize quickly
the first series of studies which resulted in interesting
findings but did not bring us closer to the goal of
differentiating the agrammatic patient in operational
terms. The methodology which all these studies had in
common was that a preselected grammatical task was presented in a highly structured framework so that the
expected response was obligatory. Most of these tasks
took the form of sentence completions or sentence repetitions or one-word responses to questions. For example,
to test the availability of the final "d" of the past
tense one of the items used was:

The baby cries every night.

He did last night too.

Last night the baby "   ".

With test items of these types we compared almost
all of the English inflectional endings with respect to
their availability to aphasics of the two contrasting
clinical types. We then used a sentence-repetition test
to compare sentences of eight different syntactic constructions in their difficulty for aphasics. With a
modification of the sentence-repetition technique, we
compared the auditory discrimination of grammatical
distinctions with the ability to produce the corresponding
distinctions expressively.

The net result of these studies was the repeated
demonstration of a universal hierarchy of difficulty among
these various constructions, which applied with few
exceptions equally to Broca's and to fluent aphasics.
Furthermore, the various syntactic constructions followed
the same order of difficulty for comprehension as they
did for expression. Thus, the pattern of clinical
agrammatism which we associate with Broca's aphasia is
not distinguished from the speech pattern of Wernicke's
or amnesic aphasia, by reference to performance on
standard grammatical operations. In this respect we
failed to support Jakobson's belief that certain grammatical operations are more vulnerable to contiguity disorder

335

than others and should therefore be differentially disturbed in the speech of the agrammatic patient, as compared to that of the fluent aphasic.

We were, however, able to draw some conclusions about what the psychological demands are which determine the order of difficulty of grammatical operations. One of our unexpected findings, partly explained in a later study, is that the easiest of our English sentence types for repetition was not the imperative or the simple present indicative, but, rather, the question beginning with an interrogative adverb. We called this the "WH question", because many of the interrogatives begin with a WH, as in "what", "why", "where", "when", "who". This is one of several findings which appear to contradict both common sense and formal theoretical models as to the order of complexity of English sentences.

Now we turn to the area in which we have observed clear differences between the agrammatic and the fluent aphasic. In the studies described here we were concerned principally with the conditions under which the function words of grammar may be omitted or confused in aphasic speech. The loss of these words, which is largely responsible for the impression of telegraphic speech, is usually referred to as one of the central features of agrammatism. However, the omission of inessential words is characteristic of many speech abnormalities, and confusion among grammatical words is also to be heard in the speech of fluent aphasics. The question in our mind, then, concerns the way in which the defective use of function words is demonstrably peculiar to Broca's aphasia with agrammatism.

It is important to remember that the function words constitute the most commonly-used group of words in the language. They are easy to pronounce and, although chiefly monosyllabic, are phonetically distinctive from each other. They constitute a closed class in that their limited number is sufficient for an unlimited variety of sentences. Thus, their selective disturbance in aphasia would appear to contradict the familiar psychological principal of frequency of usage. In the material which follows we present evidence that factors of stress and position in the rhythmic pattern may determine when a function word is retained and when it is dropped. We moved from fortuitous findings, to begin with, to controlled experiments testing explicit predictions.

336

The first fortuitous observation occurred in the forty-item Sentence Repetition Test mentioned above, which was administered to fifty subjects--twenty-seven Broca's and twenty-three fluent aphasics. The fluent aphasics in this sample were consistently judged as having greater conversational ability than the Broca's aphasics, and a question might therefore be raised as to propriety of comparing the two groups. However, if we accept the provision that a repetition span test for unrelated words serves as a basis for equating the groups, we find that they are precisely equal. The task required in this experiment was much closer to one of repetition span than to one of conversation.

While the Sentence Repetition items had not been composed with any consideration as to their opening words, it turned out that in thirty items the initial word was an unstressed function word, and the number of initial omissions for the Broca's aphasics is much greater for unstressed words and significant beyond the .01 level, as compared to the omissions of the fluent aphasics.

We have evidence, then, that while the two groups of subjects have equal repetition-spans for words spoken as a list, with equal emphasis, they perform very differently on meaningful sentence groups of about the same number of words, where the first word is an unstressed grammatical morpheme.

The saliency-seeking model of agrammatism

At this point I will digress to develop what we can call a saliency-seeking model of agrammatism. From an earlier study of the length of interpausal word-groups in Broca's and fluent aphasia, we know that the natural distribution of this feature is markedly bimodal. Broca's aphasia, which is marked by short runs of words, rarely exceeding four words in length, does not blend gradually into fluent aphasia. Rather, there is a decided gap between the very short-phrased Broca's aphasics and the long-phrased fluent aphasics. While Broca's aphasics are in fact more restricted in communication than most fluent aphasics, it is fallacious to regard Broca's as merely a more severe level of impairment.

337

On the basis of the characteristic shortness of word-groups and the observed tendence to open each group with a stressed word, the following explanation was suggested for a part of the symptomatology of agrammatism: the underlying defect in this form of aphasia is an increased threshold for initiating and maintaining the flow of speech, either after a silence or as a continuation of sequences already in progress.   Further, we suggested that in order to produce any speech the patient with this disorder must find the salient point in his intended utterance, which is ordinarily the significant noun or verb.   As a result, his speech issues in short bursts, each centered about a salient verbal element, with rarely more than one unstressed morpheme before or after it.   The normal melodic intonation and rhythm are thus destroyed.

This formulation has the advantage of wrapping up with one explanation both the short-phrased speech pattern and the ungrammatic quality of the syntax.   However, it creates a problem of defining a new construct called "saliency".   The intuitive definition which is suggested is that saliency is the psychological resultant of the stress of the informational significance, of the phono-logical prominence, and of the affective value of a word. While stress and informational or nominal quality usually coincide, this is not necessarily the case.

In explaining the omission of the small function words, we can point to two components of saliency which they lack: namely, nominal quality and, in most cases, stress.   In our hypothesis concerning the underlying speech difficulty of the agrammatic aphasic, we suggested that a salient or psychologically-forceful word was needed in order to initiate speech, which might then run on for a few syllables.   This leads to the testable prediction that the same word which is omitted at the beginning of a construction should be retained when it follows a stressed word.

We took the occasion to test this prediction when a patient came to the aphasia unit with a classically-agrammatic style of speech.   In conversation, this man could produce brief answers consisting almost exclusively of principal nouns and verbs.   While he found these with difficulty they constituted his only speech production. His verbs were uninflected, showing no distinction between tenses.   Although his articulation was often stiff, he

338

did not have any consistent mispronunciations. He showed
very clearly the pattern of repeating model sentences in
agrammatic form, omitting the little words and inflectional
endings. Thus, his repetition duplicated the defects of
his spontaneous speech, in spite of the immediate availability of a model sentence in his memory.

For the experiment, a series of three-word groups was
constructed. The principal focus was on the patient's
ability to repeat, in context, a function word in the
first or second position, under various conditions of
stress and, holding the stress constant, in various
grammatical constructions. The basic models of stress
and syntax are illustrated in Table 1. One of the comparisons possible from this set of sentences is the contrast
between the simple interrogative and the negative interrogative. [See Table 1.] Here, the greater grammatical
complexity represented by the negative is pitted against
the expected facilitating effect of having the initial
function word stressed, as it is in the negative interrogative form.

Examination of the results from the administration
of 114 items reveals that there were many more omissions
of unstressed function words in the first position (70%
omissions out of 70 items). There were only six omissions
in 44 items for a medially-placed unstressed function
word, whether the first word were a verb, adverb, modal
or auxiliary verb, or a noun.

Other unanticipated differences emerged, which
seemed to be attributable to the rhythmic pattern. For
example, the pattern in the sentence "Can Jim come?" led
to 83% omissions of the initial unstressed word alone.
The pattern in the sentence "Can he come?" led to only
9% omissions of the initial word alone but an additional
52% omissions of the first two unstressed words. We
might better interpret the results as showing the
patient's need to find the first stressed word to begin
talking. Looking within the group of sentences having
similar stress patterns, we find no differences between
interrogatives and declaratives with respect to the
retention of the unstressed function words.

With respect to the question of the difficulty of
the negative versus the simple interrogative, we found
the complexity of the negative interrogative is apparently

Table 1.

Proportion of correct reproduction of function words in various contexts of stress, position, and syntactic function, by one of Broca's aphasics (Patient L), a group of Broca's aphasics, and a group of fluent aphasics. (Test word is underlined)

Proportion Correct for Patient L	Sentence types	Mean Score for Broca's Aphasics	Mean Score for Fluent Aphasics
2/17 (12%)	<u>Do</u> birds fly?	5.7	7.7
	<u>He</u> feels good.	---	---
1/11	<u>Can</u> he dance?	---	---
15/53 (28%)	<u>He</u> can dance.	---	---
	<u>In</u> the house.	---	---
	Dogs <u>can</u> bark.	8.4	8.6
72% (32/44)	Where <u>is</u> Jack?	---	---
	Close, <u>if</u> open!	---	---
6/11	<u>Can't</u> he dance?	8.5	8.4
----	<u>Don't</u> birds fly?	7.5	6.7
6/6	Cows eat grass.	---	---

24%

more than compensated by the facilitating effect of
placing a stressed word in the first position so that it
is reproduced correctly 6 times in 11, as opposed to 1
correct out of 11 tries at the simple interrogative. The
negative interrogative represents one of the few instances
in which an opening function word appears as a stressed
word, as is also the case with WH- questions. In no case
were any of these words omitted. Among the stimulus
sentences were six of the type having three successive
stressed words, as in "Cows eat grass". These were all
perfectly reproduced, showing that memory span could not
by itself be invoked to account for our patients' failures
in other sentence types.

Group administration of stress test

While the stress test just described produced
impressive results on a single patient, we still lacked
evidence that it would differentiate a <u>group</u> of Broca's
aphasics from a group of fluent aphasics. Accordingly,
a shortened version of the test was administered to twelve
fluent and ten Broca's aphasics.

For the group, as in the individual case, the initial
unstressed function word was the least often correctly
produced by the Broca's group, but one of the easiest
forms for the fluent aphasics. The very easiest form for
both groups was the sentence with a medial unstressed
copulative or modal verb. Comparing the simple interrogative with two forms of negative or interrogative, we
find that the Broca's patients perform better in both of
the negative interrogative forms. The difference in favor
of the negative interrogative form for the fluent aphasics
was statistically insignificant. Furthermore, an analysis
of errors shows that virtually all of the errors made by
the fluent aphasics on the negative interrogative consisted of the substitution of the unstressed simple
interrogative opening word, showing that the fluent
aphasics have a predilection for beginning with an
unstressed function word, which contrasts with the
inability of the Broca's aphasics to operate with a
stress pattern beginning that way.

One observation, which we presumed to be specific to
our first agrammatic patient, now turns out to be a
universal feature. This is the facility for reproduction
of the middle word in sentences of the stress pattern
similar to "Dogs can bark."

In these experiments with the prosodic variables of stress and rhythm, we have attempted to account for what appeared to be linguistic changes in aphasic speech as artifacts of what is essentially a sublinguistic defect--a sort of raised threshold for the initiation of any speech sequence. There is, however, another group of grammatical defects that are not so easily disposed of, and which we might call "conceptual agrammatism". In these cases the patient does not necessarily omit grammatical particles, but he interchanges prepositions, confuses genders of pronouns, confuses tense forms, and confesses that he does not recognize the difference between them upon hearing them spoken. Upon analyzing the performance of one such patient recently, the general formulation came to mind that he failed to distinguish linguistic signs which represented contrasting positions on some dimension, whether time, space, or gender. This formulation of conceptual agrammatism is very close to what Luria has called "loss of appreciation of 'logical-grammatical' relationships," and which he attributes to aphasia caused by parietal lobe injury. Luria's formulation, like ours, permits this defect to exist either side by side with, or independently of, the grammatical disturbances of Broca's aphasia to which we have devoted the main part of this presentation.

Footnotes

[1] Based on work supported in part by USPHS grants MH 4187 to Clark University and NB 06209 to Boston University Medical Center.

[2] This paper is a condensation of a chapter entitled "Studies on the Grammar of Aphasics," which will appear in the forthcoming book <u>Developments in Applied Psycholinguistic Research</u>, edited by Rosenberg and Koplin (Macmillan).

[3] The author is a member of the research staffs of both the Boston Veterans Administration Hospital and the Boston University Aphasia Research Center.